This England's Second Book of

BRITISH DANCE BANDS

The Singers and Smaller Bands

Compiled for *This England* by Edmund Whitehouse

This England acknowledges the help and assistance of many enthusiasts,
without whom it would have been impossible to compile and check the
enormous amount of material contained in this book.
Some entries came from contemporary magazines, others from readers' recommendations,
Brian Rust's *British Dance Bands On Record*, some from *Memory Lane*
(especially articles by Chris Hayes and Doug Wilkins), and some from Don Wicks *The Ballad
Years*. Other useful pictures and information came from Percy Bickerdyke, Eric Holmes,
Derrick Francis, Ray Pallett, Arthur Jackson, Henry Stonor, Barry and Iris McCanna,
Peter Wallace, John Wright, Peter James, Edward Towler, Bob Martin, Mike Carey,
Geoffrey Bond, Harold Kaye, Ted Rowley, Charles Hippisley-Cox, Mike Thomas, Billy Amstell,
Ken Mackintosh, John Stavordale, Dimitri Kennaway, Millicent Phillips, Betty Taylor,
Jo Marney, Sandra Haynes, Alan Griffiths, Rosemary Squires, Frank Lockyer, Vic Charters and
John Andrews. Many other contributors are also gratefully thanked for their assistance,
especially the ardent membership of the Internet-based "British Dance Bands Group".
In addition, *This England* is pleased to recognise
the staff production and design team whose dedicated
work made it possible to piece everything together:-
Ann Augur, Keren Bowers, Maureen Compton, Sally Hunt,
Paul Makepeace, Christine Manifold, Susan Beaty, and Peter Worsley.

Published by This England Books,
Alma House, 73 Rodney Road, Cheltenham,
Gloucestershire GL50 1HT. Tel: 01242-537900

Printed in Great Britain by Polestar Wheatons Ltd., Exeter

ISBN 0 906324 37 8

Contents

Foreword

I was delighted when Edmund Whitehouse invited me to say a few words about *This England's Second Book of British Dance Bands — Singers and Smaller Band Leaders.* To the best of my knowledge, nobody has ever attempted a book on this subject before and it is a natural and worthy successor to their earlier splendid volume on the major band leaders first published in 1999.

To have been associated with the great British Dance Band era for so many years has been a great privilege for me. During that time — more than 50 years — I worked with many wonderful people and this book mentions a significant percentage of them. With more than 1,000 indexed entries the work is a masterpiece and one which I heartily recommend to all those with even the faintest of passing interest in British Dance Music. It is a sobering thought that during its heyday, four out of every five marriages began with a meeting on the dance floor!

What makes the book so valuable is not just the biographical information but the superb illustrations and photographs which recreate the events so vividly. They brought back many happy memories for me and I know they will for you too. Look inside and allow yourself sufficient time to wallow in the magical musical nostalgia of yesteryear. It has been great fun and *This England* magazine is to be congratulated on recreating it.

KEN MACKINTOSH

△ Ken Mackintosh

**"The amateur works hard until he gets it right —
but the professional works hard until he can't get it wrong.**

Introduction

Our first highly popular volume of *British Dance Bands* concentrated on the many well-known band leaders, and this second volume is an attempt to describe all the important dance band vocalists of the 20th century – more than 600 in total! It is readily admitted, however, that to have included everyone would have been quite impossible. It was also difficult to distinguish between a genuine dance record and a more commercial popular song, so — using several defining guidelines — a compromise had to be achieved.

Also contained in this book are more than 350 minor band leaders not described in Volume One. These were the backbone of the country's live dance music, certainly pre-war, and to a large extent during the immediate post-war period as well. Many of them doubled as singers and this has been acknowledged where significant. It is obvious, however, that hundreds, if not thousands, of other amateur and semi-professional bands also existed, but no-one could ever hope to catalogue them all, especially with fading memories due to the inexorable march of time.

Much interesting information cropped up during our extensive research, but what surprised us most was the apparent disappearance of so many well-known pre-war singers after hostilities ceased in 1945. Dates of birth and death have been included, where known, but some have been difficult to obtain or confirm, with at least one famous band leader credited with being born on three different dates during a 10-year period!

What is not in doubt is that several famous stars began their career as humble dance band singers. While some of the more important ones have been allocated a chapter to themselves, others certainly deserved it but space would not allow.

Every major expert in this distinctive field has been consulted, but in a book of this nature some errors and omissions are almost inevitable. We would therefore be pleased to hear from anyone with new or up-dated information.

If you enjoyed those rhythmical "Dance Band Days" we hope this second volume will bring back happy memories of a time when live music rarely involved amplifiers, certainly not computers or electronics, and when an "amorous affair" meant walking your girl back home in the late evening and kissing her goodnight on the doorstep!

EDMUND WHITEHOUSE

Lew Stone at the Monseigneur

Lew Stone used to arrange Ambrose's music. Then he united with Roy Fox and formed the Monseigneur Band. Now he plays the piano and conducts his eleven music-makers and makes people dance delightedly

LEW STONE CONDUCTS HIS BAND FROM THE PIANO AT MONSEIGNEUR

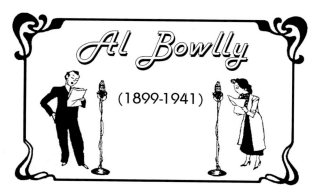

Al Bowlly

(1899-1941)

The cult of the star vocalist is largely a post-war phenomenon with wealthy publicity agents being responsible for the marketing and packaging of their "products". But for a cruel stroke of ill-fortune American superstars Frank Sinatra and Bing Crosby might well have been joined by a singer who came to Britain from southern Africa in the late-Twenties. Al Bowlly was destined to become everyone's darling — until cruelly cut down in his prime during the London Blitz.

Born in Lourenço Marques (now Maputo), Mozambique, Al's date of birth was 7th January — but which year was it? Most sources say 1899, some say 1898, but his brother, Mish, always insisted it was 1900. Whichever is correct, however, he was certainly brought up in Johannesburg, South Africa, where he was apprenticed to a barber whose customers he serenaded on the banjo, guitar and ukelele. He also played the piano and in 1923 went on tour with Edgar Adeler's band, eventually finding himself in England via Asia and mainland Europe — but not without a certain amount of controversy. Being a strongly-opinioned person he often became embroiled in arguments and on one occasion was left standing on the platform of a railway station while the rest of the band departed without him!

Early on he played with Fred Elizalde and his orchestra but soon found himself out of work when the sedate management of the Savoy Hotel decided that Fred's band was much too "hot" for their customers. They rarely played waltzes and that did not suit the well-heeled patrons at all. They complained, so Fred and his band had to go.

Various stories have been told about Al busking at London cinema and theatre queues, and being spotted and taken straight to the recording studio. Some may be true but others apocryphal. He certainly figured prominently with Ray Noble's HMV orchestra, however, and became a household name on the back of its

many recordings. He also sang with Roy Fox at the Monseigneur restaurant and had all the girls swooning at his relaxed, sincere voice. His prowess as an amateur boxer (he once had a nearly fatal showdown with Al Starita shortly after he arrived in England), also dissuaded lesser males from making disparaging remarks to his face.

Among the many songs he helped to make famous were two world-beaters by British writers and composers. *Goodnight Sweetheart*, by Jimmy Campbell and Reg Connelly, was possibly Ray Noble's best-known melody, while *South of the Border* (1939) was actually as British as they come, written by Jimmy Kennedy and Michael Carr. Al went to the United States in 1934 and appeared with Ray Noble in New York, becoming known as "Britain's Ambassador of Song" — not bad for someone from Portuguese East Africa! Noble's band included a young Glenn Miller on trombone and a significant number of records were made. Al returned twice more to the States, the second time for an operation on a severe throat infection, which was performed in New York during November 1937. He then returned to Britain and embarked on a new spate of successful recordings.

Al Bowlly sang, played and recorded with many top bands including Lew Stone, Jack Jackson, Billy Cotton, Len Fillis, Geraldo, Howard Godfrey, Nat Gonella, Harry Hudson, Arthur Lally, Sydney Lipton, Percival Mackey, Mantovani, Oscar Rabin, Carroll Gibbons, Debroy Somers, Jay Wilbur and Maurice Winnick. Always in demand, his main challengers for the top crooning spot were probably Sam Browne and Denny Dennis, but few would ever bet against Al coming out top of the annual opinion polls.

Like most contemporary popular musicians of the period he took part in several films, some as an instrumentalist, others as a main singer, but never in a starring role. Before he went to America it seems he appeared in "Up for the Cup", "The Mayor's Nest" and "Up for the Derby" (all starring Sydney Howard, 1931, 1932 and 1933 respectively), plus "The Chance of a Night Time" (1931, Ralph Lynn) and "A Night Like This" (1932, Ralph Lynn and Tom Walls). Across the water he appeared with Ray Noble's band in "The Big Broadcast of 1936", although whether he sang solo is open to debate. Confusion reigns as to what other films he appeared in but he certainly made some Pathe "shorts". Unfortunately, the first

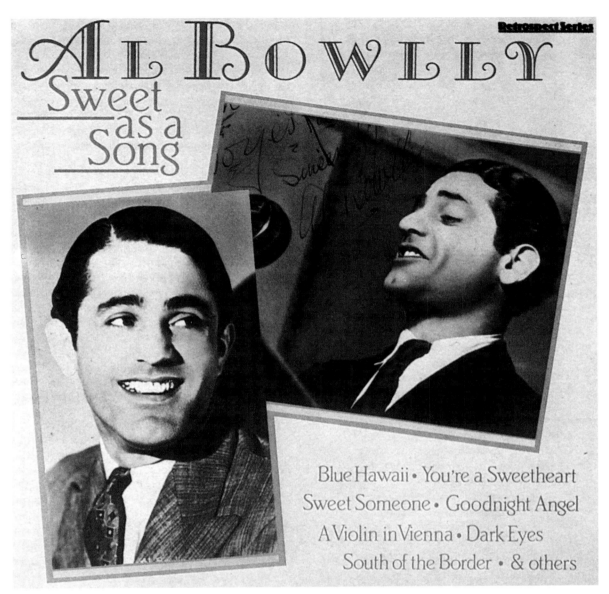

AL BOWLLY
Sweet as a Song

Blue Hawaii • You're a Sweetheart
Sweet Someone • Goodnight Angel
A Violin in Vienna • Dark Eyes
South of the Border • & others

items to be cut from old films are usually the solo songs and therefore we may never know for sure just how many films he did actually appear in.

War came at the height of his career but he continued to perform and sing all over the country, including army camps and munitions factories. On 17th April, 1941, the Luftwaffe unleashed one of their many raids on London and among the casualties was Al Bowlly, killed in his flat by a land-mine. He was found trapped against the inside of the front door but without a mark on him. One of his closest friends and neighbours in the same block of flats in Jermyn Street, pianist Monia Liter, was away at the time and so escaped the severe blast which would otherwise have wiped out two famous

dance band personalities. Monia had been an accompanist and a close friend from Al's youth abroad, arriving in England at the same time.

Despite his premature death, Al's name lives on. His voice was instantly recognisable and was often compared to the world's best. He always sounded sincere and had a special way of getting his song across to the audience, whether on stage, radio or recording studio. His swarthy complexion and smooth matching vocal sound were a unique combination and his memory still looms large — and not just among those old enough to remember him when he was alive. His much-loved rendition of *The Very Thought of You* makes a suitable epitaph for someone who became a legend in his own life-time, and will remain so for evermore.

Sam Browne

(1898-1972)

Of Lithuanian Jewish extraction, Sam was one of 11 children — the second son, born on 26th March, 1898 to Lewis and Kate Browne of Stepney, where he initially went to school. His father later moved the family to Tottenham to open a shoe repair shop where young Sam could often be found helping out. His subsequent pre-war rise from rags-to-riches was unfortunately paralleled by a post-war reversal in fortunes which left him in complete obscurity, ironically renting a basement room near the mighty Alexandra Palace from where the fledgling television network first began broadcasting.

After leaving school Sam Browne joined the Merchant Navy where he quickly learnt to play the drums *en route* to North America. He also enjoyed singing and mastered musical theory so thoroughly that band leaders were later delighted to hire a singer who could read a tune at first sight. Small time engagements gained him an enviable reputation as possibly the first ever full-time professional dance band singer, which catapulted him into the big time when he received an unexpected telegram while performing in Stockholm. He returned to Britain immediately and began his first big professional engagement touring with Jack Hylton's show band, using a glass megaphone so people could actually see as well as hear him! However, it was not long before the microphone replaced the megaphone!

Despite the glamour, long stints in Europe took their toll and, after little more than 12 months, Sam decided to leave Jack Hylton to seek a more permanent job in London. He found one with Ambrose with whom he spent many years happily resident at the Mayfair Hotel, and also at Ciro's and the Embassy Club. During this time he made a huge number of records not just with the maestro but also with many other bands including Syd Roy, Harry Hudson, Billy Merrin, George Scott-Wood, Lew Stone, Jay Wilbur, Billy Cotton, Jack Harris, Bertini and Primo Scala. Everybody wanted Sam Browne and he probably sang with more bands than anyone else, Sam Costa probably running him a close second.

With new-found fame came a new-found fortune. His first car was a Model-T Ford, quite a rarity in north London and eagerly viewed and clambered over by the local young rascals. This was soon part-exchanged for a Rover, which in those days was a prestigious marque second only to the more-expensive manufacturers Bentley and Rolls-Royce. Whenever they were live on the wireless Sam acted as the compère to Ambrose's broadcasts from the Mayfair Hotel and, despite a shy nature and nerves which were never evident to the public, enjoyed a fine reputation as one of the country's leading crooners, vying constantly for top place in the public's affections with Al Bowlly and Denny Dennis.

Unfortunately, Sam spent money as fast as he earned it, mainly through betting on horses and greyhound racing, being a regular visitor to the White City Stadium in West London where, in retrospect, he really did "go to the dogs". It was a pity that his parents refused his offer of a luxury home saying that he might need the money in the future. He did … but by then it had all gone. At the time it was "easy come, easy go", as indeed it was for many others, including Ambrose himself, but nobody could have foreseen the disastrous effect which the war would have on virtually everyone in the dance band profession.

In 1935, at the height of his fame, he appeared in a Royal Command performance at the London Palladium, accompanied by fellow singing star Elsie Carlisle with whom he had a highly successful relationship on-stage, but a love-hate one off it. Almost 20 years later he appeared in another Royal Command performance, but this time with Ted Heath and other "old-stagers" who were still in harness.

Sam's career nearly came to a sudden end in

1941, when he was travelling by train from Paddington with Evelyn Dall and Max Bacon to appear at the Bristol Hippodrome. Without any warning, he was hit by three bullets fired from the trackside which lodged in his jaw and neck. Only the retarding effect of the window saved him from instant death, although a fraction of an inch either way would still have proved fatal. The bullets were extracted and eventually kept as souvenirs by his second wife, Olga. Sam's first wife and mentor, Terry, had died young in 1931 which proved a terrific blow to his morale. Although he married Olga a couple of years later and by whom he had two daughters, Carol and Myrna, the marriage broke down in the early-Fifties.

Back in the Thirties Sam had received several offers to tour America but preferred to stay at home with his friends. When war arrived he appeared with Ben Lyon, Bebe Daniels and Vic Oliver in the radio programme "Hi Gang" and later sang with Ken Mackintosh and Jack Parnell. He also ran an eight-piece choir called the Sam Browne Singers, but post-war austerity and the changing popular musical scene soon found him down on his luck.

Sam knew the writing was on the wall for singers like him and despite his fellow musicians truthfully telling him he still sounded great, he refused to continue singing past his best. Having previously tried running a club in Soho and a confectionery stall on the Isle of Man, he then made a big mistake by accepting a job in a betting office where he got into financial trouble and served a prison term for alleged embezzlement.

At this point he went to ground and simply disappeared. Amazingly, he only came back into public view when a hoaxer imitating him for a documentary film was dramatically exposed as a fake. So successful was this "double", both in looks and performance, that he successfully passed himself off in several places and was only rumbled when he insisted he had made his first record in 1931 instead of three years earlier. The film producers became suspicious and decided to set a trap by enlisting the help of band leader Lew Stone. The hoaxer clearly failed to recognise Lew and, when subsequently challenged by phone about alleged tax evasion — which was not true, although he could not have known it — readily confessed his guilt. He, too, then disappeared!

Sam was finally tracked down by an old friend and the documentary was duly completed, although it was not a commercial success. He happily responded to enquiries about his glorious past but there was little left of the present and almost nothing of the future, because, despite his faithful landlady looking after him, Sam Browne died alone on 2nd March, 1972, something of a recluse. It was a sad end for someone who made such a vast number of recordings and gave so much pleasure to literally millions of people. Estranged from his wife and two daughters with whom he had lost touch, he was buried in the Jewish Cemetery at Rainham in Essex.

Much of Sam Browne's early career was spent with Ambrose. Here is an unusual picture of the band during filming for the 1936 movie "Soft Lights and Sweet Music", which also starred Evelyn Dall, Turner Layton, Donald Stewart, Elisabeth Welch, Max Bacon and the Three Rhythm Brothers.

Elsie Carlisle

(1897-1977)

Elsie Carlisle was known as "Britain's Radio Sweetheart" — and no dance band singer ever deserved the title more. One of the first girl vocalists to broadcast, this lively wide-eyed Lancashire lass had a tremendous following in the Thirties but her magic lingers on today only in the minds of connoisseurs of vintage dance band music. A whole generation has grown up knowing nothing about a lady who was one of Britain's top singers for almost 20 years — because after the war she deliberately walked out of the spotlight and into the shadows of obscurity.

Despite her humble beginnings Elsie was a class act. Her range was remarkable — from blues to buffoonery — yet it was said that her voice made strong men weak and small boys perspire! Whether chortling through comic duets in the recording studio, or just standing soulfully in a lonely theatre spotlight, Elsie Carlisle combined cheeky elegance and piquant charm. Whatever the song, she sprinkled it with gold dust.

Elsie's voice was honed in the music halls and developed by broadcasts with Ambrose and his orchestra with whom she sang from 1932 until 1936. He it was who encouraged petite Elsie to form a double-act with suave Sam Browne, then one of Britain's best-known crooners. Together they sang such rib-ticklers as *No, No, A Thousand Times No!* and *Home James and Don't Spare the Horses*. Yet Elsie could also massage the heartstrings with such timeless vamp songs as *Body and Soul* and *Ten Cents a Dance*. Delight and despair were thus dappled in one glorious voice.

Details of her early life are sketchy but it is

believed she was born Amy Brunton in Didsbury, south Manchester, on 21st January 1897. As a six-year-old she was singing and dancing at local concerts, and by the time she was 12 had become top box-office draw in a revue. Four years later she was starring in advertisements. Then a BBC official, who happened to be a guest at a luncheon, heard her sing and thought she was something special. He asked her to perform in front of a microphone and regular broadcasting dates followed.

Primarily an actress, Elsie made her professional stage debut at the Metropolitan Music Hall in July 1920, followed by years of provincial touring. Her recording career began in 1926 when she had the good fortune to have Carroll Gibbons as her accompanist. Further early recording experience was gained with Jay Wilbur's band.

She was a radio guest on BBC's "Dancing Time" with Sidney Firman's London Radio Dance Band, and in March 1929 opened in C.B. Cochran's prestigious London production of Cole Porter's musical "Wake Up and Dream", in which she sang *What Is This Thing called Love?* She was accompanied on one memorable occasion by Cole Porter himself, and at other times by Leslie Hutchinson, better known as "Hutch", who had been promoted from the pit orchestra! The cast also included Jessie Matthews, Tilly Losch and Sonnie Hale. Anna Neagle was then in the *corps de ballet* and the show was Elsie's first taste of national success. She was on course for stardom.

One critic called her "the epitome of the know-it-all flapper, the coyer English cousin of Americans Ruth Etting, Annette Hanshaw and Helen Kane". A born comedienne, she at times used the pseudonyms Sheila Kay, Amy Brunt and Lallie Lack, while an original stage presentation of the comedy song *Gertie, the Girl with the Gong* cast her as an over-zealous policewoman called "Constable Car-oil", booking any motorist who was a fraction over the newly imposed 30 mph speed limit. She also resurrected her "tripe and clogs" Lancashire brogue to sing the bouncy *Say Si Si*, in Gracie Fields-style with the Jack Harris band.

RADIO PICTORIAL, March 17, 1939. No. 270
Registered at the G.P.O. as a Newspaper

LUXEMBOURG
NORMANDY
PARIS : LYONS : EIREANN
PROGRAMMES
Mar. 19—Mar. 25

CASH
PRIZES
for
LISTENERS
NO ENTRANCE FEE
See Page 25

RADIO PICTORIAL

THE MAGAZINE FOR EVERY LISTENER

3D.

EVERY
FRIDAY

★
RADIO
in the
NEXT WAR
Professor Low's
Remarkable
Prophecies

Visiting
BERTHA WILLMOTT
Radio's
Old-time Songstress

ARE FILMS
FAIR TO
RADIO STARS?

Private Letter to
My Sons by
Mrs. JACK JACKSON

Specially featured :
DOROTHY CARLESS
CLARENCE WRIGHT
MARY LAWSON
BILLY MERRIN
MURRAY & MOONEY

B.B.C.
PROGRAMME
GUIDE

Elsie
CARLISLE

△ By the time Elsie Carlisle appeared on the front cover of "Radio Pictorial" in March 1939, both she and the magazine were heading for an early retirement. Ironically, just like many other popular singers, she was at the height of her fame but the outbreak of war signalled an end to the old order. For Elsie it meant switching from a solo career to star in three series of a radio programme called "Carlisle Express". After the war she acquired a ballroom in Tooting then simply vanished from the scene to become a publican.

A mixture of cool elegance and Northern candour, Elsie lived in considerable style in a flat behind the Dorchester Hotel off London's exclusive Park Lane. Described as a "diminutive blonde who could project pretty little romantic songs, light comedy, brittle sophistication and highly suggestive blues-style numbers with the same sense of form" she was seen in action by long-serving dance band musician Billy Amstell at the London Palladium, who said: "She was a lovely person who wore lovely dresses — there was no doubt about it, she was the star". Yet she could also be as hard-nosed as any man when it came to negotiating the poisonous tendrils and prickly paths of the show business jungle.

For her double-act with Sam Browne she had to make sure he knew all about stage craft — so she did the job herself! "Relax when you embrace me. You're supposed to be holding me tenderly, not as if I was a seat board!" They were the perfect duo and humorist B.C. Hilliam ("Flotsam" of Flotsam and Jetsam fame) penned the following cunning limerick:

> *A crooner named Elsie Carlisle,*
> *Is a girl with a very nice stisle;*
> *But the cheek that she gets*
> *From Sam Browne in duets —*
> *Now how can this chap be so visle?*

In 1933 Elsie featured in the comedy film "Radio Parade" and two years later scored a big hit at the RadiOlympia exhibition. In 1936 she topped *Melody Maker's* nation-wide female vocalist popularity poll with almost 5,000 votes. American blonde bombshell Evelyn Dall, Elsie's successor with the Ambrose band, came second. In 1937 Elsie explained jokingly how the lines on her face were caused by foot trouble — having to run around with six dogs on one pair of feet. Her dogs and an occasional game of golf were her main forms of relaxation.

In October 1940 the first programme in a new radio series was broadcast. "Carlisle Express" was described as "a weekly train call from Elsie Carlisle and a distinguished gathering of fellow passengers". Initially featuring Charles Shadwell and the BBC Variety Orchestra it was followed by an improved second series with comedy from Wheeler and Wilson as "Wear and Tear" the permanent porters, Charlie Clapham as "Spiller" the restaurant car attendant and Bobbie Comber as "Bertie" the engine driver. A third series featured the locomotive-friendly Jack Train, who co-starred with fellow "ITMA" stalwart, Dorothy Summers. Elsie hosted all three series and kept up morale-boosting stage performances right to the end of the war.

In conjunction with her brother Billy, in 1949 she opened "Elsie Carlisle's Tooting Ballroom" which, according to contemporary newspaper reports was the fulfilment of a lifetime's ambition. Two years later she made a guest appearance with Ambrose on television but then, despite being one of Britain's top radio idols, she suddenly disappeared from view and spent the next 30 years in almost total privacy, part of which time was spent running the Old Rose Inn at Wokingham in Berkshire.

She was always on hand to offer advice to any budding entertainer who sought her out, but her business affairs were now managed largely by her son. Nevertheless, she remained a commercially astute woman right up until her death on 5th September, 1977, aged 80.

Sam Costa

(1910-1981)

The crooner with a 'smiling moustache'

No one could forget Sam Costa, famous as much for his looks as his voice. Initially a singer he went on to become a comic and highly successful post-war disc jockey, a real character and clown who everybody loved. Complete with a bristling pointed moustache, first honed as complete handlebar version during his RAF days but later trimmed back, he was the genuine professional article.

"Uncle Sam" was born in Stoke Newington on 17th June, 1910 and was educated at Highbury Grammar School. Early efforts as a clerk ended in him being shown the door for continued late arrivals but this only served as a springboard for him to form a dance band with some friends. Led by Maurice Burman, later a drummer with Roy Fox and Geraldo, they began at the Dreamland Ballroom in Margate where Sam doubled on piano and vocals. Sid Millward then took Sam and Maurice with him to Monte Carlo following which Sam decided to go solo. His natural qualities soon found him work with so many bands that he eventually rivalled Sam Browne for the biggest collection!

Among the best-known orchestras which Sam worked and recorded with during the Thirties were Maurice Winnick, Lew Stone, Jack Jackson, Geraldo, Jay Wilbur, Lionel Falkman, Bert and John Firman, Jack Harris, Sydney Kyte, Harry Leader, Joe Loss, Terry Mack, Bram Martin, Ronnie Munro, Lou Preager, Johnny Rosen, Arthur Salisbury, George Scott-Wood, Debroy Somers, Nat Star, Maxwell Stewart, Peter Yorke and Carroll Gibbons — a quite astonishing list.

It was during the war that Sam's charismatic qualities showed through and turned him into a national celebrity. After working as a resident vocalist for the BBC in Bristol — at a fraction of his previous pay as a top crooner — he secured a small part with Tommy Handley in "ITMA". After joining the RAF he teamed up with Denny Dennis and Cyril Stapleton but then fell in with two natural comedians called Kenneth Horne and Richard Murdoch. When asked if he had any acting experience he only had to mention "ITMA" and he was immediately included in a review which progressed well beyond the confines of the wartime RAF.

Playing the role of a cheeky Cockney office boy his flippant catchphrase "Good morning sir, was there something?" became a household institution in the popular programme "Much-Binding-in-the-Marsh". He had first come

△ *The cast of "Much Binding-in-the-Marsh" in 1947. Sam Costa (top right) talks to Richard Murdoch while Kenneth Horne (bottom left), peruses a script with Maurice Denham, who took the parts of more than 60 lesser characters.*

This picture of Sam and his then fiancée, Esther Comer, was taken shortly before they were married in 1938. She was Sam's secretary as well as his wife for more than 40 years — and handled all his extensive fan mail.

across it at an "olde worlde" teashop run by two elderly ladies and it put him so much in the public eye that he became an integral part of the show. Playing a subservient but eminently likeable foil to Horne and Murdoch, he was often downtrodden but never squashed, always plotting but never quite coming out on top. The programme ran for ten very successful years and it proved a perfect platform for a new career.

Sam was a "natural" and after helping record companies to market their products in a burgeoning new post-war market, he — like Jack Jackson — became a hugely prosperous radio disc jockey. Although he appeared in several films he never liked television, much preferring a microphone from which he radiated infectious enthusiasm and cordiality every time he spoke. Although he often appeared on early sessions of "Juke Box Jury" it was on radio where he felt most at home and from which he gave listeners the greatest pleasure.

Like George Elrick, he was immensely well-liked and respected as a presenter of "Housewives' Choice" and also fronted his own "Midday Spin" both for the BBC and for Radio Luxembourg. On Sundays he could be heard on both morning "Breakfast Time" and the evening "Glamorous Nights". Invariably he serenaded listeners with *Sam's Song*, his unofficial signature tune, and at the end of each show his chirpy and cheery "Thank you for the pleasure of your company" always made everyone feel they were important. To Sam they were, because without them he was nobody. His wife and support for more than 40 years, Esther, had the unenviable task of personally replying to all his considerable fan mail.

After a lifetime of good health Sam was mysteriously taken ill in 1981 and rapidly went downhill. He died from a brain tumour on 22nd September but one can easily visualise him in Heaven saying "Good morning sir, was there something?"

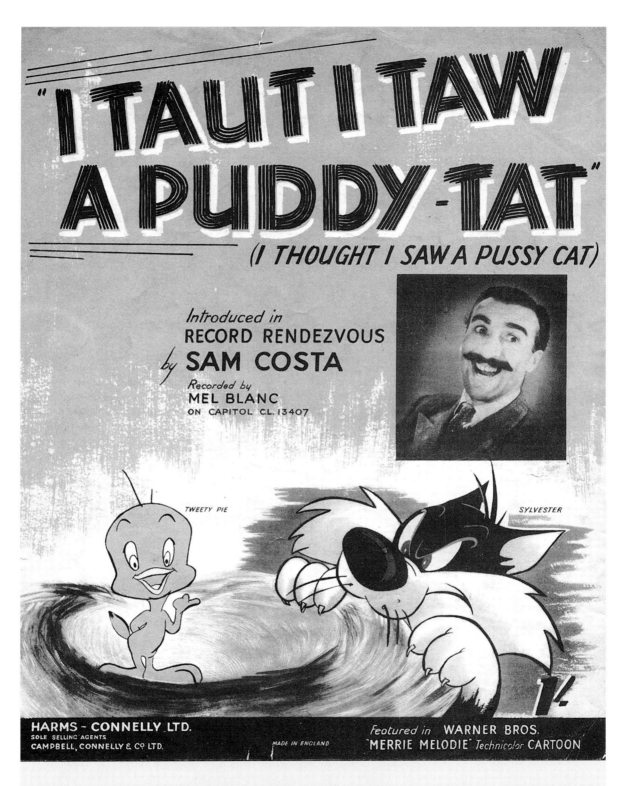

△ This hilarious hit song, recorded by Mel Blanc in 1951, was based on the cartoon characters of a lisping little bird called "Tweety Pie" and a growling pussy cat called "Silvester". It was first introduced to British audiences by Sam Costa in his "Record Rendezvous" programme. Sam had the happy knack of making all his listeners feel as though they mattered to him — which of course, they did.

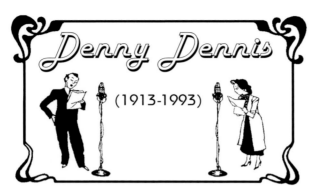

Denny Dennis

(1913-1993)

Together with Sam Browne and Al Bowlly, Denny Dennis made up a trio of singers who during the Thirties dominated the airwaves and recording scene. Like many other famous songsters, however, in later life he became something of a forgotten figure and, despite a successful tour of America with Tommy Dorsey in 1948, ended his days in relative obscurity in the Furness District of Lancashire.

Ronald Dennis Pountain was born in Derby on 1st November, 1913 and trained as an electrician with the LMS Railway. When his older brother Eric (later known as Barry Gray) moved to London as a professional drummer, Denny jumped at the opportunity to occupy his brother's chair with the local New Mayfair Dance Band, the pianist of which had been Ronnie Binge, later to find fame as the composer of *Elizabethan Serenade*, and orchestrator of Mantovani's *Charmaine*-style cascading strings.

Ron soon changed his name to Dennis and began to model his singing voice on Bing Crosby. The sound was so pleasing that it brought an audition with Roy Fox who was impressed but recommended 12 months refinement. Alhough initially dismissing a show business career Dennis was persuaded to join Freddy Bretherton's band at the Spider's Web roadhouse near Watford. Word of his melodic singing soon got around and one evening Jack Jackson arrived in his Packard car and promptly signed him on a successful short-term recording and broadcasting contract. Within a matter of months Roy Fox gave Dennis a second audition and this time signed him permanently — and also changed his name to Denny Dennis. He was just 20 years old. Fame and fortune were around the corner, but not before the latter was heavily dented when a large pay packet was stolen backstage at the London Palladium, prompting drummer Maurice Burman to act as Denny's future financial adviser.

Being young and naïve, Denny was often the butt of practical jokes and once unpacked his newly-pressed tuxedo only to discover it full of dead fish! Although he tried to kill the smell with deodorant it only made things worse and the performance at Blackpool's Winter Gardens went ahead with him feeling very uncomfortable. When Denny subsequently left his suit out overnight to air, it poured with rain! On other occasions he would find his shoes filled with shaving cream. He accepted most of the jokes in good humour but was not impressed that news of his fate was sometimes passed around the other bands.

Denny was very much at home in the private surroundings of the studio and night club, but less so in bigger auditoriums and theatres, where he sometimes became quite nervous. In 1935 he appeared in the film "Radio Pirates", the storyline of which pre-dated pirate radio stations by nearly three decades! During the same year Roy Fox signed 14-year-old Mary Lee from Scotland and her duets with Denny were always a highlight of the show. By the time Fox disbanded in 1938 Denny was a big name star and had made more than 200 records. He was always high up in public opinion polls, often coming out ahead of Al Bowlly, Sam Browne, Brian Lawrance, Sam Costa, Les Allen etc. Life seemed very rosy and his fan club published a magazine called, appropriately, the *Denizen*.

Denny always took singing seriously and studied for a time under the widow of classical conductor Percy Pitt, who felt sure he could have been an operatic bass. He was much in demand and even received an unofficial approach from Henry Hall's manager, which he was unable to accept because of his contract with Roy Fox. Surprisingly, Henry Hall and Denny Dennis never actually met each other, quite remarkable when one considers how well-known they both were.

After turning down approaches by both Joe Loss and Peter Fielding, Denny then accepted a generous offer from Ambrose. By now married to Betty Faye, he was looking forward to being based at the Mayfair Hotel and was utterly dismayed when his new boss decided to leave London and go on tour, so in 1939 he embarked on a solo career and appeared on both Radio Luxembourg and Radio Normandy. For a time he and his wife lived a life of luxury, but then the war intervened. Life was difficult for everyone and Denny took work wherever he could get it, including singing in a stage version of Arthur Askey and Richard Murdoch's "Band Waggon" which turned Tommy Trinder into a star. He was then engaged by the BBC to operate from Bristol and found himself working almost round the clock, although he still found time to perform elsewhere and was in Sheffield when his son was born.

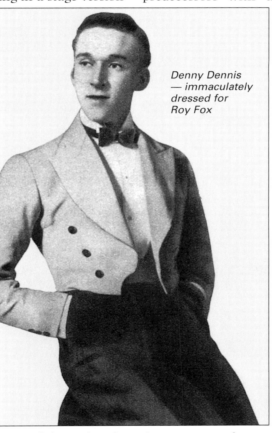

Denny Dennis — immaculately dressed for Roy Fox

Then out of the blue came a marvellous offer to join Paul Whiteman's band in America — but permission was refused by the Ministry of Labour, and also for a similar offer by Sammy Kaye. Instead, Denny joined the RAF where he discovered several people impersonating him, many of whom were far from scrupulous in other directions. He was once threatened with "exposure" by a female fan whom he had never met from a place he had never visited!

Associations with Cyril Stapleton and Sam Costa took him to Iceland where he received a phone call from fellow-singer Chick Henderson who was billeted nearby. Before they could meet, however, Chick was posted back to Portsmouth where he met a most untimely end. Many more wartime performances and broadcasts took place with the Squadronaires, Skyrockets, Ted Heath, Stephane Grappelli and George Shearing. When broadcasting with the latter he also stood by the piano and told George which key to play the next tune in! He nearly came unstuck altogether, however, when he was briefly put on the BBC's banned list, singled out like several others by a complicated set of rules which discriminated against various singers and songs but which was happily overturned before it did any permanent damage.

Sadly, Denny's marriage was one of the many matrimonial casualties of the war. Life went on, however, and he had a hit record with *Bluest Kind of Blues* followed by an offer to tour and record with Tommy Dorsey in America. His predecessors with the band included both Frank Sinatra and Dick Haymes, and when Denny arrived in New York in November 1948, he was greeted by George Shearing and his wife. During the next few months life was lived at a hectic pace and was also extremely expensive. It was fun but Denny was not earning the kind of money hinted at by the British papers. The Americans took to him, however, and his voice was likened to a mixture of Bing Crosby, Frank Sinatra and Perry Como — praise indeed, although Denny did not like being dubbed as "Britain's Bing Crosby" because he never modelled himself on anyone.

He met all the big stars, including Louis Armstrong who actually recalled a brief encounter with him in Nottingham some years before when Denny was still called Dennis Pountain! Trumpeter Charlie Shavers, the only black member of the band, took him under his wing, but racial prejudice in those days only allowed them to perform together when the band was playing away from the Deep South. Their close friendship was happily renewed when Charlie later toured Britain.

Unfortunately, after only 14 months, Denny was forced to return home by a combination of personal and financial problems. He could have made it in America, of that there is no doubt,

△ *Roy Fox's band in the Isle of Man, 1934. Left to right: Harry Gold, Art Christmas, Hughie Tripp, Maurice Burman, Denny Dennis, Freddy Welsh, Peggy Dell, Les Lambert, George Rowe, George Gibbs, Sid Buckman, Jack Nathan, Ivor Mairants, and Rex Owen, with the leader sitting in front.*

The Ups and Downs of Denny Dennis

▷ *In 1948 Denny visited America and sang with the Tommy Dorsey band. It promised to be an exciting time but was unfortunately cut short after only a year, when he was forced to return home because of personal and financial problems. Had he stayed longer and fulfilled his potential then there is no knowing where his career might have gone. As it was, he was never to reach the heights again and, after going on tour with the Frazer Hayes Quartette, he slipped into obscurity.*

BACK FROM U.S.A. TOUR WITH TOMMY DORSEY

DENNY DENNIS

Radio's Most Popular Vocalist

—— AND THE ——

FRAZER HAYES QUARTETTE

with
ANNABELLE LEE

FIRST VACANCY JULY 3

◁ *This rather optimistic looking poster only served to conceal — temporarily — the financial difficulties which Denny Dennis was in at the time. The Fraser Hayes Four (or Frazer Hayes Quartette as they were first known) were still in their infancy. After briefly disbanding, they reformed during the mid-Fifties and became famous after appearing with Kenneth Horne in the radio comedy programmes "Beyond Our Ken" and "Round the Horne". Denny, meanwhile, was quickly approaching bankruptcy in 1952. The Quartette here consists of, left to right, David Mason, Annabelle Lee, Jimmy Fraser and Tony Hayes.*

△ A youthful Denny Dennis is pictured behind the microphone with the Roy Fox band in the HMV studios in the thirties. Fox is on the right and the other personnel are: Maurice Burman (drums), Jack Nathan (piano), George Gibbs (bass), George Rowe and Jack Bain (trombones), Sid Buckman and Les Lambert (trumpets), Rex Owen (baritone sax), Art Christmas (alto), Harry Bolen (violin), Ivor Mairants (guitar). Hidden by DD are Hughie Tripp (alto) and Harry Gold (tenor). Denny's double-breasted suit was made by Harry Gold's father, an East End tailor.

but he did not stay long enough to fulfil his potential and life back in Britain became very awkward. A combination of missed opportunities, poor BBC coverage, and a reluctance to tour, soon put him in financial straits. Ultimately he had no choice but to take to the road and teamed up with the Fraser Hayes Four. At one point he also advised a young Max Bygraves to do more singing!

In 1952 Denny was declared bankrupt, his pride forbidding him to borrow the relatively small sum of money he needed from a number of friends who would have helped him out. Sid Phillips maintained his faith in the ageing singer, however, but by the mid-Fifties his star was definitely in the descendancy. Rock 'n' Roll had taken over and the name of Denny Dennis meant little or nothing to the new teenage generation. A brief period followed with Harry Leader plus a contract with Woolworth's cheap Embassy recording label where the songs often went out with misleading pseudonyms — although not in Denny's case.

It would be wrong, however, to assume that life was all gloom. In 1960 he was discharged from bankruptcy and still sang the occasional song. He also compered at a club called the Owl

near Selby in Yorkshire, home to many famous stars over the years, and also to Donald Peers with whom Denny very nearly came to blows when Donald finished his stint and decided to stay on-stage and join in all Denny's songs as well. After leaving the Owl, Denny was involved in a series of jobs and, following another failed marriage, ended up living as a paying guest with an old friend.

There were sporadic guest appearances around the country and also in London itself but his nomination to become a Freeman of the City of London was blocked because of his former bankruptcy — a harsh decision. He was not forgotten by everyone, however, and appeared and sang at occasional *Memory Lane* gatherings. He died on 2nd November, 1993 leaving behind many fond memories and a recently-completed biography by Mike Carey called *I'll Sing You a Thousand Love Songs*.

This England acknowledges the kind assistance of the Denny Dennis Music Society, 5 The Square, Darley Abbey, Derby DE22 1DY.

George Elrick
(1903-1999)

The BBC's regular morning radio programme "Housewives' Choice", which began in October 1945, never had a more popular presenter than Scottish-born singer George Elrick. Yet he nearly came unstuck when he sang a home-made ditty to the closing signature tune one day, without realising that the microphone was still switched on. He expected his cards, but dozens of housewives wrote in to say they wanted more! From then on he always signed off by singing "I'll see you all again tomorrow morning" to the familiar tune *In Party Mood*.

It was typical of this lively and loveable man who was born at Aberdeen on 29th December 1903, one of nine children. Educated at the granite city's famous Robert Gordon's College, his early ambition was to become a surgeon and he thought running a dance band might finance his training. Instead it turned him into a national celebrity, thanks to Carroll Gibbons who met George in 1931 just after he had won the title of Scotland's best dance band. "Come south to London" was his advice, and George accepted it.

While struggling to make the big time he met and married Alice, a London girl who was often mistaken for her friend, the prima ballerina Margot Fonteyn. Their son, Ian, was born in 1934 and their happiness was complete . . . for the time being. After a short spell with Ambrose, George became drummer-vocalist with Henry Hall where he built up a reputation for singing bright and breezy numbers such as *The Music Goes Round and Around* and *A Nice*

Cup of Tea. By 1936 he was receiving hundreds of letters asking for signed photographs.

A year later, when Henry Hall left the BBC, George toured the variety halls with a band loaned to him by Lew Stone. Among his musicians was saxophonist Harry Lewis who later married Vera Lynn. During the war they entertained the troops at home and abroad but after victory was announced George disbanded the orchestra and went solo. Christopher Stone — the first BBC disc jockey — suggested he should also try his hand in that sphere and so George joined Sam Costa and Jack Jackson in a similar change of career. In addition to appearing on "Housewives' Choice" he also managed Mantovani's orchestra from 1952-72, with whom he made many foreign tours.

Beneath the glamour, however, there was personal tragedy. In 1954, the year George was elected King Rat of the show business Grand Order of Water Rats, his son Ian, together with a fellow soldier, was killed by a car which mounted the pavement as they were walking back to Catterick Camp in Yorkshire. Despite the shock of losing their only child, outwardly George and Alice kept smiling and he continued with "Housewives' Choice" despite the deep grief inside. In 1973 he was elected King Rat for the second time and was later awarded the Freedom of the City of London.

Married for more than 60 years, George died in December 1999, just short of his 96th birthday.

He had been in show business for more than 70 years and was popular with everyone he came into contact with. As a young man he had chosen a signature tune which stood him in good stead and aptly summed him up:

When you're smiling, when you're smiling,
The whole world smiles with you . . .

Smiling is what "Mrs. Elrick's wee son George" did best and as a result — despite his own personal tragedy — he brought great happiness into the lives of a vast number of people.

This picture of George Elrick and his band was taken during the late-Thirties. The girls singers are Shirley Lenner (left) and Edna Kaye. Immediately on George's left is Vera Lynn's husband, Harry Lewis.

▷ Twice elected "King Rat", George is seen here wearing his sash, alongside his wife Alice. He was also awarded the Freedom of the City of London.

▽ Alice in 1937 with their only son Ian, an only child. Their life was full of happiness until tragedy struck him down during the early-Fifties.

21

Chick Henderson
(1912-1944)

Chick broadcasting in 1938. He had thousands of ardent fans, but few of them knew his real name was Henderson Rowntree.

As the air raid sounded at about 11pm, 31-year-old Sub-Lieut. Henderson Rowntree and other RNVR officers, including the Padre, thought they had better go down to the air raid shelter just outside the Royal Pier Hotel, Southsea, near Portsmouth. Rowntree took three of the five paces to safety but then a chance in a million occurred and he never competed the short journey. A rogue fragment of shrapnel from an ack-ack barrage pierced his heart and killed him instantly. The handsome young naval officer had risen from the ranks and gained his commission only 13 days before. He had also survived being sunk at sea so it was a tragic end to a promising career.

Chick Henderson was born at Hartlepool in County Durham on 22nd November, 1912, and between 1935-1942 his quiet charm, shy smile, steady gaze and smooth crooning re-sulted in almost 300 recordings. He also had an enormous fan club and was even seen as a rival to Frank Sinatra. Chick was a nickname he acquired possibly because he was the ninth and youngest of his mother's brood but he was, also fond of chicken, which in those days was a rare delicacy.

Training in the choir of the Abbey Church of St. Hilda at Hartlepool stood him in good stead for singing all the popular songs of the day which he learnt at an early age. The North East was particularly badly hit during the Depression but Chick sang everywhere he went. As an apprentice marine engineer he also sang at work and his first public appearance was in front of a mass of heaving youngsters at a Hartlepool night-spot called the Rink Ballroom, a large covered skating rink.

Accompanied by Jan Ralfini's band, in 1934 he won a talent contest after which Jan smart-ly signed him up for a season in Rhyl. But argu-ments over pay forced Chick and several mem-bers of the band to walk out and so he headed back for Hartlepool where he ended up on the dole. Like many others he then tried his luck in

London and after finding a job in a factory at Slough, touted his singing talents around Tin Pan Alley where he was rewarded with a generous contract by Harry Leader, who also allowed him to work freelance with other bands. He sang on Harry's first record for the Eclipse label and then a chance broadcast with Bobby Howell was heard by Joe Loss who was looking for a new singer. The only snag was that he was supposed to play the guitar, so was told to gently strum a dummy one and look busy!

At the time it was not uncommon for "vocal refrain" to appear on a record label instead of the singer's name and Chick was paid just £4 for the 1939 Joe Loss recording of *Begin the Beguine*, a tune which sold a million copies. Joe got all the credit and eventually the gold disc, but it caused considerable friction between singer and band leader. Normally a mild-man-nered man, Chick — by now supported by a large fan club — was incensed and walked out to join Harry Roy at the Café Anglais.

On 30th April, 1940, Chick Henderson married Pamela Stevenson, an attractive dancer from the Astoria Ballroom in Charing Cross Road, and their daughter, (Lynda Anne), was born on 5th July 1941. Needless to say her father doted on her, but by then he was in the RNVR and had already been rescued after his ship *HMS Cormorin* caught fire and sank off Scotland. One of his rescuers was Peter Scott the naturalist and artist who later painted the scene. Despite the fact that he could not swim, friends particularly remembered Chick's coolness in the crisis.

Known to his close friends as "Hendy", he later served aboard *HMS London* based at Chatham and took advantage of voyages to Canada to step ashore and sing on Radio CBY with Russ Jerrow and his orchestra. Back on leave in Britain, he finally patched up his differences with Joe Loss, with whom he made his final recording in 1942 — aptly titled *What More Can I Say?*

In fact Chick had a great deal more to say but sadly not on record. He was remembered by those who knew him as a curious mixture — a comedian, perfectionist, artist and disciplinarian, who belonged to the North but made his name in the South. Always ready with a quip or a quote there is no knowing where he might have ended up but for that cruel stroke of fate on the Hampshire seafront.

▽ *Chick Henderson*

Mary Lee
(Born 1921)

"Would Miss Mary McDevitt please come to the Empire Theatre on Friday night and bring her parents with her?"

The microphone announcement at the local store in Glasgow came as a shock because 13-year-old Mary had, unknown to her parents, skipped off school to take part in an audition for Roy Fox's band. She had not expected anything to come of it, but the American band leader had already decided her voice was outstanding and expected her to win the forthcoming event — which she did. It was agreed she would sign a contract on her 14th birthday when she joined the band at the Streatham Locarno, London, in September, 1935 — complete with chaperone! She was advertised not as Mary McDevitt, however, but as "Little Mary Lee".

Bobby Joy and Mary Lee both did sterling service as teenage vocalists for Roy Fox in his pre-war heyday.

Born on 13th August, 1921, to a traditional working-class family in Glasgow, Mary had a happy childhood but was suddenly catapulted into the limelight in the most extraordinary manner. For three glorious years she described how she was "groomed in every way — speech, dress, manners — you name it, I had it." Surprisingly, however, she was never groomed in singing because her voice was so natural that Roy Fox banned her from listening to records of Ella Fitzgerald and Peggy Lee, in case they spoilt her style! He also banned his boys from using bad language in her presence.

Records and radio programmes came a-plenty and with his star-studded line-up, Roy Fox was at the peak of his career. Mary rubbed shoulders — not literally because she was always treated with great respect – with Syd Buckman, Harry Gold, Les Lambert, Jack Nathan, Maurice Burman, Ivor Mairants and many others. She also sang duets with the band's male vocalist, none other than Denny Dennis. Immaculately-dressed and with Rolls Royces on hand, Roy Fox even had a racehorse

named after his signature tune, *Whispering*. But Mary's idea of heaven was not to last. After three years, most of which time she later admitted passed over her head as though in a dream, everything suddenly fell apart and the group disbanded.

The next three unhappy months were spent with Jack Payne's band although she never actually spoke to him, all transactions being done through his manager. Escaping at the first opportunity, she then joined jovial Jack Jackson with whom she enjoyed a very happy time. Unfortunately, she never recorded with either band. Eventually she tired of touring and took a position at a Soho night club. There she was occasionally accompanied by a young blind pianist called George Shearing. One night she was unexpectedly asked to sit at a particular table with what she described as some "charming boys". It was a noisy Friday evening but when she got up to sing, a loud voice shouted "Give Mary a chance!" The whole, club went deathly quiet, for the "boys" turned out to be the famous and much-feared Messini Gang!

⊲ Among Mary Lee's predecessors with Roy Fox were the Cubs, left to right, Ivor Mairants, Les Lambert and Harry Gold, and also Peggy Dell (below). The band leader treated Mary with great respect but, according to Harry, when Peggy handed in her notice Fox was furious and forbade anyone from contributing to a leaving present for her, on pain of being sacked from the band. When they publicly shook hands at the end of her final engagement, Harry overheard Fox wish Peggy "All the bad luck in the world!" Happily, she joined Jack Hylton and toured North America with him.

A short spell with Ambrose followed, although it took some time before she was paid, mainly owing to the band leader's fondness of gambling large sums of money. Some time later, when rehearsing for a broadcast at the Mayfair Hotel, a young 15-year-old girl arrived and sang beautifully. Her name was Anne Shelton and as a result it turned out to be the last time that Mary performed with Ambrose.

War then broke out and she hurriedly had to leave her Paignton engagement where she was appearing with the comedians, Jewell and Warriss. On the train back to Glasgow she hid in the toilet compartment as much as possible, because she had never seen so many soldiers before and was unsure on whose side they were! After a few more engagements in Bristol, where most of London's variety acts and orchestras had moved to, it was decided that Scotland was a safer bet. There she stayed for the next ten years, apart from two brief sorties. Firstly, she went to the Middle East with Harry Roy's band but was taken ill and forced to return home. Secondly, she took part in a show called "Stars of the Air" with Sam Browne, Max Bacon and Gloria Brent. The organiser was businessman Joe Collins, father of Joan and Jackie Collins.

Mary then married Scottish comedian Jack Milroy, and had a son, Jim, and a daughter, Diana. From 1952 onwards she appeared regularly with her husband, who was also half of a comedy duo with Rikki Fulton, called "Francie and Josie". During the Eighties they were honoured by the Variety Club of Great Britain, at which time she was also invited by Alan Dell to sing at the Royal Festival Hall, where she met up again with Roy Fox who was in the audience. With Jack she also appeared in the 1993 Royal Variety Show in front of Prince Charles and Princess Diana. Still active in Scotland, Mary has been a recent presenter on Radio Clyde and, together with her husband, appeared on the Millennium Hogmanay Show.

Meanwhile, "Little Mary Lee" she may have been, but at 80 in the summer of 2001, Mary Lee could claim to have grown-up.

Vera Lynn

(Born 1917)

△ The ever-popular "Forces' Sweetheart", Vera Lynn epitomised the British bulldog spirit during the war. Here she flashes a typical smile in uniform, with her "ENSA" (Entertainments National Service Association) epaulette clearly visible on her right shoulder.

There were three voices, above all others, which epitomised the struggle against Hitler during the last war. The first was Churchill, the second was Tommy Handley of ITMA, and the third was the "Forces' Sweetheart" — Vera Lynn. Churchill was serious, Handley was funny, but Vera was homely and welcoming. Many was the tear shed abroad by a serviceman during the dark days of conflict when he heard her sweet voice on the radio reminding him of home.

Born Vera Margaret Welch in East Ham, London, on 20th March, 1917, she was taught music hall songs by her grandmother. Although on stage by the age of seven, her teachers would not let her sing in the school choir because her voice was considered too deep — just like her near-contemporary, Anne Shelton. Nevertheless, she continued in show business as part of Madame Harris's "Kracker Kabaret Kids", a mouthful which caused her to change her name to Vera Lynn — her grandmother's maiden name.

Soon after leaving school she was heard by band leader Howard Baker who signed her as a crooner, and within 18 months she made her first record on 17th February, 1934. Called *It's Home* it was actually only a single Teledisk printing for the use of band leaders who wanted to try out a song cheaply. However, Vera made several anonymous recordings for the 8" discs sold by Woolworth's for sixpence before the war, and in August 1935 she recorded *Red Sails in the Sunset* with Joe Loss. Only a short time beforehand she had been taken on by Billy Cotton but he terminated her contract after only three days, saying she would never make the grade — at least that is the reason he gave, but perhaps he thought she might prove too popular — who knows?

After successfully auditioning for Charlie Kunz she was asked to sing for Bert Ambrose and the postal response was so great she was given a regular slot in his shows. By the time war broke out in September 1939 she had become a star and was able to afford a luxury she had always wanted — a house with an inside bathroom!

◁ Vera was married to Harry Lewis from 1941 until his death in 1998. Here they are with George Elrick, and his wife, Alice (left). In 1937 Harry was a member of the band loaned to George by Lew Stone, in order to keep the men employed while he was busy as musical director at the London Hippodrome for the Bobby Howes and Cicely Courtneidge show, "Hide and Seek".

⊲ *Vera Lynn as tens of thousands of servicemen still remember her — leading wartime community singing.*

Crosby. In November of the same year the BBC offered her a 30-minute radio programme called "Sincerely Yours — Vera Lynn". It proved so popular that she received more than 2,000 letters a week, many of which she answered by hand. By visiting maternity hospitals she was also able to pass on details of new arrivals to delighted fathers over the airwaves.

But not all the top brass approved and some thought the programme would undermine morale by causing homesickness among the troops. Some wives even thought Vera was carrying on with their husbands because she sent them signed photos! Most people took no notice, however, and ballads became her trademark. Actually a modest person, she regarded her success in a down-to-earth manner by saying "I just sang songs that were easily understood. I was never the sophisticated glamorous type, just an ordinary girl. They used to call me 'the girl next door' and that pleased me more than anything else."

Vera Lynn made three films and toured Burma with ENSA in 1944. She retired briefly when her daughter, Virginia, was born in 1946 but it was soon back to normal and she found new fame in Scandinavia with the Gracie Fields song *Wish Me Luck As You Wave Me Goodbye*, likewise in Holland with *Land of Hope and Glory* which sold a million copies and earned her a gold disc.

In 1940 she became engaged to Harry Lewis, then a saxophonist with Ambrose and soon to become a member of the Squadronaires. They married in 1941 and after she branched out into Variety, according to one newspaper, she began outselling the Mills Brothers and Bing

⊲ *Popular with the Royal Family, Vera was, understandably, a special favourite of the Queen Mother (below).*

Vera appeared at Servicemen's reunions until well into her 70s, and led the singing outside Buckingham Palace for the 50th anniversary of VE-Day in 1995.

In 1949 the BBC refused to renew her contract, saying she was "out-of-date" but she proved them wrong by having her best year ever with shows in London and New York, and broadcasts on Radio Luxembourg. Her recording of *Auf Wiederseh'n* with a chorus of servicemen also became another best-seller. When she became the first British singer to top the charts simultaneously on both sides of the Atlantic, she received many lucrative offers from America but, true to form, preferred to stay in England.

When a children's charity threw a surprise party for her, the Duke of Edinburgh heard about it and invited himself. In 1968 Vera was awarded the OBE and in 1975 was made a Dame of the British Empire. At 71 she became a Freeman of the City of London and the following year sang *The White Cliffs of Dover* on Harry Secombe's "Highway" television programme. It was Sunday, 3rd September, 1989, the 50th anniversary of the outbreak of war. Her fame had never waned. Not bad for a little London girl who once heard a fellow pantomime cast member say "She'll never get anywhere — she's too common!"

Husband, Harry, died in April 1998 but this did not stop Vera from fulfilling ex-servicemen's and other commitments. She never really went out of fashion and was a permanent fixture at wartime Remembrance Services in the Albert Hall right through to the end of the century. There in the audience were her adoring fans, all servicemen and women well into pensionable age.

Like Churchill, Vera was in the right place at the right time. Remarkably, she has carried on being in the right place ever since.

We'll meet again
Don't know where,
Don't know when,
But I know we'll meet again,
Some sunny day.

If those words cause a lump in your throat then you probably remember the last war — and Vera Lynn's reassuring voice at the height of Britain's greatest hour of destiny.

28

Cavan O'Connor
(1899-1997)

A bell rings in the theatre's bars and the intermission is over. The people hurry to their seats for the start of the second half which will feature the star of the show. The orchestra strikes up the opening bars of a tune that everyone knows because they have heard it so often before on the wireless ... and always sung by the same tenor voice. On to the stage strolls a man in open-necked shirt and corduroy trousers, with a battered trilby on his head and a jacket slung over his shoulder. He hardly has chance to sing the first few bars of the song before the entire house explodes with a roar of applause ...

I'm only a strolling vagabond,
So good night, pretty maiden,
goodnight.

It was, of course, the unmistakable voice and garb of Cavan O'Connor, the "Vagabond of Song", appearing at one of a string of provincial theatres just after the war.

It may come as a surprise to some that despite his Irish accent he was not born in Ireland but in the village of Carlton near Nottingham, on 1st July, 1899. His mother was

△ *Cavan O'Connor pictured as a student at the Royal College of Music*

English but his father, William O'Connor, was from Dublin. A painter by trade, Mr. O'Connor had a light tenor voice and a twinkle in his eye ... attributes he undoubtedly passed on to the youngest of his four children — Clarence Patrick being the boy's real name, later known to the world as Cavan. Queen Victoria was still on the throne when baby Cavan's lusty voice first woke the neighbours, long before the streets echoed with the news and celebrations of the Relief of Mafeking in May 1900.

Like many of his chums Cavan left school at 13 and went down the mines as a pit boy. Not liking that, however, he became a "lather boy" in a local barber's shop for half-a-crown a week before beginning an apprenticeship with a local printer. When the Great War was declared in August 1914, he volunteered for the Royal Navy, saying he was 17. But the Senior Service required a birth certificate to prove age during wartime so the 15-year-old had no chance of going afloat. He had set his heart on joining the Forces, however, and since the Recruiting Sergeant for the Royal Horse Artillery asked fewer questions, he was soon on his way to Flanders as a budding Gunner Signaller.

As a young soldier in khaki he often sang in makeshift Army concerts near the front, and after his demob decided to try for a career in singing. He won a four-year British Empire operatic scholarship to the Royal College of Music and in 1925 emerged to make his public debut at London's Old Vic. By then he had adopted the name of Cavan — a shortened version of Cavanagh which was the name of a friend. As he later explained, he could hardly enter show business with a name like Clarence!

Later the same year he made two Gilbert and Sullivan records for the Vocalion label on the strength of which he earned himself a twelve-month recording contract. By the following year he was in the chorus at the Royal Opera House, Covent Garden, singing in French, Italian and Spanish. He went on to appear in other London shows, mainly of a light classical nature such as John Gay's "The Beggar's Opera" at the Lyric, Hammersmith, and also appeared as a named singer in Viennese operetta at the famous Gaiety Theatre.

While at the RCM he fell in love with a fellow student, pretty Rita Tate, niece of opera singer Dame Maggie Teyte. After a three-year courtship they married in June 1929 and were blessed with three sons — Michael (a musician), Garry (a writer) and John (a landscape and portrait painter). They remained devoted to each other until Cavan's death in January 1997, a total of almost 68 years!

△ *The "Vagabond Lover" as he is best-remembered. On film or stage with an open-necked shirt, wearing a battered trilby hat and a coat slung over his arm.*

Operatic progress was somewhat slow so Cavan decided to broaden his horizons and amended his voice to accommodate dance band music. In the late-Twenties he recorded with Carroll Gibbons and the Savoy Orpheans, Ronnie Munro, Harry Bidgood and Jay Wilbur. By the Thirties he had appeared with many other top bands including Ambrose, Ray Noble, Debroy Somers, Jack Hylton, Sid Phillips, Bert and John Firman, Geraldo, Maurice Winnick and a whole host of lesser names. In addition, because of the rivalry between bands and different record labels, he also sang under a vast array of pseudonyms including Cliff Connolly on Rex records, Shaun Cassidy on Regal, and Alan O'Sullivan on Columbia.

In 1934 he was the vocalist for Fred Hartley's Novelty Quintet in a series of BBC weekly broadcasts although, under a ploy used by programme makers and record companies to keep their costs down, his name was not given. "Unknown" singers commanded a fee of two guineas (£2.10) but once they became recognised then their fee was doubled — hence a multitude of pseudonyms to stop a singer becoming too popular.

A year later came a turning point when Eric Maschwitz, then Head of Variety at the BBC, conceived the idea of a weekly programme featuring an anonymous singer called "The Vagabond Lover". The carefree gypsy-sounding fellow quickly won the hearts of listeners,

△ *Cavan topped the bill at theatres all over Britain in a career that lasted over 60 years. He didn't retire till he was 90!*

When asked the secret of his longevity and successful voice Cavan attributed it to a good wife, a good cigar, a sip or two of whisky, and practising his scales regularly every day. Out of all his 800 recordings he still enjoyed his signature tune which comes from an operetta where a person known simply as "The Stranger" visits an inn and is asked for his name by one of the local girls. He replies:

I'm only a strolling vagabond
So goodnight pretty maiden, goodnight.
I'm bound for the hills and the valleys beyond,
So goodnight pretty maiden, goodnight.
I follow Fortune that beckons me on
I catch at her skirts and the lady is gone,
But that's just my lot, if so right.
I'm only a strolling vagabond
So goodnight pretty maiden, goodnight.
Goodnight . . . goodnight . . .
Goodnight pretty maiden, goodnight.

Just before he died Cavan reflected on his life and recalled the days when he sang to deafening applause all around the country and abroad. Many is the time he also sang for charity, benefiting in particular London's Great Ormond Street Hospital for Children . . . and by his side was Rita, the lady who accompanied him on every footstep of his long vagabond journey.

particularly the ladies, but the BBC, with one eye on their costs, kept resolutely silent and refused all requests to identify him. A sharp-eared radio critic then blurted it out to the Press, however, and Cavan O'Connor became famous overnight. His picture soon appeared on the front cover of *Radio Pictorial* and he embarked on a nation-wide tour of the Moss Empire circuit. He also appeared in two films — a musical short called "Honeymoon Express" and a full-length 1936 Irish drama starring John Loder, called "Ourselves Alone".

During the war Cavan broadcast regularly from the BBC in Bristol until the studios were bombed out. That did not stop him, however, because along with "ITMA" he moved to Bangor in North Wales, where he appeared every week on the Jimmy O'Dea show "Irish Half Hour". When hostilities ceased he again took to the Variety circuit and topped the bill at many different northern theatres. Cavan also kissed the Blarney Stone but what happened to him in later life?

In 1974 he toured South Africa and New Zealand where he packed in the audiences at the age of 75. Fours years later he recorded a new LP, accompanied on the piano by his wife, Rita, long after their Golden Wedding! In 1982 he was still topping the bill at theatres as far apart as Eastbourne and North Shields — and even appeared on stage with Rita after his 90th Birthday! While celebrating their Diamond Wedding in 1989 they received a congratulatory telegram from the Queen, delivered by a motor cycle despatch rider!

▽ *Cavan O'Connor pictured at the age of 93, still wearing his old trilby hat and proudly showing the sheet music of the song which made him famous.*

Monte Rey

(1900-1982)

During the early-Thirties, Geraldo's orchestra was called the Gaucho Tango Band and so realistic were they, with slicked-back dark hair and Latin clothes that, following a Royal Variety Performance, the Prince of Wales (later the Duke of Windsor), addressed them in Spanish! When Geraldo explained that none of them could actually understand the language and admitted he was really a Londoner from the East End, he evoked the instant royal response: "The devil you are!" But Geraldo himself was once deceived in exactly the same way.

In 1933, desperate for a Spanish tenor to sing with his band in a forthcoming radio series called "Chateau de Madrid", he approached a lady friend for help. She said she knew just the person but also realised that if Geraldo was to  discover his true identity then he would never get the job. Quick as flash, she made up a name for the young Scotsman who was sitting next to her, and introduced him as "Monte Rey"! The ruse worked — for a time.

James Montgomery Fyfe was born in Lanarkshire on 5th October, 1900, but decided to adopt an extra "f" for stage purposes, thus giving him the same appellation as a distant cousin — Will Fyffe, the famous Scottish comedian — who also hailed from the Clan Macduff. Montgomery was his mother's maiden name but her son was to be remembered neither for that, nor for grand opera on which he had set his heart after becoming infatuated with Enrico Caruso while still only a teenager.

From early beginnings with the Glasgow Operatic Society he moved on to London where he met the Duchess of Montrose who was sufficiently impressed with his voice to sponsor

him for three years' training in Italy and Germany. He described Dresden as the most beautiful city he had ever seen but, like his fledgling operatic career, it was later reduced to ashes. When sudden illness robbed him of an opportunity to appear at the Monte Carlo Opera House, he returned instead to London and had his tonsils removed by a Harley Street surgeon. After his recovery, the doctor asked him to perform at his house where he was heard by a top Italian singing teacher who offered further operatic voice training for nothing. It was a fortuitous meeting.

Several engagements followed at society events and then one day he received a note from what he took to be an admirer, inviting him to tea with Lady Cunard. In fact the fan turned out to be a young singer called Vera Scott, with whom he got on extremely well. When she suggested they form a double-act he jumped at the idea and they subsequently performed with considerable success at several concerts and tea parties during the Thirties.

Vera's family was a wealthy one and it was their custom to dine at the Savoy Hotel where the Gaucho Tango Band was in residence. It was here that the pseudo-Romany band leader Gerald Bright was first introduced to would-be opera singer Montgomery Fyfe — or in show business parlance, Geraldo first met Monte Rey. The former — despite the totally false information he had been given — showed great interest in the latter and invited him for an audition the following day.

Snappily dressed in a black jacket, white waistcoat, pin-striped trousers, silk shirt and large cravat, and carrying a bowler hat and rolled umbrella, the newly-created Monte Rey arrived at the front entrance of the posh hotel and calmly announced himself. But the doorman was singularly unimpressed and simply replied "Round the back for the band". Monte was not put off, however, and being able to read music, comfortably performed the new song which Geraldo thrust in front of him. He was hired on the spot and immediately adopted his new but initially secret identity.

With a mixture of Scottish and fake foreign accent, Monte played the part to perfection — well, almost. For some time he got away with

RADIO PICTORIAL. April 9, 1937. No. 169. Registered at the G.P.O. as a Newspaper.

"DICTATORS OF THE AIR" Brilliant New Series
LUXEMBOURG—NORMANDY—LYONS :: OFFICIAL PROGRAMMES

RADIO PICTORIAL
THE MAGAZINE F

EVERY FRIDAY

3ᴰ

Monte REY

In April 1937, Monte Rey appeared on the front cover of Radio Pictorial, *the journal which publicised all the independent radio stations and programmes.*

the deception, but when he fluffed a note and let rip some choice language in his native tongue the Scottish drummer, Alec Ure, stared at him dolefully and said "I always knew you were a bloomin' Scot!" Nevertheless, because his first broadcast brought in so many interested enquiries, Monte Rey he became — and so he stayed for the remainder of his life.

His dapper appearance, operatic training and natural acting ability, meant that each time he went on stage he cut a dashing debonair image which his audiences simply adored. In his pocket he still carried a contract to appear with Sir Thomas Beecham in opera at the Old Vic but Geraldo knew he was on to a good thing and made sure that his new singer was well rewarded. Life was now such great fun that dance band singing became Monte's preferred option — at least for the time being.

Because he was never actually resident with Geraldo at the Savoy he was able to freelance with Joe Loss, but this often meant performing four shows a day — two with each band. Racing from one venue to the other between appearances, he was sometimes forced to change from his Latin gaucho clothes into a dinner jacket while still in the taxi — and then do exactly the opposite on the return journey! He also sang for bands led by Reg Edwards, Phil Green and Charles Shadwell, and even appeared in the "Ovaltineys" show on Radio Luxembourg. All of a sudden, at the end of 1934, Geraldo changed his image, stripped away his Spanish veneer and became a traditional dance band leader. Thus he no longer required a pseudo-Latin singer.

This caused only a minor glitch, however, because Monte's reputation was now so well-established that by the time war arrived he was a successful full-time ballad singer with Joe Loss. But in 1941 he married his wife, Maisie, who encouraged him to go it alone. Like many popular singers, he then went off to entertain the troops before embarking on a ten year solo career. Playing to packed houses throughout the United Kingdom, he wisely reserved each Sunday as a day of rest but gradually became aware that many previously well-known names were down on their luck. He thought hard about the future and accurately predicted a change in popular music which would not suit him.

Recognising that a famous artist is only as good as his last performance he abruptly retired in 1952, while still at the height of his fame. Then, acting on impulse rather than rationale,

he decided to make a clean break and destroyed everything he possessed — records, theatre bills, personal scrapbook, the lot — a decision he later bitterly regretted. Fortunately, his sister kept her own archives so at least something was salvaged.

So rapid was his disappearance from the limelight that for a time many people believed he had died. In fact he was living with his wife on the Isle of Arran in Scotland where the Duchess of Montrose had once promised him a home. He initially obtained work as a freight clerk on the pier where the ferry boats connect with Largs and Ardrossan, but then retired again to enjoy the quiet and solitude which only an island setting can bring. After 16 years virtually cut off from the outside world, his wife suffered a stroke and in 1971 they decided to return home to Galleywood near Chelmsford in Essex, where they had once bred dogs on a small farm. This time they moved into more modest surroundings in a sheltered old peoples' complex where, with his wife making what he described as "a miraculous recovery", Monte was very happy.

Still looking remarkably young for his age, he died in August, 1982, leaving behind a legacy of almost 200 records, of which his signature tune *Donkey Serenade*, is perhaps the most famous. His life had been an eventful one, but had it not been for the quick-thinking of a young lady at the Savoy Hotel then "Monte Rey" would never have existed.

While singing with Geraldo, Monte bred show dogs and is seen here with two pet schnauzers.

Anne Shelton (1923-1994)

Pat Sibley — born in November, 1923 — had such an unusually deep voice at school in Dulwich, south London, that her teachers refused to let her sing in the choir — just like Vera Welch in north London a few years earlier — and Kathleen Ferrier in Lancashire a few years before that. Pat later became Anne Shelton and Vera later became Vera Lynn. They also became good wartime friends despite persistent rumours to the contrary. Meanwhile, Kathleen Ferrier became perhaps the greatest classical contralto of the 20th century.

Pat's mature voice was heard by Billy Ternent who invited her to sing with Jack Hylton's band, of which he was then deputy leader. So in January 1936, accompanied by her mother and still wearing her school gym-slip, Pat turned up at the studio to record *Moanin' Minnie*, just two months after her 12th birthday! Soon after leaving school she appeared as a "discovery" on BBC's "Monday Night at Eight" where she was heard by Ambrose. He immediately invited the now 16-year-old to join him at the Mayfair Hotel and in no time at all — as Anne Shelton — she became a wartime favourite of Winston Churchill, Bing Crosby, Glenn Miller and millions of servicemen.

Anne's deep voice eventually became unmistakable, but not before a soldier wrote to Ambrose complimenting him on his new "male" vocalist! He received a signed photograph of Anne by return!

Her popularity earned her a BBC programme of her own. Entitled "Introducing Anne", it ran for four years and was very popular overseas. A special weekend programme, "Calling Malta", proved a great morale booster when the small island was under attack by Hitler, and in 1942, when the King awarded the island the George Cross, Anne was one of the first to congratulate them.

Wartime saw several unusual incidents and also practical jokes. Once, Anne got locked in the ladies' room when she was due on air and after nobody heard her cries for help, she climbed out of the window and arrived somewhat unkempt. The announcer apparently made the most of the situation! On another occasion a stage-hand told her that Bing Crosby wanted to see her at the All-Services Club. Anne's response was "Tell him I can't come because I'm going to have tea with the King". Eventually she was persuaded it was not a joke and when they finally met, the great American crooner expressed great surprise at her youth.

Churchill described her voice as "warm and compelling" while Glenn Miller said she was the only suitable British singer for his band. He invited her to join him on his fateful flight to Paris, but fortunately she had to decline for contractual reasons. What happened to the plane is still a matter for conjecture, but Anne retained a lasting memory in the form of a solid gold bracelet which Glenn said matched her "pure gold" voice. Ambrose was a great encouragement and trained her to sing *My Yiddishe Momme* — which she once performed in Hitler's private theatre in Hamburg! Her other big wartime hits were *Lilli Marlene* and *Coming In On a Wing and a Prayer*. Meanwhile, the proceeds from *I Don't Want to Walk Without You* all went to the Merchant Navy's comfort fund and she worked with charitable organisations for the rest of her life.

In 1945 Anne went solo and on her 25th birthday, 10th November 1948, she recorded a

Entertainment during World War Two

△ George Formby (above) was a huge star and was helped on the way to stardom by the backing of Jack Hylton's band on his early records and films. His saucy lyrics and cheeky humour endeared him to all troops. Gracie Fields (above right) had a cheerful temperament and a truly magnificent voice but having an Italian husband was difficult, so Churchill advised her to go abroad and "earn dollars" for the war effort.

△ Singing during wartime was as natural as making a cup of tea for someone in need. "ENSA" stood for "Entertainments National Service Association" and quickly boasted many top stars among its ranks, despite some claims that it actually stood for "Every night something awful". Many entertainers were already in the Services and so a second organisation was formed called "Stars in Battledress". A great many singers toured the globe giving their services free and both George Formby and Gracie Fields covered huge mileages in both hemispheres and across several continents. They, and others like them, contributed a great deal to successful Services morale.

◁ Anne Shelton — like her friend Vera Lynn — was regarded by the top brass as one of Britain's secret weapons. Both had radio programmes of their own and one of Anne's was broadcast specially for the benefit of the tiny but strategically important Mediterranean island of Malta. When King George VI awarded it — and the two neighbouring islands of Gozo and Comino — the George Cross (hence the appropriate appellation "Malta G.C."), Anne was one of the first to congratulate them over the airwaves. Here she is seen with Ronald Shiner planning a wartime broadcast.

duet with Vera Lynn. Touring in Britain was succeeded in 1950 by a tour of America, and in 1956 she had a big hit with *Lay Down Your Arms*. But the advent of new electronic music made it harder to find suitable material and like most of her kind, she faded from the public eye. Nevertheless, she continued to entertain at charity concerts and ex-servicemen's reunions and in 1989 appeared with the New Squadronaires.

In 1990 she lost both her husband of 37 years, Lt.-Commander David Reid, and also her sister and secretary, Jo. Ironically, the same year she was awarded the OBE for services to charity. Always a large lady, Anne latterly found difficulty with her weight and died from a heart attack on 31st July, 1994, aged 70. Like Vera Lynn, she had been a great inspiration during the war and was fondly remembered by all who knew and heard her.

△ *Anne Shelton appeared on the front of many sheet music covers like these.*

Dance Band Vocalists

**means the person was pictured in Volume One of
This Englands' Book of Bristish Dance Bands
*means the person was mentioned in the text
of Volume One

Lou Abelardo* — American who came to England in 1929 and as well as making some records under his own name, sang and recorded with Ambrose, Van Phillips, Debroy Somers, Ray Starita and Jay Wilbur. He returned home two years later.

Tony Adaire — Recorded with Gerry Moore during the late-Thirties.

Don Adams — Made a small number of wartime recordings with Billy Thorburn.

Gerald Adams — Also a singer of more serious music he recorded some dance records with Stan Greening and the Edison house label orchestra during the Twenties.

Bill Airey-Smith (1901-1982) — Barnsley-born drummer-vocalist with several bands, including Alfredo, Marius B. Winter, Howard Jacobs, Edgar Jackson, Harold Ramsay's Rhythm Symphony Orchestra and, during the war, Ben Frankel. Ran his own group at night clubs during the Thirties and Forties. Later worked for the Crazy Gang at the Victoria Palace before retiring to become a publican.

Wynne Ajello (died 1992) — Perhaps better-known as a more serious soprano-cum-variety artiste she recorded a couple of records for Panachord and also on the early-Thirties cardboard Durium label. Ill-health cut short her career at the start of the war.

Chesney Allen — (see Flanagan & Allen).

Jill Allen — Sang with Sid Phillips during the late-Forties and early-Fifties and also appeared with Maurice Winnick. In 1949 she sang in the Jack Warner and Kathleen Harrison film "Vote for Huggett".

Jimmy Allen — Recorded with several early-Thirties bands including Percy Chandler, Arthur Rosebery, Jerry Hoey, Jack Leon, Jock McDermott and Allan Selby. He later sang with Billy Thorburn's wartime group The Organ, The Dance Band and Me.

Judy Allen — (see Judy Dean).

Les Allen** — (1902-1996) Extremely popular singer who went freelance after joining Henry Hall in the early-Thirties, during which time his good looks and the band's charisma produced more than 50,000 items of fan mail in less than two years! Performed with numerous different bands as well as running his own group, releasing hundreds of records both as a soloist and band member. Born in London but brought up in Canada, he returned to England during the late-Twenties where he spent the next 20 years before finally settling in Toronto. In 1954 he came over for a reunion with Henry Hall and the BBC Dance Orchestra.

Rose Alper — Recorded with Joe Loss in 1938 under the name "Violett".

Dorothy Alt — (see Dorothy Ault).

Vicki Anderson — Sang with the short-lived Courtley-Seymour band during the mid-Fifties.

Joan Anderson — Sang with Teddy Foster, Edmundo Ros, Harold Geller and Nat Allen.

Bob Arden — Real name Monty Sharpe. While still only a teenager he made several wartime recordings with Joe Loss after Chick Henderson left to join the Navy. Later became an actor and appeared in several films.

Phil Arnold — Prolific American freelance vocalist of the late-Twenties, recording with many bands, including Jay Whidden, Ambrose,

Les Allen

Harry Bidgood, George Fisher, Harry Hudson, Percival Mackey, Carroll Gibbons, Debroy Somers, Ray Starita and Jay Wilbur.

Tony Arnold — (see Paul Vaughan).

Gerry Arthur — Trombonist and vocalist with Herman Darewski, Savoy Hotel Orpheans and during the war with Jack Payne.

Robert Ashley — Better-known as a ballad singer but also recorded with Louis Levy. Began his cine-variety career at the Paramount Cinema, Tottenham Court Road in January 1937.

Dorothy Ault (born 1917) — Canadian who make her mark during a brief stay in England during 1939 when she recorded with Jay Wilbur and Lew Stone, usually billed as Dorothy Alt. She also appeared on television with Eric Wild's Teatimers, the first regular dance band to feature on the small screen. Retired back to Canada.

Fred Austin — Recorded with Debroy Somers during the late-Twenties.

Bachelor Girls — Formed in 1944 the original members were Rita Williams, Maria Perilli and Donna la Bourdais. Maria and Rita were soon replaced by Paula Green and Elva Sloane.

Max Bacon — Drummer and vocalist with Ambrose and Ronnie Munro and also sang with the Blue Mountaineers. Appeared in the film *King Arthur Was a Gentleman* and toured in a variety act with Sam Browne and Mary Naylor.

George Baker (1885-1976) — Hugely famous as a Gilbert and Sullivan baritone for more than 50 years and especially renowned for his rendering of the "patter" songs, he also recorded several records with various dance bands, including Jack Hylton, Arthur Lally, Joe Loss, Ray Noble, Carroll Gibbons, and Debroy Somers.

George Barclay** (1911-1989) — A farmer's son from Aberdeen who sang with Arthur Mouncey before coming south to London with Archie Alexander's band during the early-Thirties, later recording with Mantovani, Charlie Kunz, Felix Mendelssohn, Victor Silvester, Harry Leader and Billy Thorburn. He also broadcast with Alf van Straten, Lou Preager and Ronnie Munro. Quiet in manner and speech, partly because people could not initially understand his broad Scottish accent, HMV nicknamed him the "Shy Singer". He successfully deputised for an ailing Harry Bentley with Charlie Kunz's orchestra at the Casani Club but occasionally ran into difficulties because Archie Alexander refused to release him from his binding contract, demanding excessive payments from other band leaders who wanted to utilise his talents. After Felix Mendelssohn died in 1952 George and his wife ran a pub before retiring to a quieter life in Peckham, south London.

Kenny Bardell (born 1927) — Sang with Ken Mackintosh for more than 20 years and also played saxophone in the band. One of many singers who broadcast on Radio Luxembourg.

△ *George Barclay — minus his usual spectacles.*

Dorothee Baronne (born 1926) — Replaced Doreen Stephens at the Squadronaires in 1948 and later sang with Ted Heath, Eddie Carroll and Harry Parry.

Tom Barratt — One of the most prolific and popular singers of the Twenties and early-Thirties who recorded an enormous number of records. Some were with unnamed house recording bands but others included Alfredo, Bertini, Harry Bidgood, Stan Greening, Jack Harris, Tommy Kinsman, Arthur Lally, Jock McDermott, Percival Mackey, Pete Mandell, Ronnie Munro, Cecil Norman, Sir Robert Peel, Jan Ralfini, Carroll Gibbons, Debroy Somers, Nat Star, Ray Starita, Hal Swain and Jay Wilbur. Also recorded under the name Tom Bailey and took part in several West End musicals. His first solo record was made in 1914 and his last in 1933. A somewhat mysterious figure who is believed to have died in Liverpool.

Elizabeth (Betty) Batey* (born 1920) — A Geordie from South Shields she sang during the war with Jack Payne then joined Joe Loss until she fractured her jaw in a fall. She was hurriedly replaced by Rose Brennan and although she stayed another six months after her recovery "Betty" then left to join Eric Winstone. Her next appearance was with her husband Harry Bence but the initial band was financially unsuccessful so she joined Harry Leader instead, later rejoining her husband when he restarted in Scotland.

Joan Baxter — In 1948 she won a talent contest and, as the "Golden Voice of Butlin's", accompanied Leslie Douglas at Filey, accompanying him to Southport the following year. She later appeared with the Blue Rockets and sang on radio.

Eve Becke** (born 1910) — Originally a pianist she was a very popular singer during the Thirties and recorded with Roy Fox, Geraldo, Jack Hylton, Charlie Kunz, Sydney Kyte, Louis Levy, Bram Martin, Ray Noble, Oscar Rabin and Jay Wilbur. She also broadcast with Carroll Gibbons from the Savoy Hotel. Initially active in cabaret as a torch singer, with the spotlight following her around as she sang, she was sometimes described as the girl with "it" in her voice. Eve's glamorous wardrobe was designed by her brother, the famous dress designer, Colin Becke. Her career suddenly changed in most unusual circumstances, however. Young Italian Count Eugenio Ugo Caneva di Rivarolo heard her singing on his radio in Milan and was immediately entranced. He later recognised her voice while at a party during a visit to London and an introduction ultimately resulted in their wedding on New Year's Day, 1935, following which she cut back her travelling to concentrate on broadcasting and filming in London. The war years were spent in Italy but Eugenio was sadly killed at Messina in 1944, aged only 34. On cessation of hostilities Eve returned to the UK where she broadcast with Louis Levy and Geraldo, and also went on tour with Jack Hulbert's organisation. She remained in London after her retirement and lived near Regent's Park.

△ *Betty Batey*

Billy Bell — Primarily a banjo, guitar and bass player with Bert and John Firman, and with Nat Star but also took the occasional vocal.

Marie Benson — Australian Marie Hariett came to England after the war and made a small number of Dixieland style recordings.

Dick Bentley (1907-1995) — After arriving from Australia in 1938 he made a record with Phil Green's orchestra before launching into a successful radio career culminating in the show "Take It From Here" with Jimmy Edwards and Joy Nichols. "Oh, Ron?" "Yes, Eth?"

Harry Bentley** (1900-1935) — Initially a drummer who originated from London's Docklands, he became a top vocalist of the early-Thirties but after his premature death from pneumonia hit the newspaper headlines, he became a largely forgotten figure. He made his name with Al Starita, Jay Wilbur, Tommy Kinsman, Oscar Rabin, Carroll Gibbons, Jack Harris, Nat Star and Charlie Kunz. He also recorded with several smaller bands but the most unusual occasion was when a desperate Billy Merrin rang and asked him to deputise immediately for Sam Browne whose voice had just given up in the middle of a recording session. Harry arrived by taxi – still dressed in his pyjamas! His real name was Harry Silverman.

Len Bermon — Drummer and vocalist with Henry Hall's BBC Dance Orchestra. Briefly led his own band at the Café de Paris in 1939 but post-war went into theatrical management.

Peter Bernard — Sang during the Twenties with Alfredo, Teddy Brown, Stan Greening and the Savoy Orpheans.

△ *When she married — in extraordinary circumstances on New Year's Day, 1935 — Eve Becke became Countess Caneva di Rivarolo. Sadly, he was killed during the war, nine years after this picture was taken.*

Gino Berni — Guitarist and vocalist with Geraldo's Gaucho Tango Band during the early-Thirties.

Anita Best — Wartime recording artist with Billy Ternent.

Harry Bentley died young

△ *The Beverley Sisters with Jack Payne during a break in rehearsals from his "Off the Record" television programme during the mid-Fifties.*

Beverley Sisters — Joy (born 1929), and the twins Teddy and Babs (born 1932), were perhaps the most successful ever British close-harmony singing group. Denny Dennis discovered them playing troop concerts while still young teenagers and knew a good thing when he heard one (or three!). He failed to persuade them to back him on tour in 1945 but Eric Winstone successfully influenced then to turn professional the following year. Surprisingly, they did not record until 1951 by which time their solo career was well under way and the dance band era beginning to wane.

Eva Beynon (born 1925) — Blonde Eva from Wales joined Henry Hall in 1943 while still a teenager and toured with him for four years. She then joined Nat Allen and Billy Ternent, broadcasting with the latter and staying until 1954.

Blue Notes — Vocal trio which recorded with Joe Loss during the late-Thirties.

Betty Bolton (born 1906) — Made her first stage appearance as a child during the First World War and was involved with the early experimental television transmissions of John Logie Baird. She later made many appearances on "Children's Hour", as an assistant to Derek McCulloch (Uncle Mac) and, during the Twenties and Thirties, made several dance band recordings with Van Phillips, Roy Fox, Sid Phillips, Al and Ray Starita, George Scott-Wood, Spike Hughes and Jay Wilbur.

Betty Bolton

42

Harry Bolton — Sang and recorded with Syd Dean during the early-Fifties.

Margaret Bond — Sang as a schoolgirl at the Streatham Locarno Ballroom and was then offered a contract by Harry Roy. Broadcast 16 times before she reached the same age and later appeared with Nat Temple, Ronnie Scott and the Squadronaires.

Issy Bonn (1903-1977) — Later a top comedian specialising in Jewish humour, his real name was Benny Levin and he was packed off to Canada by his father to prevent him from entering show business! When his father died, however, he returned immediately to England and began singing with Percival Mackey's band in the late-Twenties. He also joined a group called the Three Rascals and performed alongside Teddy Brown the huge American xylophone player and band leader.

Webster Booth (1902-1984) — Better-known for his ballad-singing duet role with wife Anne Ziegler, he also recorded separately with Ambrose, Jack Hylton, Ray Noble, Hugo Rignold and, jointly with Anne, for Carroll Gibbons. He also appeared on the early-Thirties cardboard label, Durium.

Issy Bonn disobeyed his father!

Eve Boswell* (1924-1998) — Eva Keleti was born into a Hungarian musical family which toured the world. In South Africa she sang with Roy Martin's band before marrying and coming to England where she joined Geraldo before launching into a hugely successful solo career.

Suzanne Botterell* (born 1913) — Well-known singing star of the Thirties who recorded with Al Collins, Lew Stone and Carroll Gibbons. She was also a dancer, pianist and composer who penned *Goodbye to Summer*. In 1938, together with Gaby Rogers and Harry Phillips, she formed a singing group called "Sue and Her Boy Friends".

Donna la Bourdais — (see Rhythm Sisters and Bachelor Girls).

Al Bowlly** — (see separate chapter).

△ *Susanne Botterell and Harry Phillips were both well-known radio singers and composers. Harry sang with Joe Loss, Bram Martin and Al Collins while Suzanne's songs included "I Need You", "Farewell to Heaven", "Goodbye to Summer" and "Here Am I".*

△ *Eve Boswell*

△ Kathie Kay and Alan Breeze singing "Any Old Iron?" from a 1963 "Billy Cotton Band Show". "Old Breezy" originally trained as an opera singer but changed genres and served his new boss for 40 years. Their eventual parting was extremely painful for them both, however. The Silhouettes form a colourful and glamorous background.

Franklyn Boyd (born 1925) — Won the 1941 All-Britain Crooning Championship on the strength of which he joined Harry Leader at the Hammersmith Palais. Toured post-war with Teddy Foster and also sang with Eric Winstone, Paul Fenoulhet, Kathy Stobart and Oscar Rabin. After going into music publishing, he briefly managed Cliff Richard. Later emigrated to Canada.

Eddie (Ted) Brandt — Late-Twenties vocalist with Ambrose, Harry Bidgood, Jack Harris, Van Phillips, Al and Ray Starita and Jay Wilbur.

Hazel Bray — Recorded with Eric Winstone during the war.

Bobby Breen (born 1927) — Originally an American boy soprano who appeared with Eddie Cantor. After coming to Britain he sang with Billy Ternent, Tony Crombie and Johnny Dankworth.

Alan Breeze** (1909-1980) — "Old Breezy" as Billy Cotton affectionately called him, served his boss for 40 years, a remarkable period of time, especially when one considers that Alan was initially trained for classical opera. It was ironic that after years of fun and frolics, often uncomplainingly being on the receiving end of Bill's acerbic Cockney humour, it was Billy Cotton Jr., then Head of BBC Light Entertainment, who decided that Alan was too old for the "Billy Cotton Band Show" on television. It was said that both he and Billy Sr. separately went home and cried — but the show went on for a time without him, until Billy's sudden death at the ringside of a boxing match finally rang down the curtain for both of them. In private life Alan owned a farm where his only son was tragically killed in a tractor accident.

Rose Brennan* — Initially spotted in Ireland by Roy Fox where she joined Billy Watson's band in Dublin and, after he heard her on a radio broadcast in 1951, was invited by Joe Loss to replace Elizabeth Batey who had just broken her jaw. Rose proved extremely popular and stayed on after Elizabeth recovered, eventually completing an unbroken 15-year spell.

Rose Brennan

Gloria Brent (1917-1998) — As Gladys Rae she sang with Howard Baker, thanks to an introduction effected by her north London neighbour Norrie Paramor, who had heard her sing with her brother's band. Harry Leader later bought out her contract and she married his pianist, a certain Norrie Paramor. She later went on to sing with Billy Gerhardi, Jay Wilbur, Teddy Joyce, Jack Harris, Billy Ternent, Jack Jackson, Bert Firman, Jack Payne, Bram Martin, Eric Winstone and Glenn Miller, before becoming a post-war solo act.

Gerry Brereton (born 1921) — Professional footballer for both Stockport and Derby County before he was blinded by an exploding shell while serving with the Commandos in Sicily during 1943. Having been a juvenile singing prodigy, after his hospitalisation he decided to try his luck as a professional and successfully auditioned for the Billy Ternent touring band. He later performed with Ken Turner in Derby, Charles Hennessy in his home town of Stockport and Tommy Smith in Oldham, before moving to the metropolis where he became extremely successful, appearing in a Royal Command performance and also recording for Parlophone and Columbia. Wartime marriage to his nurse, Kay, resulted in their Golden Wedding in 1993.

Bobbie Britton — Michael Day first performed during the early-Fifties with Charles Shadwell before auditioning to replace Dickie Valentine in Ted Heath's band. Ted recognised the potential of Michael's voice and changed his name, thereafter announcing him as "The voice of Britain (Britton)"!

Abe Bronson — Recorded with the Savoy Havana band during the mid-Twenties.

Elizabeth Brooke** — Alias Princess Pearl of Sarawak who married Harry Roy in a glamorous wedding in 1935. She also made a number of recordings with her husband's band.

Bob Brown — (see Debonaires & Stargazers).

Georgia Brown (1933-1992) — Unmistakable husky-voiced jazz singer with Harry Gold and his Pieces of Eight and later with Ted Heath, she went on to become an international solo star, particularly outstanding as Nancy in Lionel Bart's initial stage production of "Oliver". As Lionel Begleiter and Lillian Klot they had actually grown up together in London's East End.

Sam Browne** — (see separate chapter).

Rannyel Bryan — (see Jackdauz).

Eddie Bryant — Recorded with Sydney Lipton during 1939/40.

Gloria Brent

Beryl Bryden (1920-1998) — A great extrovert in a predominantly man's world, Beryl's washboard playing and singing during the early post-war traditional jazz boom became almost legendary. She appeared with several different British bands, including Freddy Randall, George Webb, and John Haim, plus the Dutch Swing College and Graeme Bell's Australian Jazz Band. On occasions she also led her own group, and was the washboard player on the famous *Rock Island Line*, sung by Lonnie Donegan accompanied by Chris Barber's Skiffle Group.

△ A teenage Beryl Bryden, destined to become Britain's "Queen of the Washboard".

George Buck — Vocalist with Harry Bidgood, Billy Cotton, Harry Hudson, Charlie Kunz, Ray Noble, and the Savoy Hotel Orpheans.

Sid Buckman* (1906-1981) — Instrumentalist and vocalist with several bands, notably Roy Fox but also with Billy Ternent, Jack Hylton and Billy Cotton.

Betty Bucknelle — (see The Three Sisters).

Ray Burns — Post-war singer with Ambrose's new band.

Terry Burton (born 1933) — She sang initially with Percy Pease and Phil Moss before hitting the big-time with the NDO (Northern Dance Orchestra) and the BBC Show Band.

Bob Busby — Joined Jack Payne and the BBC Dance Orchestra in 1928 and stayed until 1933 when he and some other members of the band formed their own group called the Barnstormers. He joined Teddy Joyce in 1934 and later became a famous light music composer.

△ *Four stars from 1939 — from top left clockwise: Ann Canning, Dorothy Carless, Ronnie Hill and Dick Bentley. Although Bentley initially came over here from Australia as a singer, he soon branched out into comedy and became famous with Jimmy Edwards in the post-war BBC Light Programme "Take It From Here". Also in the series were Alan Dean, the Keynotes, Joy Nichols and Alma Cogan.*

Sheila Buxton (1931-1994) — Before becoming a big solo star she first sang with Phil Phillips in north Manchester and then graduated to resident vocalist with the BBC Northern Dance Orchestra under Alyn Ainsworth.

Len Camber — Sang with Geraldo from the war period onwards. Surprisingly, together with Lew Stone's blind singer Peter Gray, his voice was considered temporarily unsuitable for broadcasting during wartime itself — a ban which was rescinded after a public outcry. Later sang in a touring double act with Terry Devon.

Don Cameron — A former member of the popular Morton Fraser Harmonica Gang he sang for several years with Ken Mackintosh.

▷ *Small, close-harmony groups were extremely popular during the Twenties and Thirties and later inspired the Beverley Sisters to great things during the Fifties. The Carlyle Cousins were formed by three friends at music school and were big names until they disappeared without trace in 1939. Six different singers made up the group at various times and this picture shows from left to right: Helen Thornton, Cecile Petrie (the founder, leader and ever-present) and pianist Lilian Taylor. Helen and Cecile were sisters. The Second World War proved a turning point for many entertainers and a sizeable number of singers simply decided not to take up the reigns again after hostilities ceased.*

Billie Campbell — Sang with Hatchett's Swingtette and Johnny Clae's Clay Pigeons during the war and also recorded with Harry Leader, Jack Payne, Primo Scala and Carroll Gibbons.

Jean Campbell (born 1926) — Sang with Cyril Stapleton and was also a member of the Keynotes and Mike Sammes Singers who broadcast regularly on the radio. She made several records and broadcast with Harry Roy, Felix King and Harry Leader.

Ann Canning — (see The Radio Three).

Les Carew — Trombonist with Jack Hylton and Ambrose who occasionally popped up as a vocalist on novelty numbers.

Dave Carey (born 1925) — Sang with Lew Stone while still only 16, then with Tim Clayton before replacing Bob Dale in Cyril Stapleton's Orchestra. There his talents led to him becoming a member of the famous Stargazers close-harmony group.

Dorothy Carless** (see also Cavendish Three) — Initially a pianist she became an extremely popular pre-war singer and broadcaster, and also recorded with several bands, including Ray Noble. In 1939 she married Eugene Pini and honeymooned in France just before hostilities commenced. Apart from making many wartime records, including more than 50 with Geraldo, she also toured with ENSA. After remarrying she emigrated to America but did return briefly during the Fifties. Older sister of Carole Carr.

Elsie Carlisle** — (see separate chapter).

Carlyle Cousins — Highly-talented female trio formed in 1930, consisting initially of "Three Little Maids from School" (actually the Royal Academy of Music) — founder Cecile Petrie ("Trissie" Thornton), Pauline Lister and Lilian Taylor (pianist). They made recordings with several bands including Ambrose, Sydney Baynes, Eddie Carroll, Harry Hudson, Charlie Kunz, the Savoy Hotel Orpheans, Debroy Somers, and Jay Wilbur. Various changes of personnel took place before the group folded after the outbreak of war in 1939. Helen "Tinker" Thornton (Cecile's sister) replaced Pauline Lister and later additions included Gladys Chapelle and Glenys Evans. Although absent for a considerable time through illness, the leader throughout was Cecile Petrie, who changed her maiden name of Thornton to that of her famous actor cousin, Hay Petrie. She also sang separately with Carroll Gibbons's Savoy Orpheans. Lilian Taylor really was a cousin to the Thorntons. All six vocalists subsequently disappeared from the scene and have never been heard of since! One wonders whatever happened to them all?

Paul Carpenter (1921-1964) — A Canadian who sang with Bob Farnon's AEF wartime band before appearing with Frank Weir, Carroll Gibbons and Paul Adam. Post-war he joined Ted Heath where his excellent diction (he played Jeff Arnold in the popular radio series "Riders of the Range") saw him compering as well as singing. He later became an actor and minor film star.

Carole Carr* (1928-1997) — It was big sister Dorothy Carless who first recommended Betty (as she then was) to Jack Payne. Despite having an untrained voice she successfully auditioned and never looked back, moving on to Geraldo while still a teenager, and soon becoming a firm favourite on both radio and television. Gifted with the ability to read and sing a new tune with no rehearsal she was much in demand and was the first girl singer to appear on television after the war. She appeared with many different bands, including Mantovani and Syd Lawrence and late in her career teamed up for a second time with Geraldo. She had her own television programmes during the Fifties and also entertained the troops during the Korean War. After retiring to Devon she occasionally came back up to London to perform on the radio with Syd Lawrence and Nelson Riddle.

Pearl Carr — In 1944, while singing with Phil Green's band, she met her future husband, drummer-vocalist Teddy Johnson whom she married 11 years later and with whom she formed a world-famous singing partnership. Their most well-known song was *Sing Little Birdie*, which came second in the 1959 Eurovision Song Contest. Prior to international fame she also sang with Leslie Douglas, Cyril Stapleton, Nat Temple, Robert Farnon, Malcolm Lockyer and Stanley Black.

Rita Carr — Sang with Lou Preager and Lew Stone.

Carson Sisters — Marie (died 1997) and her younger sister Laura formed an act initially known as Sisters in Harmony. Later, as the Carson Sisters, they made several records including one with Sam Browne and the Ambrose orchestra in 1931. They also sang with Sydney Lipton and both became Mrs. Greenspan when they married two brothers!

Harry Case — Guitarist and vocalist who recorded with Joe Loss during the Thirties.

Kay Cavendish — (see also The Radio Three & Cavendish Three) (1910-2000) — Originally a classical pianist known as Kathleen Murray she became a popular pre-war singer with Lew Stone but is perhaps better-remembered for her contributions to three close-harmony groups - The Six of Us, the Radio Three and The Cavendish Three. Her later solo career as pianist and singer began when a chance wartime recording at the BBC brought her a record-breaking show she called "Kay on the Keys". It ran for more than 400 performances featuring her signature tune, *Kitten on the Keys*.

△ *Carole Carr*

A prolific performer for ENSA, she travelled more than 10,000 miles across Europe and the Mediterranean and, during the highly successful post-war years, appeared on both radio and television. She explained her love of all kinds of music as follows: "Most lovers of classical music close their ears to jazz and vice versa. What starts as ignorance becomes prejudice and passes into snobbery. By linking together in my programmes two extreme aspects of music, I hope to break down some of this prejudice."

Cavendish Three — Late-Thirties close harmony group consisting of Kay Cavendish, Pat Rignold (sister of band leader Hugo Rignold), and Joy Worth (later replaced by Dorothy Carless), who appeared on Radio Luxembourg and recorded with Jay Wilbur and George Scott-Wood's Six Swingers.

Sylvia Cecil — Sang and recorded with Ambrose, Eddie Carroll and Jay Wilbur.

Mary Charles — Recorded with Lew Stone during the early-Thirties.

Harold "Chips" Chippendall* (1909-1999) — Born in the Everton area of Liverpool, Harold Chippendall later changed his name to Chipppendale. His mother was always known as "Mrs. Chips" so her "chip off the old block" naturally gained the same title. Worked as a local Co-op grocer before singing with Wilf Hamer's band, often duetting with the leader's wife, Mary. While performing in Nottingham he was recommended to Billy Cotton, with whom he toured for 18 months. He then appeared with Sydney Lipton, Jack Harris, Carroll Gibbons and Debroy Somers before being called up in 1944, when he performed with Archie McCulloch in Glasgow. After hostilities ceased he returned to Liverpool and appeared with Mary Hamer, who had taken over her husband's band after he died suddenly in 1936. He then joined the Cliff Adams Singers and appeared with the BBC Show Band before officially retiring to Devon, where he became resident singer at the Balmoral Hotel, Torquay. Father of singer Toni Eden.

Wendy Claire (also spelt Clare) (born 1919-1966) — Thirties and wartime singer with Harry Roy and Lew Stone. When she was selected to tour South Africa with the former, her father's employer gave his iron foundry a day's holiday in celebration! Once married to Stanley Black.

Diana Clare — (see Esther Coleman).

Helen Clare (born 1916) — Bradford-born redhead who went to Australia as a child, returning home in her teens. After being spotted on a North Region radio broadcast she sang with many bands during the Thirties. Initially with Conri Tait at the Grand Hotel, Harrogate, she moved to London where she hit the big time with Billy Thorburn, Van Phillips, Carroll Gibbons and Jack Jackson. During the Fifties she was a regular on the radio programme "Songs from the Shows".

△ In 1938 Roy Fox's "Young Ladies" consisted of dancer Audrey Foster (left), "Glamour Girl" Primrose — actually Primrose Orrock (centre) — and the 17-year-old "veteran" singer, Mary Lee. Primrose Orrock later married band leader and saxophonist, Harry Hayes.

△ The Cavendish Three rehearsing in the bathroom! Pat Rignold (left) and Joy Worth survey the music and also the soap-suds in which Kay Cavendish is relaxing.

Brian Clark — Sang with Teddy Foster and was highly-rated by the *Melody Maker* which considered him to have great talent.

Petula Clark (born 1932) — Before her meteoric rise to fame as a child actor and popular singer, she began band singing at the tender age of just eight.

Norma Clarke (born 1924) — Only 4 feet tall she sang with Jack White and his Collegians at the Astoria Dance Salon both before and during the war. She later kept a hotel at Worksop in Nottinghamshire, the town of her birth.

June Clyde (born 1909) — Popular American singer, dancer, actress and film star who came to England in 1934 and appeared in several dance band and musical films including Jack Hylton's "She Shall Have Music", Buddy Rogers' "Dance Band" and "Let's Make a Night of It", "Charing Cross Road" and "Land Without Music". She also recorded with Billy Cotton

Archie Coates — Post-war singer with Felix Mendelssohn's Hawaiian Serenaders.

△ *Two very different types of singer but Tommy Handley and Peggy Cochrane were both true professionals.*

Peggy Cochrane** (1902-1988) — An infant prodigy who grew into an extremely versatile young lady capable of singing in several different languages. She was also a pianist, composer, actress and dancer. Played in Jack Jackson's 1934 Dorchester Hotel band then, in 1940, secretly married Jack Payne. When he returned to her in later life — after estrangement — a broken and bankrupt man following a series of unsuccessful ventures, she nursed him until his death in 1969. In between times she was resident entertainer at London's Charing Cross Hotel and, after her husband's demise, played all across the south coast of England. Recorded and broadcast as a pianist in her own right.

Alma Cogan (1932-1966) — She packed a great deal into a tragically short lifespan and, in addition to her glittering career as a solo artist, in the early days she sang with the bands of Wylie Price, Dennis Hale, Grisha Farfel and Joe Burns.

Co-Harmonists — Mid-Thirties recording group with Jay Wilbur.

Michael Cole — Sang with Jay Wilbur during the late-Thirties.

Esther Coleman — Initially a solo artist who created a minor sensation by changing her name to Diana Clare during the Thirties and recording with both Harry Roy and the Savoy Hotel Orpheans, before switching back to her more common name for variety events.

Sid Colin — Sang with Geraldo, the Jackdauz, the Squadronaires and Lew Stone before becoming a successful BBC producer. He also wrote a book called *And the Bands Played On!*

Lynn Collins — Experienced singer who performed with several bands, including Harry Kahn during post-war ocean cruising.

Eddie Collis — Drummer and early vocalist who began his career in the band of his cousin, Leslie Jeffries. From there he progressed to Syd Roy and made several recordings with other bands during the Twenties and early-Thirties, including Alfredo, Bert Firman, Ray and Al Starita, Sydney Kyte, Ray Noble, Jack Payne, Ronnie Munro, and Carroll Gibbons. He also appeared with Oscar Rabin but his extrovert approach to singing went out of fashion as the crooners started to hold sway during the late-Thirties.

Bobbie Comber (1886-1942) — Essentially a comedian who recorded pre-war with Harry Bidgood, Harry Hudson, Charlie Kunz, Arthur Lally, Ray Noble and Jay Wilbur.

Jean Conibear — (see Rhythm Sisters).

Steve Conway (1920-1952) — Known as "England's romantic singer" he became a professional after successful appearances in talent contests near his home in East London. At the end of the war he sang with Ambrose, Lew Stone, Joe Loss and Maurice Winnick, and is especially remembered for his association with Peter Yorke and his Concert Orchestra, with whom, he made many Sunday lunchtime broadcasts. He was once blamed for housewives spoiling the Sunday roast when they became engrossed with his voice! Not dissimilar in sound to Bing Crosby, his most famous song was *Good Luck, Good Health, God Bless You* but childhood illness had caused a weak heart and he died after surgery aged only 31. Another song was *Daddy's Little Girl* which his daughter Janice believed was all about her.

Jack Cooper* (1911-1977) — Briefly replaced Sam Browne with Ambrose during the mid-Thirties — until Sam returned after touring with Elsie Carlisle and the Rhythm Sisters. His Christian name was actually Bert (short for Herbert) but because the Ambrose band already had Bert himself wielding the baton, plus Bert Barnes on piano, he was quickly renamed. He began his career with Tommy Kinsman in 1933 and later sang with Jack Jackson at the Dorchester Hotel, Louis Levy and Fred Hartley. He also recorded with Joe Loss, Primo Scala and Jay Wilbur. A loner, he became

an electronic engineer and married late in life – but died a reclusive widower in a central London flat.

Mae Cooper — Scots girl who sang pre-war with her brothers Dave and Nick (Kidd), as the Cooper Trio. Then joined Ivy Benson and later married Carl Barriteau, with whom she sang until ill-health intervened. Later emigrated with him to Australia.

Sam Coslow — American songwriter who made a few recordings during the Thirties with Geraldo and Henry Hall.

Sam Costa** — (see separate chapter).

Diana Coupland — Initially with Teddy Foster, Felix King and Frank Weir, she joined Geraldo during the late-Forties and became well-known to radio listeners during her time with Stanley Black. She also sang with Carroll Gibbons at the Savoy, Cyril Grantham at the Dorchester and with both Nat Allen and Paul Adam. Later found fame on television, especially with Sid James in "Bless This House". Married to singer Monty Norman whom she met while singing with Stanley Black.

Crackerjacks — Close harmony wartime singing group with Jack Payne's band consisting of Nadia Doré, Carole Carr, Jane Lee, and Betty Webb. Betty later changed her name to Lizbeth Webb and became famous in musicals, especially with Georges Guetary in Vivian Ellis's *Bless the Bride*. Not to be confused with the Krakajax hot tempo dance band.

Ken Crossley* (died 1987) — Sang with fellow-Midlander Billy Merrin and also recorded with Billy Thorburn and Mantovani. Sang and toured during the early war years with Henry Hall then, after surviving a Japanese prisoner-of-war camp, appeared post-war with Nat Allen and Wally Chapman. Also managed Maddison's record shop.

Joe Crossman (died 1989) — Once described as Europe's greatest saxophone and clarinet-player, he also dabbled as a vocalist, notably with Lew Stone, for whom he also acted as general announcer. Also played and sang pre-war with Ambrose (with whom he began his career), and Jack Hylton. During the war he played for ENSA, Harry Roy, the RAF Fighter Command dance orchestra, and later for Maurice Winnick (once deputising as leader when his boss was busy buying up radio programmes in America, notably "Twenty Questions"), Geraldo (on board the *Caronia* cruise liner), the Nitwits (after Sid Millward died), before finally leading his own quartet on several world cruises. Lew Stone once asked him if he recognised the vocalist on a 30-year-old record and when he said he didn't, was somewhat surprised to learn it was himself! Retired to Florida in 1983.

George Crow** — (see Jackdauz, and also Services Bands in Volume One).

Gene Crowley (1913-1989) — Began his career with Claude Bampton then moved to Bram Martin before freelancing in 1938. Appearing several times a week on radio during wartime he performed with many top bands including Jack Jackson, Maurice Winnick, Carroll Gibbons, Sydney Lipton, Sydney Kyte (for whom he occasionally deputised as leader), Phil Green and Billy Bissett. Appeared on 75 editions of the show "Intermission" with Charles Shadwell's orchestra. He then enjoyed a highly successful variety career ending his time as a pianist and entertainer on cruise liners.

Peggy Cochrane

Diana Clare was also
known as Esther Coleman

Helen Clare

Gene Crowley and Tressa Dale
both sang with Bram Martin.

Two pairs of sparkling eyes —
June Clyde and Brian Lawrance.

Harry Roy (centre) with pianist Ivor Moreton (left) and
Bill Currie (timpani). Currie often doubled as the band's
vocalist and announcer.

"Romeo of the Radio" — Jack Cooper.

▷ Bobbie Comber was one of a number of comedians who made a considerable contribution to the dance band vocal repertoire.

The Cubs — Roy Fox's vocal trio which consisted of Ivor Mairants, Les Lambert and Harry Gold.

Bill Currie** (1908-1969) — Real name William Fryer, he was Harry Roy's timpani player and vocalist throughout the Thirties, also acting as compère on many occasions. His versatility explains his longevity with the band which was only brought to an end by the war, when he enlisted in the army and saw active service in Italy. In 1947 he became one of a close-harmony quartet called The Men About Town but later emigrated to Australia. He died in the New Hebrides group of Pacific Islands.

Betty Dale (see also Rhythm Sisters) — Golden-haired Glaswegian girl who toured Scotland singing and tap-dancing. At the age of 16 she joined Jimmy Bell's band at the Glasgow Marina Palace and three years later went off to America for four years where she broadcast as a soloist. After 12 months in Gibraltar she returned home to Britain and sang with Billy Cotton, Syd Lipton, Ambrose and Joe Loss. Apart from her career with the Rhythm Sisters (*q.v.*) she also sang at the Glasgow Plaza with Alex Freer.

Bob Dale (born 1921) — As 16-year-old Walter Winn he began his career singing with Bob Walker in Grimsby and, shortly afterwards while with Billy Thorburn, sang under the name of Wally Windsor — the Duke of Windsor being a topical point of conversation at that time! Later under his new name of Bob Dale, he appeared with many famous bands including Denny Boyce, Oscar Rabin, Cyril Stapleton, Geraldo, and Syd Lawrence. He also recorded several sides for the Woolworth brand name "Embassy" label.

Teresa (Thressa) Dale (see Rhythm Sisters) — Younger sister of Betty Dale who sometimes sang as Tressa Marshall. Appeared solo with Bram Martin.

Evelyn Dall** — Trained in America as a young singer and dancer and went on stage in a knockabout comedy routine called "Fields, Marvin and Dall". Worked on the Felix Ferry Show in Monte Carlo before coming to England during the mid-Thirties when she replaced Elsie Carlisle with Ambrose. A large, well-endowed lady, her looks and mannerisms earned her the nickname "The Blonde Bombshell". On one occasion, she was requested to sing for the Royal Family at Buckingham Palace where, despite misgiving in some quarters, she went down extremely well. According to Billy Amstell in his autobiography *Don't Fuss Mr. Ambrose*, it was not uncommon for some of the band to play wrong notes when she appeared on stage, simply because they took their eyes off the music and focussed on her instead. Bert Ambrose allegedly never understood where the mistakes were coming from or why they occurred! Appeared in the film "Miss London Ltd." (1943) and with Arthur Askey and Anne Shelton in "Time Flies" (1943). Unfortunately for British audiences, with whom she was extremely popular and regularly brought the house down, she eventually returned to America where she married and settled down to a life of domesticity.

△ The "blonde bombshell" — Evelyn Dall.

△ *This prophetic cutting was published in February, 1939. How right they were to suggest that Beryl Davis would go on to become one of the best dance band vocalists of the 20th century but they would have been surprised to know she would still be singing more than 60 years later.*

Chappie D'Amato** (1897-1976) — He really was a cheerful Chappie and a versatile instrumentalist and singer, notably with Jack Hylton and Jack Jackson. He also ran his own band.

Bebe Daniels (1901-1971) — Popular wife of Ben Lyon, another former Hollywood film star. She appeared in a huge number of silent movie "shorts" before settling permanently with Ben in Britain and stayed throughout hostilities, earning great praise from the British public who loved their wartime radio show "Hi Gang" (co-starring Vic Oliver) and later "Life With the Lyons". In addition to being an actress Bebe was also a most accomplished singer.

Maxine Daniels — Maxine (real name Gladys) began her career with Denny Boyce's band before going solo in the mid-Fifties. Modelling herself on Ella Fitzgerald she also appeared with Humphrey Lyttelton's band.

D'Arcy, Bert — (see The Ramblers).

Yvette Darnac (1896-1999) — French-born actress and singer who emigrated to England and became a regular solo broadcaster on commercial radio such as Luxembourg, Paris and Normandy during the Thirties. She also performed with Jack Payne and recorded with Joe Loss.

Louis Davids — Recorded with Ambrose during the early-Thirties.

Ivor Davies — Recorded with Billy Reid's accordion band and sang with both Eddie Carroll and Sydney Lipton during the late-Thirties and early-wartime period.

Beryl Davis** (born 1924) — She was actually born backstage at the Palace Theatre, Plymouth, where both her theatrical parents were performing at the time. Her father, Harry Davis, fronted the Oscar Rabin band for 20 years, most of which time his versatile young daughter was the lead singer — until they both emigrated to America — where he became a car salesman and she began a new singing career. Amazingly, she first appeared on stage at the age of only three and began singing professionally at eight. Before her teenage years had evaporated she had already appeared with Phil Green, Ted Heath, Geraldo, Stephane Grappelli, the Blue Rockets, Squadronaires and Skyrockets. She was also Letter "I" in the Ovaltineys show on Radio Luxembourg and sang at Windsor Castle for the 16th birthday party of Princess Elizabeth in 1942. In America she set up home in Palm Springs, California but was always on the move. Popular with Bob Hope she replaced Doris Day for 12 months alongside Frank Sinatra and sang, among others, with Louis Armstrong, Ella Fitzgerald and the orchestras of Les Brown and Benny Goodman, touring with the latter in Asia when it was reformed after Benny's death. Back home she appeared with both the new Glenn Miller and Syd Lawrence Orchestras, and was still going strong as the 20th century came to an end.

Chappie D'Amato

Dawn Davis — Recorded with Charlie Kunz, Harry Leader and Ray Noble. In 1941 she briefly led her own touring group called the Master Swingers. Composed mainly of members of the late Teddy Joyce's band it only lasted a few months, however.

Helen Davis — Regularly performed with Felix Mendelssohn's post-war Hawaiian Serenaders and also with Don Smith's Stardusters in Nottingham.

Marion Davis (Keene) — In 1948 Oscar Rabin appointed her to replace Annabelle Lee and immediately shortened her name from Davison. She later replaced Julie Dawn in Eric Winstone's band and appeared with Jack Parnell before marrying Ronnie Keene, changing her name for a second time, and going solo.

Marjorie Daw — South African-born singer who joined Oscar Rabin after appearing on "Opportunity Knocks".

Jimmy Dawn — Vocalist with Andy Ross, MD of BBC Television's "Come Dancing" series.

Julie Dawn* (died 2000) — Born an Italian Cockney named Juliana Maria Theresa Mostosi, she first sang as a child with Alf van Straten's band at Quaglino's Restaurant, Anglicising her name shortly afterwards. In 1939 she broadcast with Billy Ternent in Bristol following which Billy handed her a large sum of cash to take back to Jack Hylton in London. Petrified, Julie slept with it under her pillow before eventually handing it over. Her Italian parents were unfortunately interned throughout the war during which, after being engaged by Harry Roy, she mischievously sang a few words of Italian during a 1940 performance in Glasgow. Harry was livid and sacked her on the spot! Following wartime appearances with Geraldo (with whom she toured northern Europe on a trip which had been personally requested by Field Marshall Montgomery), Billy Thorburn, Ken "Snakehips" Johnson, Lou Preager, Harry Leader and a lengthy and highly successful spell with Eric Winstone, she later sang with Joe Daniels and Cyril Stapleton's showband. She also broadcast on "Night Ride", "Music Thru' Midnight" and Charlie Chester's "Soapbox". Latterly she had her own personal slot on the Radio 2 programme "You and the Night and the Music" and hosted "Julie Dawn's Penfriend Programme" specifically aimed at people who lived alone.

Norma Dawn — Sang and broadcast with Teddy Joyce in the late-Thirties.

Colin Day (born 1935) — First appeared with Denny Boyce before joining the ill-fated David Ede who took over Oscar Rabin's band.

▷ *Like mother, like daughter. Barbara Lyon (top) later emulated her mother, Bebe Daniels (below) as a band singer. Her career, however, was much shorter.*

Tessie O'Shea made a joke of her own weight.

Vera Lynn became the "Forces Sweetheart".

Margaret Eaves sang with
Herman Darewski.

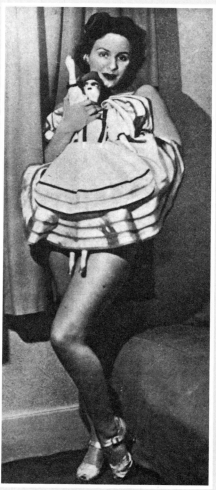

Helen McKay sang with Lew Stone
and Ambrose.

Stella Roberta was Mantovani's sister.

Joy Worth was a member of the Radio Three.

Pat Hyde's hair, when unravelled, reached her ankles!

Betty Dale was a member of the Rhythm Sisters.

Joe Loss discusses a song with Frances Day.

Norma Dawn

Yvette Darnac emigrated to
England from France.

Hughie Diamond

Frances Day (1908-1984) — Blonde American film star whose real name was Frances Schenk. She became famous in England during the late-Twenties and early-Thirties and sang with many bands, recording with both Ray Noble and Carroll Gibbons.

Jill Day (born 1930) — Born Yvonne Page, but under the name of Jill Page she toured immediately post-war with Harry Roy, then went on to sing with Syd Dean and Cyril Grantham before Geraldo changed her name to Jill Day, under which guise she finally went solo during the mid-Fifties.

Jimmy Day — Post-war singer with Leslie Douglas.

Alan Dean (born 1924) — Sang with Art Thompson, Jack Wallace, Harry Roy, Ambrose, Oscar Rabin, Harry Leader, Frank Weir, and Jimmy Leach. In the late-Forties he formed a short-lived be-bop band which included Ronnie Scott on tenor sax, and also became a founder member of the famous Keynotes singing group. Later emigrated to America.

Judy Dean (also known as Judy Allen and Jan Fraser) — Sang with George Evans, Freddy Randall, Harry Roy, Oscar Rabin and the Fraser Hayes Four.

Vicki Dean — (see Valerie Kleiner).

Debonaires — Late-Forties group who sang with Ambrose and had their own late-night radio show. The members were Nadia Doré, Bob Winnette, Helen McKay and Bob Brown.

Frances Dee — Recorded with Billy Ternent.

Peggy Dell** — Taught the piano by her father who was a musician at the Dublin Empire under the family name of Tisdell. She preferred singing, however, and by the age of 14 was promoting sheet music at Woolworth's by singing the latest numbers to potential customers. She then formed her own band which played regularly at Fuller's Café, before joining Charlie Harvey who toured England and gave her the big break she needed. Roy Fox liked her singing and promptly signed her for his band after which she toured America with Jack Hylton, and continued singing with him after he returned to the UK. Post-war she returned to her native soil and led a small band at Dublin's Portmarnock Hotel.

△ Dawn Davis was one of many singers who "disappeared" after the last war.

Nina Delmonte** — Toured and sang with Primo Scala's Accordion Band during the Thirties.

Denny Dennis** — (see separate chapter).

Johnny Desmond — USAAF sergeant who sang with Glenn Miller's AEF band.

Terry Devon (born 1922) — Joined Billy Thorburn while still only 15 and later appeared with Art Gregory, George Scott-Wood, Oscar Rabin, Woolf Phillips, Vic Lewis, the Stardusters and Tito Burns, eventually marrying the latter. Also a member of the Keynotes (*q.v.*).

Roy Dexter — Guitarist and vocalist with Nat Gonella's New Georgians.

Hughie Diamond* (born 1920) — Remarkably, he could sing in no fewer than 20 different languages and recorded with Eddie Carroll, Maurice Winnick, Jack Harris, Teddy Joyce, Joe Loss, Jack Payne, Harry Roy and Lew Stone. Well over six feet tall, he continued singing at private functions until the end of the 20th century. Once, when appearing in Coventry with Jack Harris just before the outbreak of the Second World War, his Scottish accent was mistaken for an Irish one and, immediately branded as one of the IRA terrorists who had been blowing up British letter boxes, was set upon by a mob. Fortunately he was spotted by Billy Amstell and his wife Tessa, who quickly explained he was a singer with their band!

Diane (born 1920) — Real name Dorothy Wick, who was discovered in a talent contest run by Roy Fox who promptly signed her for his band under the title of "Diane". She later sang with Tommy Finnigan in Edinburgh then Oscar Rabin when Beryl Davis became overburdened with freelance work. Married Oscar's eldest son, Bernard, on Boxing Day 1941. Retired to Rustington on the Sussex coast.

Lonnie Donegan — During an intermission in recording schedules with Chris Barber's band in 1956, he recorded an American folk song called *Rock Island Line*. It was only for fun but knocked the popular music trade for six and became a classic which spawned the short-lived Skiffle craze which had fans jiving alongside rock 'n' roll all over the country.

Dan Donovan** (1901-1986) — Qualified motor mechanic who began as a band leader in his native Cardiff but is better-remembered as a highly successful singer, particularly with Henry Hall and Debroy Somers (with whom he also played the baritone sax), although he also recorded with Sydney Kyte, Bertini, Harry Bidgood, Charlie Kunz, Mantovani, Oscar

△ *Terry Devon married band leader Tito Burns.*

Rabin, Nat Star and Jay Wilbur. A chance audition with Debroy Somers in London brought him wealth beyond the dreams of a coalman's son — £26 a week being a small fortune in 1930. Four years later he joined Henry Hall as a replacement for Les Allen and became established as a firm favourite with thousands of fans, one of whom kept a daily scrapbook which she eventually presented to him. Among his many party pieces was *The Ghost of No. 10* in which he impersonated several well-known band leaders of the time. When Henry Hall went on tour in 1937 so did Dan, but now as a soloist commanding high fees. He then formed his own band again but was never far from the microphone, even during the war when he had a narrow escape from Holland when the Nazis invaded. In conjunction with his Serenaders, his post-war radio shows from South Wales proved so popular they were repeated at national level. When his wife became ill he returned to Cardiff where he eventually retired after a short stint as a pub licensee.

Nadia Doré — Member of Jack Payne's pre-war Crackerjacks female vocal quartet she later sang with Geraldo, Paul Adam, Harry Parry, Ambrose and the Debonaires.

Fred "Buck" Douglas (1886-1955) — Prolific recording artist with several bands during the Twenties and Thirties including Wag Abbey, Stanley Barnett, Bertini, Billy Cotton, Stan Greening, Tommy Kinsman, Arthur Lally, Percival Mackey, Pete Mandell, Oscar Rabin, Carroll Gibbons, Nat Star and Jay Wilbur. Father of band leader and singer, Leslie Douglas.

Leslie Douglas** (see also Four in Harmony) — Band leader in his own right but he also recorded separately as a vocalist with several other bands, including Henry Hall, Teddy Joyce, Carroll Gibbons, Nat Star, Billy Thorburn and Jay Wilbur.

Julie Dawn

Sally Douglas — Glaswegian who replaced Dorothy Carless with Geraldo in 1944 and then toured northern France and Germany entertaining the troops. After the war she joined Cyril Stapleton, before replacing Doreen Lundy at the Skyrockets. Later a resident singer with Ronnie Pleydell where she met and married Jimmy Young, who occasionally deputised as leader when Ronnie was away.

Evelyn Dove (died 1987) — Rich blues-style sounding singer who recorded with Louis Levy and Billy Cotton at the outbreak of war and subsequently enjoyed a cabaret and broadcasting career.

Betty Driver (born 1920) — Should have appeared as a teenage dancer in George Formby's first film "Boots, Boots" in 1934, but George's wife Beryl was jealous and had her take cut out! She switched to singing with Henry Hall during the war with whom she stayed nearly eight years. Later graduated to variety and broadcasting, running her own shows and recording with Sid Phillips. When the pop music scene altered during the late-Fifties she switched to acting instead and, in July 1969, became a regular as Betty Turpin on television's long-running "Coronation Street", a role she held for more than 30 years.

Vivian Duncan — One half of the Duncan Sisters cabaret act. Sang with Stanley Barnett's 12 Million Airs band at the Café Anglais during the late-Thirties.

△ *Dan Donovan was an excellent mimic as well as a singer and band leader.*

△ *A teenage Betty Driver had her name in the final credits of George Formby's first film but never actually appeared in it! However, she later became a big television star in "Coronation Street".*

(From top to bottom):

Girvan Dundas died young during the war.

Nadia Doré was a pre-war Crackerjack!

Evelyn Dove sang the blues.

Fred Douglas also performed in old time music hall on Radio Luxembourg.

Girvan (Tommie) Dundas (1908-1944) — Born Eileen Caroline Dundas she was the daughter of a variety artist who introduced her to his act when she was only three years old. Sang with Charlie Kunz and Harry Roy and became the second wife of Charlie Smirke, the famous flat race jockey who won the Derby four times. The marriage, however, was a commercial and unhappy one and ended in divorce. She died after working with ENSA during which time she contracted cancer. "Tommie" was a nickname for Girvan, the place of her birth in Ayrshire, Scotland.

Johnnie Eager (born 1924) — Cut his musical teeth with Fred Hedley's semi-professional band in Wimbledon, before moving on to Sid Phillips and Ted Heath.

Robert Earl — Sang during the Forties and Fifties with several bands, including Sydney Lipton and Nat Temple.

Jim Easton — Saxophonist, clarinettist and occasional singer with Roy Fox, Nat Gonella, Jack Hylton, Brian Lawrance, Maurice Winnick and Lew Stone.

Rex Eaton — Recorded during the war with Ambrose.

Margaret Eaves — Sang and broadcast with Herman Darewski's band during the Thirties.

Eddie & Rex (see Brian Lawrance & Jack Lorimer).

Toni Eden (born 1936) — Daughter of "Chips" Chippendall" and christened Antoinette, while still only a teenager she successfully auditioned for Ted Heath — who promptly changed her name and took her on tour to Europe. She later branched out into a solo stage career.

Roy Edwards — Post-war singer with many bands, including Geraldo, Oscar Rabin and the Squadronaires.

Linda Ellington — Scots girl who, following a recommendation from Steve Race, joined Johnny Dankworth in 1950. Later sang with Kenny Baker.

Chris Ellis (born 1928) — EMI World Records/Retrospect record producer during the Seventies and Eighties who later sang with Tiny Winters's recreated 1930s band called the Café Society Orchestra. Also sang with the New Paul Whiteman orchestra.

June Ellis (born 1927) — Began her career with Stan Atkins in Welling, Kent then worked with Ivy Benson, Al Tabor, Joe Daniels and Ken Mackintosh.

George Elrick** — (see separate chapter).

Dolly Elsie* (1907-1961) — Younger sister of Jack Hylton but changed her name so as not to live in his shadow. She first broadcast with Bertini in 1933 and then married his drummer, Norman Vickers. Big brother was never far away, however, and she sang with his "second" orchestra, the Billy Ternent-led touring band and also with Jack himself. During the war she broadcast with Billy Cotton from Bristol and with organ-playing Charles Smart, and his son Harold during their early morning programmes. When Jack hung up his conducting baton after several of his band were called up in 1940, she became Billy Cotton's first permanent girl singer, Vera Lynn having been shown the door after only seven days a few years earlier! After a number of successful variety engagements she retired after the war but succumbed to cancer while still relatively young. She was remembered with great affection, and especially for her Rochdale accent which was as distinctive as her older brother's.

Maurice Elwin* (see also The Ramblers) (1896-1975) — Modest but prolific recording artist and composer, Norman Macphail Blair had more than 60 pseudonyms! He recorded, among others, with Bertini, Harry Bidgood, Herman Darewski, Bert Firman, Jack Hylton, Arthur Lally, Ronnie Munro, Debroy Somers, Carroll Gibbons, Nat Star and Jay Wilbur. During the mid-Thirties he opened a school for voice coaching and trained many famous names, including Maureen O'Hara, Annette Mills, Julie Dawn, June Malo and George Barclay. He also assisted Al Bowlly, Les Allen, Jack Plant and Cavan O'Connor — no mean achievement! Devoted to his wife, Zena, after she died in 1968 he gave over the rest of his life to helping aspiring composers.

Don Emsley (born 1923) — Glaswegian guitarist and vocalist who worked with ENSA in wartime Europe before being signed by Billy Ternent on his return home. Also freelanced with the Keynotes.

Paul England — Recorded during the late-Twenties with Jack Hylton, Ronnie Munro and Allan Selby.

Clive Erard (1913-1988) — Member of Ambrose's Thirties singing group called the Rhythm Brothers and also Syd Lipton's Three-T's. After emigrating to America he became a member of the Merry Macs who also appeared in this country. Versatility was the name of his game and he also played both the piano and accordion, as well as being an accomplished tap dancer and one-time band leader in the north of England. Also a member of the Manhattan Trio with Frank and Jack Trafford.

Dusty Evans — Sang with Cyril Grantham's Dorchester Hotel band during the early-Fifties.

Howell Evans — Maesteg-born and discovered by Henry Hall, he sang with the band for 18 months before joining the RAF. He later went on to work on stage and television and, in 1985, teamed up again with a former singing colleague while taking a small role in "Coronation Street" — because famous "Rover's Return" barmaid Betty Turpin, began her professional career as Betty Driver (q.v.), a bright young singer who also appeared with Henry Hall.

Maureen Evans — Broadcast with Billy Ternent towards the end of his career.

Rudy Bayfield Evans — Recorded with the Savoy Havana band during the mid-Twenties.

Terry Fahey — (see Mackpies).

Jean Farrar — Recorded with Harry Roy during wartime.

Harry Fay — Recorded with several bands during the Twenties and Thirties, including Harry Bidgood, Billy Cotton, Herman Darewski, Bert Firman, Stan Greening, Percival Mackey, Ronnie Munro and Leon van Straten.

△ Maurice Elwin was a friend to many.

Jewel Faye (see also McCarthy Sisters) — Recorded as a soloist with Jack Hylton in 1936.

Joe Ferrie* — Trombone-playing vocalist who featured with several bands including Billy Cotton, Roy Fox, Geraldo, Jack Jackson and Lew Stone.

Miff Ferrie** — (see Jackdauz).

Gerry Fitzgerald** (1908-1964) — An extremely popular pre-war vocalist from Toronto who came to Britain in 1934 and recorded with several bands including Len Fillis, Eddie Carroll, Sydney Kyte, Howard Godfrey, Louis Levy, Sydney Lipton, Ray Noble, Lou Preager, Debroy Somers and Jay Wilbur! Also appeared in the 1937 Hitchcock thriller "Young and Innocent". In many cases he also recorded under a pseudonym. After wartime service as a squadron leader in the RAF he married and returned home to Canada but died young.

Bud Flanagan — (see Flanagan & Allen).

Flanagan & Allen — Members of the Crazy Gang who made a number of novelty recordings with Henry Hall, Jack Hylton and Debroy Somers during the Thirties. Bud sang more than Ches whose voice only really allowed him to perform a supporting role. Somehow the two always hit the mark, however, and were a hugely popular double act, even when they came out of post-war retirement.

Jackie Flood — (see Jackie Lee).

Patti Forbes — Sang with Oscar Rabin and Ken Mackintosh before emigrating to America.

Four in Harmony — Henry Hall's young singing group in the late-Thirties, consisting of Bob Mallin, Anita Riddell, Leslie Douglas** and Bernard Hunter. An extremely lively combination with Leslie going on to become a band

leader in his own right. Anita also sang with Claude Bampton, Bernard with Ambrose, Phil Green and Jack Payne, while Bob doubled as the band's guitarist and married Yolande Mageean from the Three in Harmony group, celebrating their Diamond Wedding in San Diego, California, in August 1999. Bernard Hunter later went on television and the stage, likewise Bob Mallin who toured the Middle East with ENSA, played alongside his father in pantomimes and also appeared in the popular early-Fifties radio programme "Riders of the Range".

Four Musketeers — Henry Hall recording group during the early-Thirties.

Fox Cubs — (see The Cubs).

Derrick Francis** (see uncaptioned picture on page 103 Volume One) — Popular on All-India Radio, in 1950 Derrick arrived in London as a 19-year-old from Calcutta to join Geraldo, alongside Nadia Doré, Eve Boswell and Cyril Grantham. He later sang successfully with Eric Delaney, the Courtley-Seymour Band, Chick Smith and Bert Ambrose.

Jan Fraser — (see Judy Dean).

Joyce Frazer — Born in Shanghai, China, she returned to England with her parents and sang with Teddy Foster before touring with the American Army Show. She later sang with Roy Richards in Margate.

Dave Fullerton — Drummer-vocalist with Arthur Young and Hatchett's Swingtette during the war. He also played in a Burton Gillis-led Henry Hall band at the Mayfair Hotel in 1939.

Deric Gaitt — Sang with Marius B. Winter during the mid-Thirties.

Sandra Gall — Vocalist with the Malcolm Mitchell Trio during the early-Sixties

Tessa Gallon — Wartime singer with Oscar Rabin.

Janet Garden — Billy Reid's replacement for Dorothy Squires in 1951.

Gaye Sisters — Immediate post-war trio used by Denny Dennis as his backing group on tour. Quickly formed when Denny failed to persuade the Beverley Sisters to join him, it consisted of Jean Barrie, Betty Currie (wife of Harry Roy's vocalist Bill Currie) and a girl called Ann from Derby!

◁ *While playing in Frank Davidson's band in Edinburgh, Joe Ferrie was invited to be best man at colleague Sydney Lipton's registry office wedding — but Syd was too busy and failed to turn up! He then suggested it took place the following day but with no licence and no ring it had to be postponed for a week.*

△ *Four in Harmony — Henry Hall's young singing group who all went on to greater things with their individual careers. Top to bottom: Bernard Hunter, Bob Mallin, Anita Riddell and Leslie Douglas.*

Mel Gaynor (born 1931) — Came to England from India and sang initially with Fred Hedley at Wimbledon before moving on to Oscar Rabin's band.

Ronnie Genarder** (1909-1972) — Later a band leader in his own right but sang with Roy Fox, Jack Payne and Syd Millward's Nitwits. Real name Ronald Gardner.

Georgina — Real name Thelma Jagger, she sang with Jack Payne after cutting her teeth with her father's band in Bournemouth. She also sang with Geraldo and toured with ENSA during the war. With Bruce Trent she formed a duo called the Singing Sweethearts.

Geraldettes — Mid-Thirties singing group with Geraldo.

Mollie Gibson — Worked with ENSA and appeared in wartime radio on "Variety Bandbox". Then joined Stan Atkins at Welling in Kent before touring with Teddy Foster alongside Franklyn Boyd. Later sang with Frank Weir.

Burton Gillis — Arranger and tenor sax player with Henry Hall who briefly led the band at the Mayfair Hotel in 1939.

Walter Glynne — Although he is much better-remembered as an operatic singer he also recorded several dance band records with Jack Hylton, and a couple with Ray Noble.

Bruts Gonella* — Trumpeter-vocalist with Billy Cotton and older brother Nat.

Nat Gonella** — Band leader in his own right but he also sang with Stanley Black, Billy Cotton, Roy Fox, Sydney Lipton, Ray Starita and Lew Stone.

Niela Goodelle — American cabaret star who broadcast on wartime "Band Waggon" and various other radio dance programmes during the late-Thirties.

Gary Gowan — Wartime singer with Oscar Rabin.

Cyril Grantham** — In addition to making early recordings with many bands, especially Geraldo, with whom he worked for many years, versatile Cyril also ran his own post-war group at the Dorchester Hotel. Also appeared with Billy Cotton, Sydney Lipton, Joe Loss, Primo Scala and Jay Wilbur.

△ *Not many dance band singers looked like this in 1938 but "Little Johnny Green" was already a veteran before he reached his teens.*

△ Walter Glynne was one of many more serious and, paradoxically, comedy singers who made records with Jack Hylton's band.

Barry Gray (1909-1941) — Derby-born elder brother of Denny Dennis and a self-taught drummer and bass player who played for silent movies at the Grand Theatre there. Went to London under his real name of Eric Pountain and played at the Streatham Locarno and Shepherd's Bush Empire. After a spell with Teddy Joyce he surfaced as a singer with Al Davison in Clapham and then spent two years at the 400 Club in Leicester Square during which time he featured with both Reginald Foresythe and Jack Harris, as well as being a house vocalist for EMI. He then appeared with Roy Fox, at the same time as his more famous younger brother (who had a lower voice), was making a name with the band. Killed in a U-boat attack while on his first voyage serving as a radio officer in the Merchant Navy.

Peter Gray — Blind wartime singer with Lew Stone, whose voice was compared to the American singer Bob Eberle but, together with Geraldo's Len Camber, and several others, it was considered unsuitable for broadcasting by the BBC. After many complaints the ban was later lifted.

Johnny Green (born 1924) — Known as the "Pocket Crosby" "Little Johnny Green" had already sung with Harry Roy and Oscar Rabin before he was even a teenager! Recorded with Billy Merrin, Geraldo and also with Harry Roy, appearing in his film "Rhythm Racketeer". Made more than 2,000 broadcasts before 1950. Toured Europe and the Middle East with Geraldo and also sang with Harry Parry. In order to avoid confusion with a band leader of the same name, he became Barry Green while touring America during the late-Forties. Made a brief comeback in the early-Sixties.

June Green — Sang with her father, Alan's band at the Brighton Dome during the war.

Paula Green** (born 1917) — Although born in Blackpool she began singing with Cecil Epsteid in Eastbourne, then worked with Michael Flome, Joe Loss, Marius B. Winter and Felix Mendelssohn. After briefly flirting with her own all-male band she went back to singing as a career. Also appeared on "ITMA".

Greene Sisters — Wartime recording act with Jay Wilbur and appeared in the 1941 film "Hi-Gang!" with Ben Lyon and Bebe Daniels. They also later recorded with the Sid Phillips Quintet.

Larry Gretton — Post-war singer with Joe Loss and Stanley Black.

Olive Groves — More of a radio singing celebrity who was a big name during the Twenties and Thirties. Recorded several times with Geraldo, Henry Hall, Jack Harris, Jack Hylton, Arthur Lally, Savoy Havana Band and Savoy Orpheans, and Jay Wilbur.

Eddie Guray — Recorded with Billy Thorburn during the late-Thirties.

Dennis Hale (1922-1960) — After demob from the army as a sergeant-major he recorded with Teddy Foster following which, as a clever raconteur, he was chosen by Eric Winstone to lead a band at the Brighton Aquarium, one of whose singers was a young Alma Cogan. The orchestra then moved along the coast to Southsea for a short spell after which, and before going freelance, Dennis became a resident singer with Oscar Rabin and Jack Parnell. Killed in a road accident in Northern Rhodesia.

The Three Herons

◁ This is a picture of Geraldo's team of singers for a Radio Luxembourg broadcast in 1939. Left to right: Cyril Grantham, Judy Shirley (eldest of the six Lenner Sisters), Geraldo himself (after his Gaucho Tango days), Gwen Catley (better-known as a singer of light opera), and Monte Rey (who originally trained for grand opera but switched musical genres to great effect). At the time, Geraldo was described as "One of Radio's busiest personalities".

Adelaide Hall (1909-1993) — "Sweet Adelaide" was a great American blues singer with Duke Ellington, but merits attention here because, after a time in Paris, she settled in Britain just before the war and, together with her husband, Bert Hicks, opened a club in London which was unfortunately later bombed-out, following which she joined ENSA. She remained in Europe and sang with Fela Sowande, Robin Richmond, Gerry Moore, Fats Waller and Joe Loss. In between times she revisited America and appeared with many different musicians and bands.

Hamilton Sisters and Fordyce — A close-harmony singing group which recorded in 1927 with both Ambrose and Carroll Gibbons's Savoy Orpheans.

Tommy Handley — Best-remembered for his witty and sarcastic quickfire wartime comedy programme "ITMA", he also made several novelty dance band recordings with Harry Bidgood, Jack Hylton and Ronnie Munro.

Kay Harding — Born Kathleen Bolton in Ilford, Essex, she toured and recorded with Harry Roy during the early stages of the war. She then appeared with Billy Thorburn, Frank Weir and Felix Mendelssohn before joining the entertainment section of the American Red Cross. She later sang with Artie Shaw when he appeared at the Grosvenor House Hotel and was then invited by Spike Jones to go to America and sing with his non-City Slickers band. At the time she was appearing with Harry Roy who sacked her on the spot, prompting Spike, and his friend Bing Crosby, to help

her empty her locker! Unfortunately, owing to contractual and domestic reasons, she never actually made it to the States but went on tour instead with Jack Jackson. She later sang with Jack Nathan and also to the American Forces based in Germany where she had a narrow escape after fainting and falling from her hotel window.

Doris Hare — Better-known as a comedienne and revue artiste, she recorded with Sydney Lipton during the early-Thirties. When war came along she appeared in a radio series broadcast from the Merchant Navy Club in London, called "Shipmates Ashore".

Harristocrats — Late-Thirties singing trio from Jack Harris' band made up of Fred Latham, Chick Smith and Freddy Williams. They also recorded for Radio Luxembourg and Carroll Gibbons.

Hawaiian Sisters — Female singing group with Felix Mendelssohn.

Adelaide Hall became a legend in her own lifetime.

△ Doris Hare — comedienne, singer and revue artiste.

According to the original caption, singer Eddie Guray (right) was sculpting a bust of his band leader and pianist, Billy Thorburn.

Chick Henderson** — (see separate chapter).

Rickie Henderson — Began his singing career with Charles Marcus in Leeds before joining Denny Boyce's band at the Wimbledon Palais and recording for Woolworth's Embassy label.

Henderson Twins — Winifred and Theresa were the identical twin daughters of plump pre-war Hull comedian Dick Henderson, and sisters of post-war comedian Dickie. They were heard regularly on "Rinso Revue" a soap-powder sponsored programme on Radio Luxembourg, and also on Radio Toulouse, Normandy and Paris. At the age of 14 Winifred fell off her bike and was unable to go to school. Theresa promptly refused to go back without her so father enrolled them instead at the London School of Broadcasting, from where they soon found themselves on the road with Elsie and Doris Waters, who quickly taught them the tricks of the show business trade. Extremely popular during the late-Thirties they recorded with Al Bowlly for Ken "Snakehips" Johnson just prior to the latter's demise when a bomb destroyed the Café de Paris in London during the Blitz. They were so alike that they often played practical jokes on unsuspecting boy friends and acquaintances and, apart from a difference over eating tomatoes, shared absolutely everything else in common, even their taste in clothes.

Leonard Henry — Better remembered as a comedian and all-round entertainer from the mid-Thirties he made a number of earlier novelty recordings with Sydney Lipton and Ray Noble.

Heron Sisters (also known as The Three Herons) — Joan, Wendy and Kay really were sisters and left the typing pool to form an attractive close harmony group which worked with Bram Martin during the mid to late-Thirties and also appeared on the commercial continental radio stations. With the addition of their two brothers they then became simply The Five Herons and from 1935-40 worked in variety alongside stars such as Carroll Gibbons, George Formby, Charlie Chester, Tommy Handley and George Robey, before wartime claimed the boys for active service. They also recorded with Al Bowlly.

Hildegarde — Hildegarde Loretta Sell was an American vaudeville and cabaret star who sang and played the piano. She appeared in Britain with great success between 1933-36 when she recorded with Henry Hall and also starred in his film "Music Hath Charms".

△ Leonard Henry was a well-known broadcaster.

Ronnie Hill (1911-1991) — Recorded with Charlie Kunz, Phil Green, Lou Preager, Ambrose, Jay Wilbur, Tommy Kinsman, Primo Scala, Dare Lea, Harry Leader and Jack Hylton. With Jack Nathan he jointly composed *Here's Looking At You*, the tune which introduced the first television programme transmitted on August 26th, 1936. He was also a member of Ambrose's Thirties singing group called the Rhythm Brothers.

Vince Hill (born 1937) — Spent 12 months with Teddy Foster's band before going solo in 1958.

Ronnie Hilton (1926-2001) — Hull-born Adrian Hill was a ballad singer whose wife finally persuaded him to stop out-singing Perry Como from the radio and enter a talent contest instead. He won and was invited to join Johnny Addlestone's band at the Starlight Ballroom in Leeds. After he came to the notice of HMV he became Ronnie Hilton and recorded every year between 1954-69, totalling more than 100 sides. Toured with the Cyril Stapleton Show Band in 1957 (alongside Marion Ryan) and again in 1958. Also sang with all the BBC orchestras. Appeared in three Royal Command performances.

Frank Holder — Came to England from British Guiana and enlisted with the wartime RAF. Sang with various amateur service bands before joining Leslie "Jiver" Hutchinson, Kenny Baker, Johnny Kerrison and finally Johnny Dankworth, where he replaced Marion Williams. After five years with both the Dankworth Seven and Big Band he went solo in 1956.

Michael Holliday (1925-1963) — Liverpudlian Norman Miller changed his name firstly to Milne, before finally settling on his stage name of Holliday. While serving at sea he met up with Trevor Stanford, alias Russ Conway, and sometimes they put on impromptu performances together. His dance band singing career began with Hal Graham in his native town, then Dick Denny at Pwllheli and finally Eric Winstone from where he launched out on a solo career, tragically cut short by his suicide after yet another bout of depression.

Leslie Holmes (1901-1960) — Famous variety artist who enjoyed a long association with Jack Payne and, together with Leslie Sarony, formed a duo called "The Two Leslies". Separately, they made a large number of comedy records with various dance bands before the war, especially Jack Hylton and Jay Wilbur, but only a handful together.

Ruth Howard — Sang with Billy Ternent.

Alberta Hunter (1895-1984) — Original black American blues and jazz singer who first came to England in the late-Twenties when she appeared at the Palladium and in the musical "Showboat" at Drury Lane. An inveterate world traveller she also sang live and recorded with Jack Jackson's Dorchester Hotel band in 1934.

Bernard Hunter — (see Four in Harmony).

Jackie Hunter — Drummer and vocalist who recorded with Jack Jackson and Geraldo, and also appeared on stage as a comedy actor.

Rusty Hurren — Post-war singer and instrumentalist with Lou Preager.

Leslie Hutchinson (Hutch) (1900-1969) — No relation to Leslie "Jiver" Hutchinson (*q.v.*), he was a famous West Indian pianist and singer who also made some dance records with Harry Roy.

Pat Hyde** (1916-1992) — Named after St. Patrick's Day, on which she was born into a musical family in Plaistow, East London. As a child she learnt to play the piano, organ, guitar, saxophone, violin and piano-accordion! Touring with her mother as a singer from the age of 12 she attended different schools almost every week. As "Pat and Ivy" the duo were a great success but Pat eventually pursued a solo career, performing and recording with a large number of bands. She also broadcast abroad in Norway, Holland and Denmark. Although only resident once, in 1937 at London's Mayfair Hotel, when she stepped in to replace Billy Bissett's wife, American Alice Mann who did not have the necessary work permit, she was much in demand elsewhere. When Billy Merrin persuaded her to sing out-front to her own accordion playing, she had to perform by instinct as she moved around the stage because she was acutely short-sighted and refused to wear glasses! Her late-Thirties decision to tour the continent was triggered when Gypsy Nina arrived from America with a similar act. Following wartime service with ENSA she went back to Europe and also performed in India and Japan. A serious accident then badly affected her career but she still managed a trip to America and performed well past pensionable age. Although she always wore her hair in a bun when unravelled it reached down almost to her ankles! Married for 31 years to band leader Peter Rush until he died in 1972.

Ellis Jackson** (1892-1990) — Came to England from Massachusetts in 1907 as part of a family variety act and played with Victor Vorzanger's band as a singer and trombonist

This 1937 "Christmas Toast" reflects the importance of dance bands and singers in the popular music of the time.

1. Bram Martin
2. Anne Lenner
3. Stella Roberta
4. Charles Shadwell
5. Sutherland Felce
6. Hildegarde
7. Leslie Sarony
8. Leslie Holmes
9. George Elrick
10. Judy Shirley
11. Paula Green
12. Billie Houston
13. Ronnie Hill
14. Vera Lennox
15. Cavan O'Connor
16. Rita Cave

Sutherland Felce was famous for his musical nonsense songs; Billie Houston did a double-act with Ronnie Hill and also with her sister, Renee; Rita Cave was a solo singer; while Vera Lennox was a popular radio actress.

from 1921-3. In 1931 he became a singer and tap dancer for Billy Cotton with whom he worked for the next 20 years.

Jackdauz** (Jakdauz, Jacdors, Jackdaws) — Successful Thirties vocal trio which began as the Jacdors — "Jack" being short for Jack Jackson and "dors" being the Dorchester Hotel where the band was playing at the time. The original members were Fred Latham**, Sid Colin* and Rannyel Bryan. Although officially disbanded the group was reformed under the leadership of Miff Ferrie**, with George Crow** joining up alongside Fred Latham, its original founder. Fred in turn was soon replaced by Harry Parry**, and all four went on to become band leaders in their own right. The Jackdauz broadcast with many different bands and recorded with Lew Stone, George Scott-Wood, and Nat Gonella. Teddy Prince later replaced Harry Parry.

Shirley Jackson — Hailing from Sheffield she sang with Frank Weir before joining the Ray Ellington Quartet during the mid-Fifties.

Dick James (1919-1986) — Born Isaac Vapnick he sang with Cyril Stapleton, the Skyrockets and Geraldo, and later owned his own music publishing company which handled songs by both the Beatles and Elton John. Founder member of the Stargazers singing group and also performed for Henry Hall as Lee Sheridan.

Ricky James — Following a brief "pop" career he sang and toured with Ivor and Basil Kirchin's band.

Susan Jeans — Joined Jan Ralfini's band in 1946, performed with Terry Thomas in cabaret and then sang with Gloria Gaye's All-Girls band. Later joined the Squadronaires.

Bryan Johnson (1926-1995) — Teddy's younger brother who was encouraged to follow

Leslie Hutchinson — better known as "Hutch".

in his footsteps by Geraldo who, after hearing him answer the telephone, thought his voice might prove suitable for a dance band. He was right and Bryan later appeared with Woolf Phillips, Lew Stone, Peter Knight and Paul Fenoulhet. In 1960 he came second in the "Eurovision Song Contest" with *Looking, High, High, High; Looking Low, Low, Low* — a remarkable coincidence and double, following second place 12 months earlier for big brother Teddy and his wife and singing partner, Pearl Carr, who performed *Sing Little Birdie*.

Don Johnson — Singing brother of ill-fated West Indian band leader Ken "Snakehips" Johnson.

Teddy Johnson (born 1919) — Formed his own dance band while still only 14 and, after being invalided out of the Navy in 1944 was signed up as a vocalist by Jack Payne. He met his future wife, Pearl Carr, while appearing as a drummer with Phil Green's orchestra, and then sang with both Roland Peachey and Jack Jackson before becoming a joint international celebrity star with his wife, whom he married in 1955. Came second in the 1959 "Eurovision Song Contest" with *Sing Little Birdie*.

Gwen Jones (1920-1993) — Thirties and wartime singer who hailed from Tonypandy in south Wales but later moved to London. Having been expelled from school for truanting in favour of attending and singing at music shows she was recommended to Oscar Rabin but was snapped up instead by Stan Atkins. She later recorded with Eddie Carroll, Geraldo, Jack White and Carroll Gibbons.

Howard Jones* (born 1921) — After a few wartime bookings with Frank Weir, Stanley Black and Billy Ternent he was offered full-time employment with Joe Loss where he remained as a vocalist until going solo in 1955.

Bobby Joy** — Young teenage singer with Roy Fox during the Thirties. After the war he swapped his soprano voice for a tenor and continued to appear with Roy Fox throughout the Forties, often doing clever professional imitations of Danny Kaye and the Inkspots — for which purpose he named the latter the Pinkspots.

June — Her real name was June Tripp but after marriage was elevated to Lady Inverclyde. Recorded with Henry Hall in the mid-Thirties by which time she was already an established theatrical name. Also sang with Joe Kaye and toured with Jack Hylton. In the 1927 production of "Clowns in Clover" she appeared with Jack Hulbert and Cicely Courtneidge and was described as "enchantingly pretty and danced like a thistledown".

◁ Wearing an unusual fashion, even for the early-Thirties, is June, later to become Lady Inverclyde.

△ Alberta Hunter starred with Jack Jackson's band.

△ Ella Logan

△ Betty Kent

△ Diana Miller

△ The calm before the storm. When the war clouds finally broke in September, 1939, all centres of musical and theatrical entertainment were temporarily closed but then hastily reopened when it was realised how badly the decision would affect morale. Ella Logan was already in America but Diana Miller got caught up in hostilities in Europe. Betty Kent retired to look after her family.

Alan Kane[**] (1913-1996) — Extremely popular singer of the Thirties and Forties and later a band leader too. Began his singing career with Jan Ralfini but changed his name from Arthur Keizelman to Arthur Kaye when he joined Lou Simmonds and Harry Leader. After succeeding Al Bowlly with Lew Stone he changed his name again, later singing with Billy Thorburn, Mantovani and Ambrose. After a lengthy post-war spell with Eric Winstone he formed his own band which was resident from 1960-1983 at the Wellington Club, Knightsbridge.

▽ Like Mary Lee in Scotland, Welsh girl Gwen Jones took time off school in order to follow dance music. Unlike Mary, she got expelled!

Kathie Kay — Worked with Jimmy Shand and Peter Yorke but was best-known for her appearances on the Billy Cotton Band Show.

Dinah Kaye — Glaswegian who sang with Harry Parry at the end of the war and throughout the Forties, later appearing with Cyril Stapleton, Edmundo Ros, Freddy Randall and Nat Allen.

Edna Kaye — Succeeded Stella Roberta with Mantovani in 1941 and also sang with many bands including Carroll Gibbons, Lou Preager and Primo Scala. Married to Stanley Black.

Harry Kaye — Wartime and post-war singer with Joe Loss, Harry Leader, Harry Roy and Billy Thorburn.

Kaye Sisters — Carol, Sheila and Shan first met as teenagers in 1955 and were initially a popular singing act during the Fifties and Sixties. After going their separate ways they came back together during the early-Nineties when they toured with the Herb Miller Orchestra, (conducted by John Miller) specialising in the sound of the Andrews Sisters.

Eleanor Keenan — Vocalist with Andy Ross, MD of BBC Television's "Come Dancing" series.

Marion Keene — (see Marion Davis).

Annette Keith — Recorded with Joe Loss and Stanley Barnett's Madame Tussaud's band.

Barry Kent (born 1926) — His big break came in 1948 when he won an Eric Winstone inspired national talent contest. Thereafter he sang with Tito Burns, George Evans, George Crow and Harry Roy before launching out into musical theatrical productions. Later retired to Bechuanaland (now Botswana) in Southern Africa.

△ Brian Lawrance was tempted back to his native Australia by an offer he could not refuse but later returned briefly to England.

Betty Kent (1913-1966) — Born Elizabeth Scott-Chisholm, and second cousin to George Chisholm, she married band leader Teddy Foster and quickly became his singer! She later performed with Jack Payne, Lou Preager, Edgar Jackson and Jack Simpson, and appeared in the 1938 Royal Command Performance. After the war she gave up a glittering career to devote herself solely to their adopted daughter but poor health and depression eventually resulted in her suicide.

Frank Kerslake — Recorded with George Scott-Wood's Six Swingers during the mid-Thirties.

Keynotes — Prolific and popular broadcasting group of the late-Forties and Fifties. Before hitting the high spots they recorded with Primo Scala and Harry Roy, and also backed Sam Browne, Denny Dennis and Anne Shelton. Among the changing personnel were founder Johnnie Johnston, Alan Dean, Pearl Carr, Irene King, Terry Devon, Cliff Adams, Harry "Miff" King, Joyce Frazer, Eddie Lester, Frank Holmes, Don Emsley and Jean Campbell.

Master David Kidd — Scottish child singer who recorded with Jack Hylton during the early-Thirties. Together with his brother Bert, they also toured with Hylton as a double act, Bert having written waltzes and songs for the occasion.

Dave Kidd — Scotsman who was born Dave Cooper and sang with brother Nick, and sister Mae, as the Cooper Trio. Later went freelance and sang with several bands.

Irene King (1924-1986) — During the Forties she appeared with Lou Preager, Billy Ternent, Stanley Black, Johnny Claes and Harry Leader. A regular with the Tito Burns Sextet on radio's "Accordion Club" she later sang with both the Keynotes and Coronets

Marjorie Kingsley (see also the Royalists) (born 1922) — Hailed from Westcliff-on-Sea in Essex and began her professional career as a 16-year-old with Joe Loss at the Astoria in London's Charing Cross Road. She then became a vocalist with Harry Roy between 1940-44 and later emigrated to the USA.

Kathy Kirby — This vivacious young lady requested an audition with Ambrose during the mid-Fifties and, so impressed was the old maestro that he took her on and supervised the rest of her successful career. In addition to Ambrose's own band, and, before going solo, she also sang with Nat Allen and Denny Boyce.

Stanley Kirkby — Sang with many bands during the Twenties and Thirties including Alfredo and Jack Payne.

Ken Kirkham (born 1935) — Following an appearance with Joe Loss in 1955 he was invited to join Ronnie Aldrich and the Squadronaires, eventually going solo in the early-Sixties.

Pat Kirkwood — Glamorous film star who made four sides with Jack Hylton at the start of the Second World War, having appeared with him in the wartime film "Band Waggon" starring Arthur Askey and Richard Murdoch.

Valerie Kleiner (born 1938) — On the strength of winning Miss Melody Maker of Butlin's 1954 she made a test record with Geraldo and also appeared on "In Town Tonight". Toured full-time with Ken Moule then changed her name to Vicki Dean and sang with the Kirchin band.

Eddie Kollis (Kolis) — (see Eddie Collis).

Cleo Laine* (born 1927) — Frizzy-haired Clementina Campbell was married to Johnny Dankworth with whose band she sang for a lifetime. Her unusual voice and perfect diction also enabled her to become a successful actress. Made a Dame in 1997.

Dawn Lake — Australian who honeymooned in London during the mid-Fifties and extended her stay long enough to perform with Ted Heath and Cyril Stapleton's Showband.

△ *Fred Latham was also a champion racing cyclist during his youth.*

Les Lambert* — Multi-instrumentalist who was also one of Roy Fox's vocal trio called The Cubs. With the Skyrockets during the war.

Lupino Lane — Famous actor and revue artist who recorded a novelty number with Henry Hall's BBC Dance Orchestra in 1934.

Ben Late — (see Swingtette).

Fred Latham** (1905-1985) — Self-taught saxophone player and singer from New Mills in Derbyshire who cycled all the way to London for a successful audition with Jack Jackson, with whom he subsequently made several records. He also freelanced with Jay Wilbur and Primo Scala before moving on to sing and record with Jack Harris. The original founder of both the Jackdauz (*q.v.*) and the Harristocrats (*q.v.*), he later broadcast with many well-known bands and also briefly ran his own group called the Cuba Swing Band. After call-up he played and sang with the Blue Mariners with whom he broadcast in "Navy Mixture". In 1940 he was on stage with Henry Hall at the Empire Theatre, Sheffield, when a bomb landed backstage. Fortunately, everyone escaped. When hostilities ceased he continued singing until 1950 when he became a publican and later an electrical engineer. A champion cyclist in his youth he thought nothing of doing 50 miles a day following his retirement in 1970.

Brian Lawrance** (1909-1983) — Very popular character, both as a singer and band-leader. Returned to his native Australia during the Second World War, although he did briefly return to Britain during the early-Fifties. A fine hot violinist, he starred in Jack Hylton's film "She Shall Have Music".

Lee Lawrence (1920-1961) — The Second World War brought an abrupt end to his operatic training in Italy so he turned to dance band singing instead. In a relatively brief career cut short by the changing pop music scene, and ultimately a premature heart attack, he sang with Ronnie Pleydell, Geraldo, Stanley Black, George Melachrino, Louis Levy, Ray Martin, Cyril Stapleton and the NDO. He died in America shortly after emigrating to make a fresh musical start.

Annabelle Lee (born 1925) — Real name Angela Lambert, she came to England from France when she was six and sang with ENSA during the war. Post-1945 she appeared firstly with Oscar Rabin and then Don Smith, a former Rabin trumpeter-vocalist, when he formed his own band in Norwich. During the early-Fifties she toured with Denny Dennis and the Fraser Hayes Four.

Benny Lee* (1916-1995) — Versatile singer with many bands who also became famous as a comedian and broadcaster. Born in Scotland he began his career as a young pre-war variety artist but comprehensively failed to make the grade as a singer. During his stag night at Glasgow in 1941, however, his mates bribed band leader Frank King to let him sing, whereupon trumpeter Johnny Claes suggested he should try his luck in London. True to his word, within a few days Johnny invited Benny to join a new band he was forming in the metropolis which unfortunately meant leaving the new Mrs. Lee north of the Border — which was regarded a safer place than London during the Blitz. Benny quickly made the grade and later broadcast with many famous names, including Ambrose, Lew Stone, Primo Scala, Jay Wilbur, Nat Temple, Cyril Stapleton, the Squadronaires, Harry Parry and Oscar Rabin. Post-war appointments came with Louis Levy and Stanley Black but comedy broadcasting then began to edge out his singing career. "Hi Gang" with Ben Lyon, Bebe Daniels and Vic Oliver was succeeded by three programmes featuring well-known Canadian Bernard Braden and his wife, Barbara Kelly. "Breakfast With Braden", "Bedtime With Braden" and "Between Times With Braden" were all extremely popular and led not just to similar television productions but to numerous other radio, television and stage shows. Benny also became a star turn as a disc jockey on "Housewives Choice" and "Midday Spin". The wheel had turned full circle and Benny ended his career the same way as he began it — as a versatile variety artist.

FAMOUS BROADCASTERS' GALLERY OF GREETINGS

THE
LENNER
SHIRLEY
FAMILY

Wish You Every
Happiness

JUDY

ANNE

MAIDIE

SALLY

IDA

SHIRLEY

MUM
and
DAD

△ *Greetings to Mum and Dad in 1937 from the remarkable Lenner Sisters.*

Four of the six sisters used pseudonyms which are explained in the text opposite. This picture shows five of the six, from left to right: Maidie, Rosa (Sally Page), Shirley, Judy (Judy Shirley), and Anne. Ida was away at the time.

Georgia Lee — Classically-trained Australian aboriginal who came to England during the mid-Fifties and sang with Geraldo.

Jackie Lee — Irish girl Jackie Flood sang with Billy Watson in Dublin before coming to England during the mid-Fifties to sing and record with the Squadronaires.

Jane Lee — Married to trumpeter Cyril Ellis she sang during the late-Forties with Harry Gold and Jack Jackson and during the early-Fifties with Sid Phillips. Also a member of the Crackerjacks.

Mary Lee** — (see separate chapter).

Linda Lee — Real name Jessie Harrison, from Peterborough, she appeared with Roy Fox after the war.

Len Lees — Versatile musician and vocalist with Herman Darewski, Fred Elizalde, Arthur Rosebery and Victor Silvester.

Joe Leigh* — Sang and recorded during the late-Twenties and early-Thirties with Fred Elizalde, Alan Green, Jerry Hoey, Harry Hudson, Terry Mack, Carroll Gibbons, Nat Star, and Maurice Winnick.

Lenner Sisters — Six in number, and all fine singers, they hailed from Leicester. They also had two brothers — Herbert who died young, and Arthur, who had a fine voice and was a song writer but who chose to become a cobbler ahead of show business! The family name was Green but father, a north country comedian, changed his name from Arthur to Tom Lenner — while his wife, Florence Wright, was also a solo artist, billed as a "famous variety star". Some of the girls changed their names too! Three became well-known dance band singers — Violet became Anne Lenner; Ivy became Shirley Lenner; and Florence became Judy Shirley; meanwhile Rose became Rosa, enjoying some early success as a dance band singer, and also going on stage as Sally Page; Ida did a double act with Violet called the Lenner Sisters, and also performed with her husband Bert Ford in a double act called "The Capitols"; while Maidie, also a fine singer, married a millionaire! Quite a family!

Anne Lenner** (1909-1997) — Best-known for her singing and recording sessions with Carroll Gibbons and the Savoy Hotel Orpheans, with whom she sang from 1934 until 1941. Initially she thought she had missed her chance when she overslept for the first recording session but Gibbons was so keen to sign her that he arranged another one three hours later! She also recorded with Joe Loss, George Scott-Wood, Frank Weir, Jack White and Jay Wilbur, and featured on a wartime session with Maurice Winnick, following in the footsteps of big sister Judy Shirley, who was Winnick's vocalist during the mid-Thirties. In addition to performing on records and radio, in 1937 Anne appeared with Eric Wild's Tea Timers, the first dance band to feature regularly on the infant television screen. She also appeared in the 1940 film "Garrison Follies" and did a variety double-act with Bob Harvey during the late-Forties called "Just the Two of Us".

Shirley Lenner (1922-1967) — She was not even a teenager (although the word had not yet been invented) when she began singing with Stan Atkins and Tommy Kinsman, and was not much older when she recorded with George Elrick and Joe Loss. During the war she worked briefly for ENSA, married and then retired in her early-twenties to be a mother. Sadly, she died in 1967, aged only 43, having been overcome by carbon monoxide poisoning while in her bath. A blocked chimney was discovered to be the cause.

Queenie Leonard — Appeared in West End musicals and recorded with Van Phillips and Percival Mackey.

Archie Lewis (1917-1988) — Jamaican-born singer who came to England during the war and recorded several records with Geraldo.

Harry Lewis (1916-1998) — Occasional crooner with George Elrick during the late-Thirties but better-known as a sax player with Ambrose, Jack Harris, Jack Jackson and the Squadronaires. Married Vera Lynn in 1941.

△ *Queenie Leonard was also an actress.*

△ June Malo married snooker player, Joe Davis.

Patti Lewis — Canadian-born she came to England on her honeymoon in 1952 at which point her husband, pianist Red Mitchell, joined Vic Lewis. Already a dance band singer, three years later Patti sang at the Festival of Dance Music at the Royal Albert Hall which was followed by an appearance on Henry Hall's "Guest Night". In 1956 she replaced Janie Marden with the BBC Showband but, after completing several more records, stage, radio and television appearances, she returned home to Canada at the end of the decade.

Kealoha Life (born 1920) — The only really Polynesian connection of Felix Mendelssohn's Hawaiian Serenaders who made several recordings with the band before retiring to South Wales.

Janet Lind (1905-1986) — Australian-born Reita Nugent came to London during the Twenties, where she appeared in various musicals alongside such famous names as Jack Hulbert, Gertrude Lawrence, Binnie Hale and Bobby Howes. During the mid-Thirties she changed her name and, after deputising for Judy Shirley, sang and recorded with Louis Levy. She also appeared with Peter Yorke and the BBC Northern Studio Orchestra, based in Manchester and led by Tommy Matthews. She married in 1935 and moved to America four years later, eventually returning to Melbourne where they started an antiques business. Janet admitted she could not read music but was note perfect after one hearing, honing a tune to perfection by singing it over and over again while relaxing in her bath!

Celia Lipton** — Sang in her father Sydney's band for three years, and also performed with Lew Stone and Jack Hylton. Eventually emigrated to America where she married a millionaire and enjoyed a lavish lifestyle, still performing well into old age.

Pauline Lister — (see Carlyle Cousins).

Renee Lister (see also the Royalists) — Wartime singer with Harry Roy. Real name Renee Lester, later changed to Suzi Miller.

Kathy Lloyd — Australian who sang with Percy Winnick's band "down under" before spending all her savings to come to England and audition for Ted Heath after she heard Lita Roza might be leaving. She was an instant success and, 12 months later was back in the Antipodes touring with the band when she met and married a former boy friend. After a brief spell back in England she decided to join her husband in Hollywood where she launched out into a solo career.

Billie Lockwood — Recorded with Nat Star, Jay Wilbur and Sydney Lipton during the early-Thirties.

Buddy Logan (died 1992) — Ella's brother who sang with both Geraldo and Lew Stone.

Ella Logan** — Glamorous Scottish-born singer who, before disappearing to make a name in America, recorded with Jack Payne, Ambrose, Len Fillis, Jack Hylton, Roy Fox and Arthur Lally.

Eve Lombard — One of Harry Roy's immediate post-war singers who stayed until 1952 before going solo.

Tony Lombardo — (see Eric Whitley).

Jack Lorimer (died 1975) (see also Rhythm Brothers) — In addition to being a sometime member of Ambrose's famous Rhythm Brothers he also recorded with Harry Leader, Brian Lawrance, Maurice Winnick and Jay Wilbur. Older brother of comedian Max Wall (Maxwell George Lorimer, 1908-1990).

Loss Chords — Clever group title for various members of Joe Loss's singers who first came together during the war.

Dennis Lotis (born 1925) — South African-born singer with an unmistakable velvet voice who hit the jackpot when he tried his luck in England during the early-Fifties. As a replacement for Paul Carpenter in Ted Heath's band, he appeared alongside Lita Roza and Dickie Valentine. He later sang with Geraldo and became a national celebrity who never really went away, performing in plays, films and a Royal Variety Performance. The end of the 20th century saw him touring with Rosemary Squires in a show called "Day by Day", based on the life of the great American star Doris Day.

Peter Lowe — Dennis Lotis's younger brother who arrived to replace him in the Ted Heath band in 1955, returning to further his career in Johannesburg two years later.

△ Who says show-biz marriages don't work? This happy engagement picture of Bob Mallin and Yolande Mageean was taken in 1939. 60 years later they celebrated their Diamond Wedding in San Diego, California, where they had lived for many years. Bob came from "Four in Harmony" while Yolande came from "Three in Harmony", one of the few occasions when seven made two!

Doreen Lundy (1925-1986) — When Paul Fenoulhet agreed to her joining the Skyrockets during the war he got more than he bargained before – because they were married in 1949. She later sang with Geraldo, Max Jaffa and Eddie Calvert.

Vera Lynn** — (see separate chapter).

Barbara Lyon (1932-1995) — Daughter of Ben Lyon and Bebe Daniels who briefly flirted with a singing career before fading from view during the early-Sixties.

Lydia MacDonald — Ted Heath's first female singer who also appeared on some of his earliest records.

Helen Mack* — Glaswegian who began with Ronnie Munro then made a name with Lew Stone before appearing with Nat Gonella, Vic Lewis, Nat Temple, Sid Phillips, Frank Weir, Ray Martin, Tommy Sampson and the Blue Rockets.

Mackpies — Ken Mackintosh's singing and recording group from the Fifties, comprising Irene Miller, Kenny Bardell, Don Lang, Terry Fahey and Ken himself.

Yolande Mageean — (see Three in Harmony and Four in Harmony).

Bob Mallin — (see Three in Harmony and Four in Harmony).

June Malo — Born Juanita Triggs in South London she went to the RCM where she studied under violinist Albert Sammons. A keen pianist she also enjoyed dancing and then began a singing career with Charlie Kunz at the Casani Club. Success followed success and she appeared with Billy Gerhardi, Joe Kaye, Chappie D'Amato and notably, Jack Hylton, with whom she toured Europe When war arrived she went with Billy Ternent to Bristol before pursuing a solo career which took in various radio programmes including "ITMA" with Tommy Handley, "Band Waggon" with Richard Murdoch and Arthur Askey, "Garrison Theatre" with Jack Warner, where she replaced Joan Winters as his "little gel" and "Hi-de-Hi" with Monsewer Eddie Gray. She later married world champion snooker player, Joe Davis, and accompanied him on exhibition tours after his retirement.

◁ *While singing on local radio in the United States, Alice Mann was persuaded to audition for Billy Bissett (inset) in Toronto. Romance blossomed and they became engaged but before they could get married she was contracted to tour with Jack Hylton in Europe. She had trouble locating him as he moved about the Continent but once back in England, Billy called a halt to her travels by tying the knot and keeping her as his own singer.*

Manhattan Trio — (see Clive Erard, and Frank & Jack Trafford).

Alice Mann — American wife and singer to Canadian band leader Billy Bissett, who appeared over here during the Thirties before moving back home across the North Atlantic. She also toured Europe with Jack Hylton and recorded with him.

Lorie Mann — Sang initially with Joe Daniels in the mid-Fifties and then moved to Oscar Rabin's band which had been taken over by David Ede following front man Harry Davis's departure to America in 1950 and Oscar's death in 1958.

Margery Manners (1925-1997) — Although better known as a variety artiste she sang with Billy Merrin and his Commanders, and also with Big Bill Campbell and his Rocky Mountaineers.

Bernard Manning — Anyone who heard this Lancashire comedian sing would have instantly recognised a trained voice which was honed during his time with Oscar Rabin.

Bob Manning — Part of Jack Payne's vocal trio who also played timpani with George Fisher, and Jay Wilbur.

Tony Mansell — Sang post-war with Ronnie Jay and Leigh Martin before joining Johnny Dankworth's new big band alongside Cleo Laine and Frank Holder. He also appeared with the Courtley-Seymour band and Denny Boyce, and was a founder-member of the Polka Dots vocal group. He is probably best-remembered for his own Tony Mansell Singers.

Janie Marden — After band leader husband Teddy White recommended she turn professional in 1955, she was quickly signed up by Cyril Stapleton for the BBC Show Band, with whom she stayed for 12 months before pursuing a successful solo career. She later sang with the Malcolm Mitchell trio and Geoff Love

June Marlow (born 1934) — Hailing from Portsmouth she was something of a childhood prodigy and sang with local bands whilst still a young girl. She also appeared on "Opportunity Knocks" while still only 13. In 1953 she joined Eric Winstone and toured three seasons of holiday camps before becoming a member of the Stargazers, with whom she made several records. She also recorded with Cyril Stapleton during the Sixties.

Rita Marlowe — Recorded with Ambrose, Stanley Black, Harry Parry, Sid Phillips and Eric Winstone during and after the war.

Jo Marney — Born in Barking, East London she was encouraged to try dance band singing by Ivor Mairants. After making her debut with Johnny Howard, she then rubbed shoulders with many big names including Sydney Lipton and Malcolm Lockyer, and also recorded various advertising jingles. Then came a very happy time with Billy Ternent's band, prior to his demise in 1977. Thereafter she concentrated on freelance work.

Tressa Marshall — (see Thressa Dale and the Rhythm Sisters).

Glenn Martin — Vocalist with the wartime RAOC Blue Rockets.

Steve Martin — Manchester tailor who sang part-time at the Ritz ballroom before moving to London in the mid-Fifties where he appeared with several bands, including Nat Temple and Lou Preager.

Kitty Masters** (1902-1994) — Salford-born Katherine Masterson made an early public appearance when, at the age of only six, she sang *The Red Flag* at a union meeting to which her father had taken her! Thereafter, encouraged by her parents, she appeared regularly on stage alongside such names as George Robey (who taught her how to handle an audience), Ella Shields and Hetty King. Her mother's ill health and necessity for constant nursing postponed her solo singing career, however, but after she obtained a local engagement in Manchester she then went round the Paramount theatres as a kind of female Lone Ranger. Dressed in a mask and billed as "The Masked Crooner" her identity was kept a secret with audiences being fooled into believing she was an American. She then went to London to seek an audition and bumped into Mantovani who signed her up on the spot. She then worked with Harry Leader and Henry Hall, famously recording *Little Man You've Had a Busy Day*, which brought her a huge fan mail. Successfully appearing with Les Allen as a double act she later went solo and worked with ENSA during the war. During the late-Forties she was a director of Starway, a small passenger airline.

Valerie Masters (born 1940) — Vocalist with the Ray Ellington Quartet during the mid-Fifties.

Dick Maxwell — Guitarist, banjoist and singer with Fred Elizalde during the late-Twenties.

Mayfair Men — Male trio which sang with Sydney Lipton just before the war. Its members were George Melachrino, Sam Costa and "Chips" Chippendall.

McCarthy Sisters — Americans, Frances, Jewel and Dorothy sang with Jack Hylton during the mid-Thirties. With the addition of Eugene Prentiss and Ben Late, they formed the Swingtette.

Suzanne McClay — Pre-war croonette with Bram Martin.

Pat McCormack (1914-1971) — Cork-born and came to England from Ireland during the Thirties when he was signed by Roy Fox to tour Australia. After the band reached the USA he spent a year in Los Angeles before returning home in 1941 to sing for five years with Joe Loss, later returning for a brief spell in the early-Fifties.

Mary McGowan — Popular singer with the Clyde Valley Stompers during the mid-Fifties traditonal jazz boom.

Helen McKay (see also Debonaires) — Red-headed croonette who recorded with Lew Stone pre-war and sang the specially-commissioned song for the opening of BBC Television in 1936.

Florine McKinney — Recorded during the mid-Thirties with Jack Jackson.

George Melachrino** (1909-1965) — Amazingly gifted and versatile, George consciously set out to master all the musical instruments of the orchestra, succeeding with everything apart from the piano and harp — a rare achievement indeed! Before he became a major band leader he also sang with several famous names, including Jack Jackson and Carroll Gibbons.

George Melly — One of only a handful of true British male jazz singers whose personality was as big as his figure. Raconteur *extraordinaire!*

Tony Mercer (1920-1971) — Prior to finding fame on the "Black and White Minstrel Show" (once voted the best programme on colour TV!) he actually cut his singing teeth with Bram Martin, Lew Stone, Roy Fox, Eric Winstone, Billy Ternent and Harry Bence.

◁ *Kitty Masters was a Lancastrian from Salford but ended up as a post-war airline director.*

△ *During the mid-Thirties, Molly, Marie and Mary were signed by Henry Hall who promptly renamed them the Three Sisters. They were not related, however, and also kept their identities a secret. All we know about this photo is that from left to right, they were Mary, Marie and Molly.*

Ray Merrell — Following National Service in the RAF he sang with Phil Phillips at Sale, Cheshire and Arthur Plant at the Manchester Ritz. He then spent three years with Eric Winstone at Butlin's before joining Cyril Stapleton in 1960.

Merry Macs — Close-harmony American quartet discovered by Jack Hylton at the Drake Hotel in Chicago. He recorded with them, then took them to New York with a view to their singing in England but at the last minute discarded them in favour of the Swingtette (*q.v.*). This proved a blessing, however, because they later went to Hollywood, recorded with Ray Noble, and toured Europe several times, making six appearances at the London Palladium (one of which was the 1950 Royal Command Performance). Founded by the McMichael brothers (Jack – the eldest who stayed only a short time — Judd, Ted and Joe) they later included Clive Erard, a former member of Ambrose's Rhythm Brothers. Among the female singers were Cheri McKay and Mary Lou Cook. They came financially unstuck on one of their later European tours, however, when Jack Hylton — by now an impresario — came to their rescue!

Jimmy Messini* (died 1969) — Real name James Mesene. His successful variety act with Al Bowlly was dramatically cut short when the latter was killed in the Blitz. Guitarist and vocalist with several bands, including Nat Gonella, Teddy Joyce, Joe Loss, Jack Payne and Billy Thorburn. Died in Montreal, Canada.

Walter Midgley — Famous ballad singer who recorded for Geraldo in 1940 under the name of Michael Eastley.

Ray Millar — Sang with Mantovani's wartime dance band.

Betty Miller — Vocalist with Sid Phillips during the early-Fifties who later ran her own rhythm group.

Dinah (Diana) Miller** (born 1916) — Real name Winifred but changed it to Dinah to avoid confusion with another Winifred in a talent contest at a Tooting cinema where she was booked to appear with Harold Ramsay's Rhythm Symphony. She also toured with his Grand Serenaders. Extremely popular pre-war also with Reginald Williams, Jack Harris, Oscar Rabin (with whom she was the vocalist during his first broadcast), Sydney Kyte and Joe Loss, and always did well in public opinion polls on female singers. Just before the war began she

▷ *Stella Moya was Nat Gonella's wartime wife and vocalist and together they had a narrow escape from occupied France.*

accepted an invitation to sing in Denmark from where she was unable to escape the Nazi invasion. Now known as Diana Miller she was later able to decamp to Norway and Sweden where she was allowed to continue performing despite her pianist being interned. Returned post-war to West End club work and broadcast with Stanley Black but spent most of her time back in Scandinavia.

Irene Miller — Began post-war with Ken Mackintosh and also sang with Joe Loss, Tito Burns, Johnnie Gray, Jack Parnell and Frank King.

Jimmy Miller* (1916-2001) — Initially a pianist and vocalist with Mrs. Jack Hylton, as wartime Sergeant Miller he later went on to lead and sing with the Squadronaires, leaving in 1949 to work with Carroll Gibbons at the Savoy Hotel.

Suzi Miller — Joined the wartime Harry Roy band under her real name of Renee Lester (incorrectly spelt Lister on records), later re-appearing in the early-Fifties with Carroll Gibbons and Maurice Winnick. She was then persuaded to change her name and recorded several songs as a solo artiste.

Annette Mills — Older sister of the actor Sir John Mills who, before she found television fame with "Muffin the Mule" during the early-Fifties, invented the dance called *Boomps-a-Daisy* which she recorded with Joe Loss in 1939. Jack Dent wrote the music.

Billy Milton (1906-1989) — Talented and versatile singer who appeared in variety revues and was an integral member of the pre-war society set which included the Prince of Wales. Recorded with Van Phillips, Percival Mackey, Ray Noble and Harry Roy.

Milton Sisters — (actually Pat Hyde and Dinah Miller, *q.v.*)

Edward Molloy — Recorded with Jack Hylton and Louis Levy during the mid-Thirties.

Molly, Marie and Mary — (see The Three Sisters).

Matt Monro (1930-1985) — Real name Terry Parsons, he sang with Harry Leader who renamed him Al Jordan during a six-month tour in 1955. After this, however, and back under his usual name, he sang with Cyril Stapleton, Bob Miller and Tommy Watt, before hitting the big time as a solo artist, aided in no small measure by Winifred Attwell.

Molly Morelle (born 1917) — Blonde Leeds-born Molly initially sang with Charlie Steel all over Yorkshire before being spotted by Henry Hall in 1938. Post-war she appeared in Sweden.

Martin Moreno — Latin-American in appearance and able to sing in Spanish he was actually a Cockney called George Richards. Performed with Stanley Black.

Dennis Morley — Vocalist with the Malcolm Mitchell Trio during the mid-Fifties.

Tony Morris — Vocalist, saxophonist and clarinettist with Jack White just before and during the war.

Jack Morrison — Recorded with Harry Bidgood and Percival Mackey in the late-Twenties.

Hugh Morton — First sang anonymously with Dare Lea's band in the mid-Thirties then came to the fore once he was identified. Later became an announcer, Children's Hour Uncle and appeared in both "Life With the Lyons" films.

Stella Moya** — Nat Gonella's second wife who recorded several pre-war sides with the band.

Kay Munro-Smith (or Munro-Smyth(e) — see Rhythm Sisters).

Ruby Murray (1935-1996) — Red-haired, blue-eyed, soft-spoken Irish star of the mid-Fifties who sadly became an alcoholic and died relatively young. Although not strictly a dance band singer, during the early day she appeared with Kenny Baker.

Mary Naylor — Sang with Billy Merrin and Henry Hall and also appeared in musicals with Tommy Trinder.

Stella Nelson — (see Stella Roberta).

△ *Florence Oldham was not the only dance band singer who appeared on Radio Luxembourg's pre-war "Rinso Review", every Sunday at 6.30pm. There were many other similar programmes.*

Max and Harry Nesbitt — Recorded with Jack Hylton and Harry Roy.

Sydney Nesbitt — Recorded with Bert Firman, Ronnie Munro and Jack Payne during the late-Twenties.

Raymond Newell — Recorded with Geraldo and several times with Debroy Somers,

Carole Newton — Vocalist with the Malcolm Mitchell Trio in the mid-Fifties.

Cyril Ramon Newton** (1892-1965) — Possibly the first ever singer to broadcast on radio – with the Savoy Havana Band during the early-Twenties.

Billy Nichols — Recorded with Oscar Rabin and Arthur Young.

Penny Nicholls* — Began singing pre-war with Billy Merrin who spotted her during one of his shows in Ramsgate. From there she won the All-Britain Tap Dancing Contest and during the war performed with Ivor Kirchin. After a brief spell with Teddy Foster she was reunited with Billy Merrin, had her own radio programme in the Midlands called "Penny Serenade" and appeared on many other radio and television shows. She also toured the country in countless summer spectaculars and Christmas pantomimes, and appeared with Cyril Stapleton's Showband.

Joy Nichols (1927-1992) — Versatile singer and variety actress who came to England from Australia after the war. After making a record with Harry Roy she became well-known as a singer and character artiste in the Jimmy Edwards and Dick Bentley radio comedy series "Take It from Here". After making several more records, including the hit song *Little Red Monkey* with Dick Bentley, and a brief spell back in Australia, she starred in her own radio show called "Shout for Joy". She also appeared on television with Henry Hall before moving to America where she appeared on Broadway.

Cyril Norman — Real name Leslie Norton, he sang pre-war with Herman Darewski.

Monty Norman (born 1928) — Married to Diana Coupland whom he met while they were both singing with Stanley Black. Originally a hairdresser "The Singing Barber" also appeared with Archie May, Cyril Stapleton, and Frank Chacksfield

Cavan O'Connor** — (see separate chapter).

Ronnie O'Dell* (born 1909) — Child prodigy from Leeds who grew into a versatile band leader, pianist, guitarist and vocalist. While still only 18 he toured the Continent with the clown Noni, then toured at home with Syd Seymour before joining Maurice Winnick at the Piccadilly Hotel. After a spell in Holland with Billy Mason, he formed his own band sponsored by Lew Stone, and during the mid-Thirties played midweek at Lewis's store in Liverpool with Saturday evenings at the Grosvenor Hotel, Chester. Also recorded with Henry Hall, Sydney Lipton, Phil Green, George Scott-Wood and Lew Stone, often using the pseudonym Ronnie Ogilvy.

Kathran "Kip" Oldfield — Canadian singer who appeared over here after the war with Robert Farnon, Laurie Johnson, Syd Dean and Ray Martin.

Florence Oldham (died 1971) — Known as the "whispering soprano" in 1926 she sang with Sidney Firman's London Radio Dance Band at the BBC and two years later recorded with Al Starita's Piccadilly Players. In 1935 she compèred Lloyd Shakespeare's radio programme called "Happy Weekend" and the following year was appearing with Joe Loss in the West End. After the war she played the music halls as a soloist.

Pat O'Malley** (1901-1985) — Made many successful records with Jack Hylton between 1930 and 1936, also recording with Mantovani, Charlie Kunz, Arthur Rosebery, Ray Starita, Jay Wilbur, and Ray Noble. Emigrated to America after touring with Jack Hylton, where he established himself in films, especially Walt Disney for whom he played the voice of the elephant Colonel Hathi in "The Jungle Book".

Eileen Orchard (1926-1981) — Sang post-war with Lou Preager where she met and married famous trombonist Don Lusher who, later took over the running of the Ted Heath band. She also recorded with Billy Ternent.

Pat O'Regan — Recorded pre-war with Josephine Bradley, Lew Stone and Jay Wilbur, during the war with Ken "Snakehips" Johnson, and sang post-war with Billy Ternent and Primo Scala.

Elva Orr — (see Three in Harmony).

Primrose Orrock (died 1999) — Married to Harry Hayes and recorded with Jack Hylton and Billy Thorburn. Once described as Roy Fox's "Glamour Girl" and also sang with Tommy Finnigan in Edinburgh.

Tessie O'Shea (1914-1995) — "Two Ton" Tessie (sometimes even "Ten Ton") was a real character of ample girth but always full of fun and laughter. In a life packed with variety and entertainment she appeared in several films and shows, and also sang with Billy Cotton's band.

Dawn Page** (see uncaptioned picture on page 103 Volume One) — Sang with Eric Delaney's new band during the early-Fifties

Gail Page — Sang with Harry Parry's Radio Rhythm Club Sextet after the war.

Jill Page — (see Jill Day).

Many of the sponsored independent radio programmes beamed in across the English Channel, especially from Radio Normandy and Radio Luxembourg, contained excellent dance music. The most famous show of all was the "Ovaltineys Concert Party" and among those taking part were Phil Green and his Orchestra, Monte Rey, Tessa Deane and Jack Miranda, while the Jackdauz were thinly disguised as the Hillbilly Uncles! Two of the original child Ovaltineys were Beryl Davis masquerading as Letter I and Millicent Phillips as Letter E. Debroy Somers starred in "Horlicks' Tea-Time Hour" while Sam Browne, the Radio Three, Arthur Young and Reginald Foresythe were sponsored by Rowntrees Fruit Gums and Pastilles in "The Melody Maker" each Friday at 6.30pm. Radio Paris was home to Carroll Gibbons and his Boy Friends.

Fiona Paige — Vocalist with the Herb Miller Orchestra, where she sang alongside the band's leader John Miller, son of Herb and nephew of Glenn Miller, on whose sound the band was based.

Barbara Palmer — Coached by Maurice Elwin she performed during the Thirties with Art Gregory, Al Berlin and Billy Thorburn, and was popular with the troops during the war. Married for 45 years to musical entrepreneur Dave Toff, who looked after her when she went blind.

Ennis Parkes** (1894-1957) — Jack Hylton's first wife and early singer who later led her own band.

Harry Parry** — (see Jackdauz).

Syd Parsons — Cinema manager of the Commodore, Hammersmith, who broadcast with Harry Davidson and the Commodore Grand Orchestra as "The Mystery Singer".

Ottilie Patterson (born 1932) — A little girl with a huge voice. Arriving in England from Northern Ireland during the early-Fifties she met, and eventually married, Chris Barber, with whose band she made several records, her deep voice accurately imitating the great American Blues singers of the Twenties and Thirties.

Bob & Alf Pearson — Although largely a cabaret duet they featured on pre-war recordings with Harry Bidgood, Benny Loban, Jack Payne and Jay Wilbur. Bob (1907-1985) and Alf (born 1910), usually introduced their act with "We bring you melody from out of the sky, my brother and I". Prize-winning choirboys from Wearside in County Durham, they moved south when their father won a contract to plaster a large development of houses alongside the Kingston by-pass at Tolworth in Surrey. There they met a salesman showing prospective customers around the show house — but Roy Plomley changed careers and later founded "Desert Island Discs". After an unsuccessful audition with Columbia records, who decided their double-act sounded too much like Layton and Johnstone, who were already under contract, they were introduced to Jack Hylton which paved the way for a full-time show business career. In 1929 they were probably the first singers to appear on a television set, as models for John Logie Baird. Later they appeared with Ted Ray in the radio programme "Ray's A Laugh" featuring the weekly "Why, it's a little girl ... What's your name?" Bob's falsetto voice then replied "Jen-ni-fer ...!" followed by an hilarious bit of banter with Ted.

Another part of the same show was Bob and Alf's comedy patter between Mrs. 'Oskins and her friend Ivy ... "Oooh, it's agony Ivy!" which was a trigger to set the whole nation laughing. Complicated? No! Funny? Yes!

Donald Peers (1910-1973) — When invited to perform at a Sunday School concert party, aged nine, Donald chose to sing *When Father Papered the Parlour*, not quite what the organisers had in mind! Rather than become a trainee teacher he later ran away from home and by the age of 17 was already a variety artist. He became well-known after an appearance on the radio programme "Music Hall" and adopted *In a Shady Nook By a Babbling Brook* as his signature tune. He recorded pre-war with Bertini on the Woolworth's Eclipse label and also with Jay Wilbur, Phil Green and Harry Bidgood. Surprisingly, following a live BBC performance at the Kings Theatre, Hammersmith in 1949, he suddenly became a national icon. Besieged wherever he went and receiving 3,000 fan letters a week, a huge number in those days, he was dubbed "Britain's Frank Sinatra". He remained at the top of the tree until the Rock 'n' Roll era arrived in the mid-Fifties but thereafter still managed to maintain a healthy audience rating whenever he performed. Unfortunately, he was badly injured when he fell off an Australian stage in 1971, effectively putting paid to his career as well as his great love of golf.

Charles Penrose — Immortalised in *The Laughing Policeman* he also made several other jolly recordings, notably with Harry Bidgood, Arthur Lally, Percival Mackey, Ray Noble and Jay Wilbur.

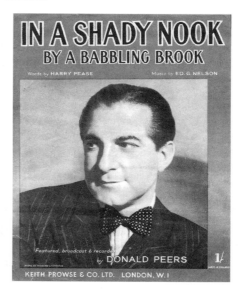

Master Joe Petersen — "Master Joe", who played the music halls and theatres, was actually Mary O'Rourke in disguise but few people suspected it. He/she made one dance band recording with Primo Scala's Accordion Band.

Cecile Petrie — (see Carlyle Cousins).

Harry Phillips — Pre-war singer with Joe Loss, Bram Martin and Al Collins.

Millicent Phillips (born 1924) — "England's Deanna Durbin" made her first radio broadcast on BBC Children's Hour from Birmingham at the age of 12, after which she became "Letter E" in the "Ovaltineys" programme on Radio Luxembourg. After winning the "new voice" contest on Richard Murdoch and Arthur Askey's "Band Waggon" show, she appeared in both the theatre production at the London Palladium and also Jack Hylton's touring version. She also had her own shows on Radio Luxembourg and Radio Normandy, worked for ENSA with Lew Stone and went on to sing with Billy Cotton, Jack Payne and Ivy Benson. In all she made several hundred broadcasts and worked with many other famous names (including a youthful couple called Morecambe and Wise — but before they became "Morecambe and Wise"!), Richard Tauber, Albert Sandler, John Hanson and Rawicz and Landauer. A later recording of 40 nursery songs found its way into a certain royal household in London where it was extremely well received by the youngest members of the family!

Norman Phillips — Saxophone player and violinist who also sang with Sydney Kyte, Ray Noble and Jay Wilbur.

△ Millicent Phillips — "England's Deanna Durbin" — began her career by winning both her own and an older vocal section at the Cheltenham Music Festival. The mother of the runner-up in the latter complained about Millicent being under-age and so the trophy was shared!

▷ Bob (left) and Alf Pearson were always immaculately dressed, but got turned down by Columbia Records because they sounded too much like Layton and Johnstone! It did not affect their career, however, and after a chance meeting with Roy Plomley, they became probably the first singers to appear on television — as models for John Logie Baird in 1929. As radio entertainers they became famous for two catch-phrases which always brought a chuckle with Ted Ray in "Ray's A Laugh" — "Jen-ni-fer!" and "It's agony, Ivy!"

Ray Pilgrim — Sang with David Ede's Rabin Band at the Wimbledon Palais during the late-Fifties and early-Sixties.

Jack Plant** (1897-1973) — Cheshire-born, he served in the First World War fledgling Tank Corps where he enjoyed entertaining his comrades. His working life actually began in a Manchester soap factory but, an excellent sportsman and athlete, in 1920 he had a trial for Manchester United football club! He then tried his luck in the concert hall but a prospective operatic career was abandoned when, at the suggestion of Maurice Elwin, he successfully auditioned for Jack Hylton in 1931. He later sang and recorded over 1,000 sides with more than 20 bands including Henry Hall (with whom he also toured for ENSA during the war), Ray Noble, Maurice Winnick, Carroll Gibbons, Roy Fox, Jack Payne, Harry Bidgood and Jay Wilbur — indeed the only famous band leaders he did not apparently appear with were Ambrose and Charlie Kunz. Among his many pseudonyms was The Velvet Voice, a nice touch for a small and gentle man who enjoyed the outdoor life and was content simply to earn enough to live on. In later life he entertained his fellow-pensioners. Also known as Carol Porter (Eclipse records) and Jack Gordon.

Eugene Prentiss — (see Swingtette).

Teddy Prince — (see Jackdauz).

Danny Purches (Born 1933) — A real-life gypsy who sang with Stanley Black and Eric Delaney before becoming a solo artist. Being a genuine nomad he often went "walkabout", especially after he had been paid! On one occasion he failed to show up for a recording session with Ray Martin's orchestra so they did the backing without him, his voice being dubbed in when he surfaced a couple of days later!

⊲ *Jack Plant first tried his luck as a footballer with Manchester United!*

The Radio Three — Close harmony group of the mid-Thirties comprising Joy Worth, Kay Cavendish and Ann Canning. They recorded with Geraldo, Lew Stone and Jay Wilbur.

Lynette Rae (born 1930) — Early-Fifties singer with Edmundo Ros who was vocally competent in eight languages. Recorded with Benny Lee when Joy Nichols was taken ill.

The Ramblers — Short-lived recording group of the late-Twenties consisting of Maurice Elwin, Bert d'Arcy and Hal Vidler.

Helen Raymond* (see Rhythm Sisters) — Member of Ambrose's Rhythm Sisters but also recorded separately with Harry Leader, Billy Merrin, Billy Thorburn and Peter Yorke.

Joan Regan (born 1929) — Recommended by Lou Preager she joined Al Feld at Brighton but, at the age of only 17, married a USAF lieutenant and moved to America. Returning to London during the early-Fifties she started her career all over again. Despite turning down an offer to succeed Lita Roza in Ted Heath's band she soon became well-known and, although mainly a solo artist, also recorded with Sid Phillips, Ray Martin and the Squadronaires. Remarkably, after suffering a brain haemorrhage, she taught herself to sing again.

Monte Rey** — (see separate chapter).

The Rhythm Brothers — Various singers made up Ambrose's vocal trio in the mid-Thirties, including Ronnie Hill, Clive Erard, Jack Cooper, George Elrick and Jack Lorimer. They also recorded with Debroy Somers, Lew Stone (where Erard was joined by Frank and Jack Trafford), and Jay Wilbur.

Helen Raymond

▷ This photo of Ambrose's Rhythm Brothers depicts Jack Lorimer (left), Ronnie Hill (centre) and Clive Erard. Below them is a shot of Sam Browne and Elsie Carlisle in the middle of their double-act.

◁ *The Rhythm Sisters changed personnel several times. This 1935 picture shows the ill-fated Jean Conibear (left), Helen Raymond (centre) and founder, Kay Munro-Smith. Jean was killed driving her car but Kay escaped unscathed from the accident and continued music-making until the age of 82!*

The Rhythm Sisters — Polished singing trio founded in the early-Thirties by Kay Munro-Smith (1907-1997) who featured initially with fellow-Glaswegians Berti Shaw and Mae Munn (Billy's younger sister). The latter were replaced in 1933 by Scots sisters Betty and Thressa (Teresa, Tressa) Dale. Two years later they in turn were succeeded by Helen Raymond (1903-1989) and Jean "Connie" Conibear (1907-1936). All went well until Jean was killed driving her own car, an accident from which Kay and Pat Taylor (*q.v.*) of the Eight Step Sisters, escaped relatively unscathed. Helen then decided to go solo so Kay selected two new partners, 20-year-old Vicky Roberts and 23-year-old Isabel March. Unfortunately Geraldo did not like Isabel's voice so a month later she was succeeded by Mavis Edmonds. Occasionally the Dale Sisters augmented the group to five but by the time the 1937 films "Around the Town" (Vic Oliver) and "Feather Your Nest" (George Formby) were made, the group was back to three in the form of Kay, Mavis and Thressa.

Kay and Mavis then became members of Molly, Marie and Mary (*q.v.*) after which Kay reformed the Rhythm Sisters yet again, this time with Vicky Roberts and a new addition called Donna la Bourdais, briefly renaming themselves the Three Sweethearts of Swing. Wartime saw Kay form a Glaswegian group called The Cheerful Earfuls which included Mae Munn.

In 1947 the Rhythm Sisters were again briefly reformed, with Kay and Mae being joined by Jeanette. Kay (or Katie to close friends) then settled down to family life although she continued music-making until the age of 82!

The Rhythm Sisters first auditioned for Jack Hylton in 1933, appeared in many shows and recorded with Ambrose, Lew Stone, Harry Leader, George Scott-Wood, Joe Loss and Jay Wilbur. Betty Dale recorded many individual records with Joe Loss, Thressa Dale later sang with Bram Martin as Tressa Marshall, and Helen Raymond recorded separately with Harry Leader, Billy Merrin, and Billy Thorburn.

△ *Foster Richardson was equally at home with both serious and popular music.*

Paul Rich (1921-2000) — Initially a guitar-playing vocalist with Harry Leader, Eddie Carroll, Ronnie Munro and Oscar Rabin, he joined Lou Preager in 1941 and stayed until 1955 thus becoming Lou's longest serving singer. He also recorded several sides for the Woolworth brand name "Embassy" label.

Jean Richards — (see Kerri Simms).

Foster Richardson (born 1890) — Nottingham farmer's son who studied at the Royal Academy of Music and was equally at home singing with Sir Thomas Beecham as he was recording during the Twenties and early-Thirties with Bert Firman, Ray Noble, Nat Star, Jack Payne, Jay Whidden and Jay Wilbur.

Anita Riddell — (see Four in Harmony).

Pat Rignold — (see Cavendish Three).

Stella Roberta** (born 1910) — Remilia Brunelda Mantovani was a Venetian, like her older brother Annunzio who was better-known simply as Mantovani, and for whose orchestra she sang during the Thirties, initially as Stella Nelson. With her ability to speak four languages and sing anything from opera to jazz, she was ideal for the orchestra's international flavour. She retired in 1941 and was succeeded by Edna Kaye.

Bette Roberts — Recorded with Joe Loss during the war.

Hilda Roberts — Sang concert pieces with Herman Darewski between 1936-9 and also appeared with him on Radio Luxembourg and Radio Paris.

Stuart Robertson — Recorded with Jack Hylton and Ray Noble.

Paul Robeson — Not many bass singers appeared with a dance band but in September 1931, at the Queen's Hall in London, the hugely popular American Paul Robeson recorded a number of Negro spirituals with Jack Hylton's orchestra.

Phyllis Robins** (1910-1982) — While still a young girl, Sheffield-born Phyllis teamed up with her talented elder sister to appear as a ukelele singing double-act billed as "Iris and Phyllis, the Juvenile Entertainers". After many pantomime and variety appearances she was invited to guest with Jack Hylton, Charlie Kunz, Ambrose and the Blue Lyres before joining Henry Hall in 1933. A year later she left to go solo, accompanied by pianist Jack Phillips. During the war she became a farmer's wife but in 1945 was involved in entertaining the troops in Berlin, although not in a singing capacity. She then did some touring, often with Iris as her pianist, plus occasional pantomimes and reviews. One of the first regular television broadcasters from Alexandra Palace, she was also the second televised subject of a one hour documentary series on top girl vocalists — only Anne Shelton came before her, with Petula Clark following behind. Although she always appeared blonde she was in fact a brunette who visited the hairdresser every day. Always immaculate in appearance, after she died Henry Hall described her as the best singer he ever had.

Ace Roland — Sang with Ray Noble during the early-Thirties.

△ *Anita Riddell*

△ *Despite her blonde appearance, Phyllis Robins was actually a brunette who visited the hairdresser every day!*

Margaret Rose — Sang with several bands during the Fifties, including the Tommy Watt Quintet, Harry Gold, Geraldo, Bill McGuffie and Billy Ternent. Married a USAF doctor/pilot and settled in Halifax.

Val Rosing* — Will forever be remembered as the vocalist on Henry Hall's classic *Teddy Bears Picnic* recorded in 1932 and used for many years as the BBC test recording because of its exceptionally wide range of notes between bass and treble. He also recorded with Billy Cotton, Howard Godfrey, Harry Leader, Percival Mackey, Ray Noble, Jack Payne, Jay Wilbur, and Jack Harris before emigrating to Hollywood and becoming a film star under his new name of Gilbert Russell. Toured during the mid-Thirties with his own small swing band.

Annie Ross (born 1930) — With show business parents and Ella Logan for an aunt it was hardly surprising she followed in their footsteps. Her first experience of dance band singing came when she was only five with, believe it or not, Paul Whiteman in America where she was staying with Aunt Ella. She then appeared as child star Annabella Logan in the popular Hal Roach-directed Thirties television film series "Our Gang". led by the irrepressible "Alf Alpha". After singing with various American bands she returned to Britain post-war and joined Reg Arnold before hopping off for a spell in France where she appeared briefly with Lionel Hampton. Back to the UK she toured with Jack Parnell and, among many other commitments, also sang with Tony Crombie and Gerry Mulligan.

Derek Roy** — Although he eventually found fame as a radio comedian during the Fifties he began as a singer with Geraldo during wartime.

Royalists — Wartime singing trio with Harry Roy, usually consisting of Harry himself, Marjorie Kingsley and Renee Lister.

Lita Roza* (born 1927) — Liverpudlian Lita tried her luck in London during wartime while still a teenager and was taken on by Harry Roy as a replacement for Renee Lister (later called Suzi Miller). From there she transferred to Edmundo Ros and Art Thompson, and then while only 18, married an American GI and moved to America. Unfortunately the marriage proved short-lived and she returned to audition for Ted Heath who was so impressed with her first live performance that he signed her on the spot. Her contemporaries included Dickie Valentine and Dennis Lotis with whom she stayed until pursuing a short-lived solo career in 1954 – the Rock n' Roll era putting paid to it by the end of the decade. During the Eighties and Nineties, however, she again linked up with the Ted Heath band, then led by Don Lusher.

△ *Val Rosing came from Russian operatic stock but found fame as a pre-war singer with several dance bands in Britain. He then embarked on another successful career during the late-Thirties — as a Hollywood film star called Gilbert Russell! He also appeared on Broadway.*

89

SOME FAMOUS SINGERS
FROM THE MID-FIFTIES

Dennis Lotis

△ Ronnie Hilton

▽ David Whitfield

Lita Roza

Patti Lewis

Joan Regan

Barbara Lyon

Danny Purches

Yana

The Keynotes minus their girl singer became the Johnston Brothers.

△ The Kaye Sisters

◁ Dennis Hale may look happy but the juke box did not do live dance music any favours during the Fifties!

▷ Marion Ryan hosted "Spot the Tune" for many years.

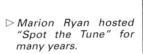

▽ Annie Ross had an excellent singing pedigree in her family.

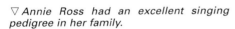

▽ Frankie Vaughan was always a popular star with his many fans.

Marion Ryan (1931-1999) — Middlesbrough-bred, shapely Marion began her career with Ray Ellington at the Glasgow Locarno in 1953 before the band moved to London where she soon hit the high spots. By 1959 she was reputed to be the highest paid singer on television and her solo career saw her top the bill at the London Palladium. She also sang with Cyril Stapleton's Showband on several occasions but will be best-remembered as the glamorous celebrity presenter of ITV's "Spot the Tune" which ran from 1956-1962. Twin sons Paul and Barry followed her into show business.

Shirley Ryan — Australian who came to Britain in the early-Fifties and, after a short spell singing in Ireland, moved to the mainland where she sang with Tito Burns, Bobby Mickleburgh and Tony Kinsey, before going solo.

Bobby Sanders — Prolific recording artist of the Twenties and early-Thirties, cutting sides with among others, Alfredo, Bertini, Harry Bidgood, Eddie Grossbart, Henry Hall, Harry Hudson, Jack Leon, Billy Mayerl, Arthur Rosebery, Debroy Somers and Jay Wilbur.

Shirley Sands (born 1927) — Sang with Cyril Stapleton's Showband at the end of the Fifties.

Leslie Sarony — Famous variety artist and song writer who, together with Leslie Holmes, formed a duo called "The Two Leslies". Between them they made a large number of comedy records with various dance bands before the war, especially Jack Hylton and Jay Wilbur, but only a handful actually together.

Edna Savage (born 1936) — Began by volunteering to sing as a teenager at a local dance when her friend was indisposed. After performing with the Northern Dance Orchestra she branched out on to a solo career but also found time to sing with Ken Mackintosh, Jack Parnell, Ivor and Basil Kirchin, Frank Weir, and Stanley Black's bands. At the height of her career she married Terry Dene, but both were really too young to make it work.

Elizabeth Scott — Sang and recorded with Henry Hall during the mid-Thirties.

Billy Scott-Coomber** (1905-1990) — Although he was born in Rawalpindi where his father was in the army, he was brought up in Ireland. A childhood hare-lip was cured by an operation and he went to art college in Dublin at the age of 16. Also a competent actor and singer he was only tempted to venture into pop music when he was offered enough money to buy a motorbike! He was overheard by John Watt, later a leading light in the BBC Light Entertainment department, who was sufficiently impressed to invite him to partner Olive Groves broadcasting from 2LO at Savoy Hill. In 1928 Jack Payne offered him £5 a week to join his new BBC Dance Band but Billy dismissed the offer as derisory. He was right because Jack immediately trebled it and so began a highly profitable relationship which ended only at the outbreak of war after Billy went solo. After the war ended he gave up singing and worked for the BBC in Manchester and later alongside two doyens of children's broadcasting, David Davis and Trevor Hill. He will forever be associated with the song familiar to all post-war listeners to "Children's Hour", *There's a Worm at the Bottom of the Garden (. . . and His Name is Wiggly Woo)*. Using his pen name of William Scott, he later gave himself over to painting and was always in demand for commissions. In all, he made more than 1,500 records with his clear diction resulting from lessons with operatic tenor, Count John McCormack.

Scovell and Wheldon — Duo who recorded with Ronnie Munro during the mid-Twenties.

▷ *Billy Scott-Coomber took singing lessons from John McCormack but is best-remembered by a generation of children for his rendering of "There's a Worm at the Bottom of the Garden".*

Harold Scruton (born 1919) — By the year 2000 he was still tickling the ivories as an octogenarian in the Regency Rooms at the Majestic Hotel in Harrogate. Leeds-born Harold sang regularly with Charlie Shadwell, Reginald King and Max Jaffa, mainly at the Yorkshire seaside resorts of Scarborough and Whitby. He also appeared at concert parties led by theatre organists Cecil Chadwick and Charles Smitton. At one point he took singing lessons alongside Anne Ziegler and a youthful Julie Andrews. Played several leading tenor roles after the war and also sang with Lionel Johns' Ladies Orchestra at St. Anne's-on-Sea, Lancashire!

Sandra Seager — Versatile singer with many post-war dance bands, including Harry Roy. She also performed as a solo act in cabaret and music halls under the title of "The Personality Girl". Later emigrated to Australia.

Cyril Shane (born 1922) — Cyril Simnock was born in London and first broadcast from an air raid shelter on the radio programme "In Town in Tonight". His voice made such an impact that he soon found himself accepting invitations to sing with Percival Mackey, Billy Thorburn, Phil Green, Oscar Rabin, and Geraldo. He was then conscripted but invalided out after being machine-gunned by a German fighter while playing cricket near Folkestone! He later sang with the Skyrockets but when they became resident at the London Palladium he left to go back on the road, where he appeared with Mantovani, Harry Roy, Ronnie Pleydell, Nat Temple and Paul Fenoulhet.

Valerie Shane — Midlander Valerie Kleiner sang as a teenager with Ken Moule and Basil Kirchin, before appearing with several jazz outfits, including Tony Kinsey and Ronnie Scott.

Beri Shaw — Real name Beryl Thomson who sang post-war with Felix Mendelssohn's Hawaiian Serenaders, the Santa Salvador rumba band and Gracie Cole. She also appeared separately with Issy Bonn and Paul Roussel as a variety vocal duo

Lynne Shaw (1922-1950) — First appeared towards the end of the war with Stanley Black, then progressed through Frank Weir, Lou Preager, Jan Wildeman, Reginald Pursglove and George Melachrino. Died from a brain tumour.

Nan Shaw — Post-war singer with Leslie Douglas.

Sandra Shayne (born 1918) — After taking lessons from Val Rosing she sang briefly with Billy Thorburn before being engaged by Jack Harris in 1938.

Lee Sheridan — (see Dick James).

△ "Personality Girl" Sandra Seager emigrated to Victoria, Australia in 1975 where, as Mrs. Sandra Haynes, she became extremely active in local amateur dramatics.

△ Sandra Shayne's mentor was Val Rosing.

93

◁ Judy Shirley (left) was the eldest Lenner Sister and literally looked after many of her younger sisters when they were growing up. She compèred a Radio Normandy programme called "Wives of the Famous" and is seen here with one of her guests, Elizabeth Brooke, alias Princess Pearl, daughter of the White Rajah of Sarawak and who married Harry Roy in a glamorous wedding in 1935. The girls are seen with piles of chicken bones in the Norfolk factory of the show's sponsor, Shippam's Pastes. Elizabeth Brooke was a competent singer with her husband's band whose signature tune was "Bugle Call Rag".

▽ The cartoon below neatly captures the impish nature of a band leader who was small in stature but always on the move, making up noisewise what he lacked in height.

Anne Shelton** — (see separate chapter).

Judy Shirley** (1906-1996) — Oldest of the six Lenner Sisters (q.v.) from Leicester and literally nurse to several of her younger siblings. After running away to London she scratched around in a number of small time variety jobs and pantomime before joining Eddie Grossbart's band. She rarely ventured out late at night but on one occasion was successfully persuaded by her friends to sing at the Cosmo Club. It changed her life because among the audience was a man with a distinctive moustache who liked what he heard and promptly sent her a message via the waiter. It was Maurice Winnick, inviting her to join his band and the note was her passport to success. Judy was actually called Florence and her stage name was a derivation of July Garland and Shirley Temple, both of whom were big name stars at the time. During the mid-Thirties she sang with Louis Levy's Gaumont British Symphony and in the late-Thirties was also the singing compere of the radio programme "Monday Night at Seven" (later "Monday Night at Eight").

Silhouettes — Female dancing and singing group on the "Billy Cotton Band Show".

Andee Silver — Post-war short-term successor to Rose Brennan with Joe Loss.

Ralph Silvester — Recorded several times with Jack Payne during the early-Thirties.

Kerri Simms — Sang with Roy and Norman Burns under the name of Jean Richards but by the early-Fifties was appearing with Johnny Gray under her new name. Later sang with Carl Barriteau and married firstly, pianist Stan Tracey and later, saxophonist Mike Senn. Toured America with Matt Monro and Johnny Gray during the early-Sixties.

Sisters in Harmony — (see Carson Sisters).

The Southern Sisters — from left to right: Betty, Sybille and Vera.

Southern Sisters — Formed in the early Thirties this rhythmical trio auditioned successfully for Henry Hall with whom they broadcast both before and during the war. Consisting of Betty Havell (Knight), Sybille and Vera they enjoyed singing together but preferred to be known as individuals. Once, while rehearsing for a concert the same evening, they had their new dresses stolen from a car outside BBC Broadcasting House — as a result of which the concert was cancelled! Sybille was quiet and enjoyed knitting, Vera was keen on gardening and driving fast cars, while Betty loved travelling, only just managing to escape from the Spanish Civil War as an evacuee on a British naval ship. After docking back in England she immediately set off for Bedford where she arrived five minutes before the show began! Their piano accompanist for a number of years was well-known light music composer Clive Richardson, perhaps best-remembered for his piece *London Fantasia* based on a bombing raid during the Blitz.

Miff Smith — Trombonist and comedy vocalist with Henry Hall who kept a second-hand music shop in Wimbledon after he retired. Also appeared on Beryl Orde's radio show "Personality Parade".

▷ *The sparkling Henderson Twins, Winifred and Theresa — but which is which on this photo is anybody's guess — were the identical twin daughters of plump pre-war Hull comedian Dick Henderson, and sisters of post-war comedian, Dickie. It was almost impossible to tell them apart and they delighted in playing jokes on boy friends by secretly swapping places.*

△ Still going strong in the year 2000, Rosemary Squires and her great friend, Dennis Lotis, are shown here in their touring show "Day by Day" based on the life of contemporary American singer, Doris Day.

Lee Street — Bass player and vocalist with Mrs. Jack Hylton (Ennis Parkes), the Blue Rockets and Billy Thorburn.

Valaida Snow — (see Valaida).

Dorothy Squires* (1915-1998) — It was dance band entrepreneur Howard Baker who first spotted her performing in South Wales while she was still only 16 years old and whisked her off to sing with him in London. After a spell with Charlie Kunz at the Casani Club she was then snapped up by Billy Reid with whom she sang for more than 20 years, initially with his London Accordion Band. She married Roger Moore but, as he was 14 years her junior and very much pursued by younger admirers, it eventually ended in divorce. She survived several major crises, financial and personal, and made a number of come-backs before dying back home in South Wales.

Rosemary Squires* (born 1928) — Bristol-born Joan Yarrow was already well known in her home town of Salisbury, where she had sung with various service dance bands, when in 1948 she was chosen to tour Germany with the Blue Rockets. Under her new name of Rosemary Squires she quickly became familiar to all the National Service troops overseas. In 1955 she turned down a lucrative offer to succeed Lita Roza with Ted Heath's orchestra, which most people thought was tantamount to professional suicide. Rosemary's subsequent career proved them all wrong, however, because she sang on the radio with Geraldo and Eric Winstone and then appeared aboard the "Six-Five Special" with Pete Murray, Josephine Douglas, Adam Faith, Tommy Steele, and Cliff Richard. In 1958 she was voted "The Most Televised Girl of the Year". Theatre and cabaret followed and by the mid-Sixties she had performed on tour with the cast of "The Army Game", Morecambe and Wise, Mr. Pastry, Alma Cogan, and Ken Dodd. By the 1980s the veritable "Jackie of all trades" could be heard entertaining on board the cruise liners *Canberra* and *Oriana*, and also in pantomime. Rosemary sold millions of records but the most unusual were

96

not available in the shops because they were familiar television jingles, including 'The hands that do dishes can feel soft as your face with mild green Fairy Liquid' and "Fry's Turkish Delight!" Yes, it was Rosemary Squires serenading the soap-suds and the seven veils, with a sound once described as "the perfect broadcasting voice". When the BBC Big Band became independent Rosemary was their natural choice as singer and she also toured with the popular Syd Lawrence Orchestra. Continuing to make regular guest appearances, she performed at the 30th birthday party of Prince Edward and, when the 50th wartime anniversary celebrations came round, again found herself in big demand, singing with the new Glenn Miller Band UK. In 1998 it was her own turn to celebrate — 50 years in professional show business — amazing but true. Rosemary's close resemblance to the international film star Doris Day was a factor for virtually the whole of her career and latterly she toured nation-wide with a show entitled "Day by Day", a celebration of the music of her famous American counterpart, with close friend Dennis Lotis as her "leading man".

Eric Stanley — Sang with Billy Merrin.

Stargazers — With their familiar introduction "The Stargazers ... are on the air!" this polished ensemble popped up regularly on radio during the Fifties. Formed in 1949 the original line-up consisted of its two founders, Dick

James and Cliff Adams, plus Ronnie Milne, Fred Datchler and Marie Benson. Over the years they played and sang with several bands including Paul Fenoulhet, Stanley Black, Billy Thorburn, Lew Stone, Malcolm Lockyer, Geraldo, Harold Smart and Cyril Stapleton. They made many hit records and also featured in the famous commercial jingle advertising "Murraymints, Murraymints, too good to hurry mints ..." Their personnel changed several times and over the years included Bob Brown, Jean Campbell, Dave Carey, Eula Parker, June Marlow, Nigel Brooks and Barbara Moore. Two Royal Variety Shows and topping the bill at the London Palladium when it was dominated by Americans, showed just how popular they were.

Marjorie Stedeford (1909-1959) — Arriving here from Australia in 1935 she shot to the top in less than a year. A regular with Jack Jackson at the Dorchester Hotel she also recorded with Geraldo, Phil Green, Jack Harris, Howard Jacobs, Mario "Harp" Lorenzi, Carroll Gibbons and Jack White. With a deep voice described as "black velvet" she enjoyed a close friendship with fellow Aussie Brian Lawrance and thrilled audiences for four years before returning back home where she was immediately placed under contract to the ABC. Sadly, she died while still young.

Doreen Stephens (1922-1965) — Began singing with Jack Hylton's band and appeared with him at the London Palladium while still

▷ There were few professional singing groups in the 20th century which could rival the versatility of the Stargazers. Although the personnel changed several times, the end result of their ensemble work was never less than outstanding. Whether making records, singing with a dance band, broadcasting on the radio or making television commercials, they were in a class of their own. This star-shaped photo shows left to right: Bob Brown, Eula Parker, Cliff Adams, Fred Datchier and Dave Carey. Cliff Adams later ran his own successful singing group which became the backbone of the popular radio show "Sing Something Simple".

TWO SINGING FRIENDS FROM LONDON

△ *Many dance band vocalists hailed from London, to where they eventually retired. Come the end of the 20th century several were delighted to discover they were being included in this book, among whom were Millicent Phillips (q.v.), and close friends Betty Taylor (above left) and Jo Marney (above right). Betty's picture dates from her happy wartime appearances with Henry Hall when she was still only a teenager. Jo sang with Billy Ternent and also recorded several commercial advertising jingles.*

only 15 years old. Wartime saw her touring the Middle East with Maurice Winnick and, after hostilities ceased, she sang at different times with the Squadronaires, Ronnie Pleydell, Felix King, and George Crow. It was her association with Billy Cotton for which she will be best-remembered, however, being a regular on his "Wakey, Wakey" radio show for many years. Her life was then sadly cut short by cancer.

Clem Stevens (1904-1981) — Trumpeter and singer with Joe Loss for six years before the war.

Donald Stewart — Recorded with Ambrose in 1935 and also appeared at the special *Melody Maker* sponsored concert at the Royal Opera House on 30th June that year, the only time such an event has been staged at that location. Partnered Renée Houston on the radio.

The Sunnysiders — Post-war vocal group which sang with Lou Preager's band, named after his signature tune *On the Sunny Side of the Street*.

Swingtette — Jack Hylton singing group of the mid-Thirties consisting at various times of the three McCarthy Sisters, Frances Jewel, Ben Late, Gene Lanham and Eugene Prentiss.

Betty Taylor (born 1923) — Began singing during the Thirties with Harry Crocker in her home town of Weymouth, then appeared with Dick Denny in Leeds (from where she did her first broadcast at the age of 14), Billy Bevan in Southport, and Bert Osborne in Portsmouth. During the war she enjoyed a stint alongside Betty Driver with Henry Hall's band. After hostilities ceased she appeared with Lou Simmons in Bournemouth, and then with Harry Gold where she developed a more blues style voice modelled on Bessie Smith. She later appeared with Sid Phillips before linking up with Harry Gold again, singing with his Pieces of Eight during the television programme "This Is Your Life" when it featured Geoff Love.

Eileen Taylor — Mancunian who won Ted Heath's first "Zinger Girl" contest. Appeared with Ted Taylor in her home town, Leon

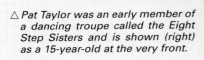

△ Doreen Stephens learned her school homework by singing it!

△ Pat Taylor was an early member of a dancing troupe called the Eight Step Sisters and is shown (right) as a 15-year-old at the very front.

▽ Valaida was a fine trumpet player and singer but later fell foul of the Nazis.

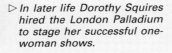

△ Marjorie Stedeford was an Australian with a deep contralto voice.

▷ In later life Dorothy Squires hired the London Palladium to stage her successful one-woman shows.

Cochrane in Torquay and in various West End clubs in London. Later sang with Sid Phillips.

Lilian Taylor — (see Carlyle Cousins).

Pat Taylor (born 1918) — Teenage member of the original Eight Step Sisters but was injured in the 1936 car crash which killed Jean Conibear of the Rhythm Sisters. She then became Jack Harris's main singer and also recorded with Geraldo. Married Jack Hylton's son.

Beryl Templeman (born 1922) — A native of India where she was a popular singer with Ken Mack's band during the war. Came to England in 1946 and toured with Roy Fox, before singing briefly with Ted Heath and, much later, recording for the budget Woolworth record label, Embassy.

Phyllis Thackray — Vocalist and tap dancer with Harry Roy.

John Thorne (1894-1939) — Prolific recording artist of the late-Twenties and early-Thirties whose real name, although he never used it, was Thomas Greenhalgh. He recorded, among others, with Wag Abbey, Harry Bidgood, Stan Greening, Leslie Jeffries, Jack Payne and Jay Wilbur. He also recorded under the names of Billy Desmond, Frank Nicholls, David Sheppard, Arthur Vivian and Marcus Browning.

Three Boys and a Girl — Wartime and post-war recording group with Geraldo's orchestra.

Three Ginx — Eric Hanley (Sam), Ivor Robbins (Rob) and Jack Joy (Jack) first met up at Southsea in 1923, while performing with rival bands. Wondering what to call themselves they were wandering along the promenade when a local sailor called out "You three silly ginks". Instead of trading insults or throwing him into the sea they saw it as an answer to their problem. Early on they were twice cheated by tour managers who went walkabout with their salaries but eventually established themselves as a highly polished close-harmony group which was much in demand on radio. They also recorded with several bands, including Ambrose, Roy Fox, Harry Hudson, Tommy Kinsman, Ray Noble, Sydney Kyte, Brian Lawrance, Louis Levy, Jack Payne, Sid Phillips, Oscar Rabin, Billy Thorburn and Jay Wilbur. During their three year residency with Sydney

▷ *The Three Ginx (pronounced with a hard "G" — not Jinx as commonly supposed) chose their name after rude comments were directed at them by a drunken sailor on the seafront at Portsmouth and Southsea.*

Kyte at the Piccadilly Hotel, Eric also played the drums and Jack the piano.

The Three in Harmony — Close-harmony female group formed in Belfast in 1934 where their appearances in a radio show called "Stop Dancing" resulted in them being invited to London where they sang with Carroll Gibbons and Charlie Kunz and recorded with Brian Lawrance, Ronnie Munro and Mario "Harp" Lorenzi. Their names were Elva Orr, Dorothy Morrow and Yolande Mageean (who married Bob Mallin from the Four in Harmony group, thus becoming "Two in Harmony" for more than 60 years!). They also appeared regularly on commercial radio and immediately pre-war in Germany with Henry Hall — after which some of the touring party got into trouble for allegedly returning Nazi salutes on stage. Gestapo and armed security were present at every rehearsal and performance, and Bob Mallin, a keen amateur photographer, had his camera temporarily confiscated when trying to take a picture of a railway train.

The Three Js — Wartime recording group with Jay Wilbur.

The Three Ginx

(top) Sam

(middle) Jack

(bottom) Rob

This rare and previously unpublished photograph of Henry Hall and the Three in Harmony, was taken on tour at La Scala Theatre, Berlin during the late-Thirties. The girls are, left to right, Dorothy Morrow, Yolande Mageean and Elva Orr.

The trip was marred — as was the England versus Germany football fixture of around the same time — by subsequent allegations that several musicians and players had returned the Nazi salute. This was never proven against the former, however, but security was certainly tight.

Yolande's fiancé, Bob Mallin, who was there as a member of the male Four in Harmony, took a harmless picture of a train and promptly had his camera confiscated! They later married and celebrated their Diamond Wedding in 1999, a fitting end to their joint music-making during the 20th century.

The Three Sisters — The original three young ladies rarely divulged their surnames but were not sisters, first meeting up during a Drury Lane theatre show, whose name they adopted for their stage act of singing and dancing — namely, "Molly, Marie and Mary". Mary Ashworth was their leader and when Henry Hall heard them while filming "Music Hath Charms", he renamed them the Three Sisters and added them to his already extensive mid-Thirties group of vocalists. Within three years Mavis Edmonds and Kay Munro-Smith (Munro-Smythe) had replaced Molly and Marie. "Mary" came from Bournemouth, "Marie" (the youngest) from Swansea, and "Molly" from Kent. One of the three was Betty Bucknelle who later sang with Phil Cardew's orchestra in the Arthur Askey and Richard Murdoch radio show, "Band Waggon".

The Three Ts — Thirties recording group with Sydney Lipton, consisting of Frank and John Trafford (q.v.) and Clive Erard (q.v.).

Top Hatters — Thirties recording group with Geraldo's orchestra, which included Cyril Grantham, Chips Chippendall and Bill Tringham.

Arthur Tracy** (1900-1997) — The "Street Singer" was not really a dance band vocalist but his remarkable career certainly deserves a mention. Born in New York to Jewish immigrants from Moldavia, he made a name as an unnamed singer whose identity was eventually leaked and revealed by the press. Toured the British Isles to great acclaim during the Thirties when he made four films, appearing opposite Margaret Lockwood, Anna Neagle and Lilli Palmer. His most famous song was *Marta*.

101

◁ *Bruce Trent came from a large family in the Channel Isles but after being persuaded to try his luck on the mainland he never looked back and sang with several different bands. He also appeared regularly on Radio Luxembourg.*

Frank & John Trafford — Inspired by Paul Whiteman's Rhythm Boys they began singing during the early-Thirties. After a European tour they joined Syd Lipton when, with Clive Erard, they were billed as the Three Ts. They later sang as the Manhattan Trio and were part of the Rhythm Brothers with Lew Stone. Also sang with Ambrose, Jay Wilbur and Debroy Somers.

Bruce Trent* (1912-1995) — Jersey-born, the youngest of 12 children but handsome and tall, Bruce initially toured England with Leslie Haskell before singing with a variety of bands including Sonny Farrar, Sid Millward, Eddie Carroll, Jack Hylton, Arthur Young and Jack Payne. Broadcast during the war with Glenn Miller but had to turn down a regular contract because of stage commitments. While in the Army he toured with "Stars in Battledress" and later became a celebrity in his own right, especially remembered as a regular of the long-running radio series "Friday Night is Music Night".

Ken Tucker (died 1999) — Sang with Jack Hylton during the Thirties. His real name was Len Smoothey but he was best known as Leslie Lowe, the title he used for general entertainment purposes.

Valaida (1900-1956) — Talented black American jazz singer and trumpet player (surname Snow) who appeared in Britain with Billy Mason before the war. She then toured Europe but was arrested in Copenhagen and ill-treated by the Nazis. Freed after spending three years in a concentration camp she returned to America and tried to resurrect her career. Internment had taken its toll, however, and she suffered considerable mental strain before her death.

Dickie Valentine* (1929-1971) — It was while doing National Service with the Army in the Middle East that he discovered people enjoyed listening to his patter — so he decided to try full-time entertainment when he was demobbed. After some initial setbacks comedian Bill O'Connor paid for him to have voice training, after which he auditioned for Ted Heath — the end result of which was Richard Bryce emerging as Dickie Valentine. In 1954, after five years with the band, he went solo and quickly became a big star. Although the changing popular music scene eventually forced him into performing more and more club work, the nation was shocked when he was tragically killed in a road accident in South Wales.

Denny Vaughan (1921-1972) — Canadian-born Denny came to England during the war and soon joined Bob Farnon's orchestra as a pianist, later performing also with Carroll Gibbons, Frank Weir and George Melachrino. He then replaced Dick James as the vocalist with Geraldo's band and also sang with Freddy Gardner. Continuing as a singing band leader he returned to America with great success but was cut down in his prime by cancer.

Frankie Vaughan (1928-1999) — Liverpool-born Francis Abelson went to the same school as Lita Roza but his family were bombed out during the war. After National Service he resumed training at the Leeds College of Art where he sang with Harry Parry's band after winning a local talent contest. He then struggled to break into show business but, initially backed by Ken Mackintosh, he finally made it as a solo artist. Genuinely popular with fellow artists he did much philanthropic work and enhanced the cause of boys' clubs around the country. Awarded the OBE in 1965 for services to charity, his long marriage to childhood sweetheart Stella was admired by everyone.

Paul Vaughan — During the Forties he sang as Tony Arnold with Nat Allen and Harry Roy and also led his own quarter at various hotels and clubs, even deputising for Eddie Calvert. During the Fifties he appeared with Tito Burns and Ronnie Scott.

Tina Vaughan — Sang with Lou Preager at the Hammersmith Palais during the mid-Fifties.

BRITISH POPULAR MUSIC DURING THE EARLY-FIFTIES

△ *There were several successful dance bands and singers who more than held their own in the first half of the Fifties, some even carrying on after the rock 'n' roll era took off during the second half of the decade. Dickie Valentine is seen (above left) rehearsing with Cyril Stapleton's showband while (above right) he is on the receiving end of Ted Heath's trombone, watched by fellow band singers Lita Roza and Dennis Lotis.*

△ *This mid-Fifties picture neatly captures the post-war popular music atmosphere with Dickie Valentine's fans sporting a variety of traditional and new hairstyles, both male and female. The Teddy Boy era was beginning to emerge, however, and rock 'n' roll would soon condemn Dickie to playing clubs up and down the country.*

Dolores Ventura — Australian-born musician who was married to composer Ivor Slaney. After coming to Britain she performed on a piano which had bells attached to the hammers and also sang with Ken Mackintosh's band on Radio Luxembourg.

Wally (Walter) Vernon — Recorded with Ray Noble at the end of the Twenties.

Guy Victor — Recorded during the twenties with Teddy Brown and Stan Greening.

Hal Vidler — (see The Ramblers).

Doreen Villiers — GI bride who married an American pilot in 1944 but who was killed soon afterwards. A favourite of the Eighth Army in North Africa to whom she broadcast on "Date with the Desert". Toured the Middle East with Geraldo in 1943 and also sang during the war with Ambrose, Stan Atkins and Harry Parry. Later emigrated to America.

Violett — (see Rose Alper).

Patrick Waddington — Recorded several songs with Harry Bidgood in the late-Twenties plus a few with Ray Noble, later leading his own group called "That Certain Trio". Emigrated to America during the late-Thirties to become a full-time actor.

Helen Ward — Helped her father with his conjuring act before joining Maurice Winnick for five years during the early-Forties. Then worked with Ronnie Munro and Dr. Crock and his Crackpots before going solo during the Fifties.

Tom Wareing — Sang with Jack Hylton during the mid-Thirties.

Jerry Warner — Sang with Norman Burns during the Fifties.

Alma Warren (born 1929) — Lita Roza's sister who sang initially with Vic Lewis as a replacement for Marion Williams — but this proved short-lived when Vic decided to economise. She then sang with Jack Nathan and Geraldo, who changed her name from Roza to Warren. Later replaced Diana Coupland with Stanley Black, before going solo.

Ray Warren — Broadcast from Northern Ireland during the Thirties, especially with Percy Waterhouse's band.

Beryl Wayne — Sang with Norman Burns during the Fifties.

Clive Wayne — Ex-Merchant seaman who sang with Maurice Winnick and Geraldo during the late-Forties and also made several HMV recordings.

Betty Webb (later Lizbeth Webb — see Crackerjacks).

Johnny Webb — Began his career with Tommy Smith at the Croydon Palais in 1943, then joined the Army. After hostilities ceased he sang with both the Blue Rockets and Billy Ternent and appeared in the musical "When in Rome" with Dickie Henderson and Eleanor Summerfield.

Elisabeth Welch (born 1908) — Glamorous American coloured jazz singer of mixed Negro, Red Indian, Scottish and Irish descent, who moved to London in 1933. Recorded with Benny Carter's late-Thirties pick-up group and appeared in many West End stage shows. Continued singing for many years after the war and was still performing in her Eighties.

Sylvia Welling — Directed and sang with the Gainsborough Dance Orchestra in the early-Thirties. Her one dance band record was called *Trust the Regulo* backed on the other side by a sales talk about Regulo gas cookers! The song came from a film called "What the Chefs Saw" produced by the National Film Corporation. Sylvia later sang with Jay Wilbur and was an established radio and early television star. For Radio Luxembourg she appeared on Horlicks Picture House with Debroy Somers, and for Radio Normandy on Rinso Radio Revue with Billy Bissett.

Danny West — Sang with Norman Burns during the Fifties.

Albert Whelan (1875-1962) — Well-known Australian music hall star who also recorded with Arthur Lally, Jay Wilbur and Stan Greening.

◁ *Elisabeth Welch knew how to sing the blues as well as croon ordinary dance music.*

△ *Eric Whitley was also called Tony Lombardo.*

Tommy Whitefoot — Sang with Henry Hall's later Gleneagles Band.

David Whitfield (1926-1980) — Hull-born and bred, a successful appearance on Hughie Green's "Opportunity Knocks" secured him a recording contract with Decca. His first single was *Marta* backed by Nat Temple but his most famous was *Cara Mia* backed by Mantovani. Known as "Britain's Mario Lanza" he sang all over the world.

Eric Whitley (1910-1991) — Violinist and singer born in Wrexham where he formed his small San Remo Band at the age of only 16. Worked as a shop assistant but sang and played piano with various local bands before joining Peter Fielding in Newcastle upon Tyne, who briefly changed his name to Tony Lombardo before it was reinstated by Teddy Joyce. Later appearances came with Carroll Gibbons, Jack Harris, Phil Green, George Elrick, Michael Flome, Harry Roy, Harry Leader, the Blue Rockets, Nat Allen and many more.

Des Williams — Winner of a talent show in 1949 and replaced Dick James when he left Paul Fenoulhet. Then joined Paul Adam before going solo. Also led the orchestra at Brighton Aquarium during the mid-Fifties.

Freddy Williams — (see Harristocrats).

Marion Williams — Joined Paul Fenoulhet in 1949, then sang with Johnny Dankworth and later Vic Lewis, with whom she toured Switzerland. In 1952 she joined Don Smith in Nottingham then Oscar Rabin in London. Succeeded Dawn Page in Eric Delaney's new mid-Fifties band where she met and married male singer, Derrick Francis. Following time off to become a mother she had second spells with Oscar Rabin, Don Smith and Eric Delaney before joining Denny Boyce at the Streatham Locarno during the early-Sixties.

Peter Williams — Made a large number of recordings with Billy Cotton during the Thirties.

Rita Williams* (1920-1971) — Londoner who had no ambition to become a professional singer until, at the age of 15, she won a competition in Bournemouth organised by Billy Merrin who promptly signed her up. She also recorded with Carroll Gibbons, Billy Thorburn, Lou Preager, Felix Mendelssohn, Ivy Benson and Billy Cotton. In addition she also cut several sides for the Woolworth brand name Embassy label.

Bertha Willmott — Known as "The Radio Comedy Girl with a Voice" she was a popular pre-war singer and recorded with Billy Cotton, Henry Hall, Louis Levy, Ronnie Munro, Jay Wilbur and Debroy Somers. Her talent was discovered when she was still at convent school where the nuns encouraged her to sing, with extra training from the London School of Music. She entertained the troops during the First World War, then turned to comedy and dance band singing.

△ *Bertha Willmott*

△ *If you want to get ahead, get a hat, which is what all these musicians and disc jockeys did for BBC Radio 2. Left to right: Keith Fordyce, Don Moss, Jimmy Young, Steve Race, David Gell, Pete Murray, dance band historian and aficionado Alan Dell, Sam Costa, Alan Freeman, and Joe "Mr. Piano" Henderson.*

Shirley Wilson (born 1934) — From a large family in Leeds she won a Ted Heath talent contest in 1954 and later sang with Don Smith at both Purley and Wimbledon.

Anona Winn** (1904-1994) — Australian radio and television star who began as a singer.

Bob Winnette — (see Debonaires).

Norman Wisdom (born 1915) — During the war, pint-sized Norman was based in Cheltenham where he was partially responsible for the formation of the local Royal Corps of Signals dance band, in which he played saxophone and also doubled as vocalist. As a singer he also appeared at the Town Hall with various other bands for the weekly Wednesday afternoon tea dances — a tradition which was revived in later years. As a joke a colleague once turned his music upside down to which Norman responded by standing on his head and playing it the wrong way up. The resultant rapturous reception confirmed Norman's natural talent for clowning, something which he delighted in for the rest of his life. It was Rex Harrison who eventually went backstage and encouraged him to turn professional and, although his commercial records of the Fifties and Sixties were largely humorous or sentimental, they were honed during his early years as an amateur dance band singer. Norman himself was grateful for this training and returned every year for the annual Signals dinner in Cheltenham. During the late-Forties he appeared in shows with both Henry Hall and Robert Farnon.

Monty Woolf — Recorded with Jack Hylton, Percival Mackey and the Savoy Orpheans during the mid-Twenties.

Johnny Worth — Post-war singer with Oscar Rabin who also recorded several sides for the Woolworth brand name Embassy label.

Joy Worth (1910-1987) — (see The Radio Three).

Clarence Wright — Before joining "ITMA", where he became famous for the catch-phrase "Good morning – nice day", he sang with John Birmingham, Harry Leader, Phil Green, Tommy Kinsman, Jack Payne, Jay Wilbur and Jan Ralfini, also making several recordings.

George Wright — Clarinettist and saxophonist who sang occasionally with Billy Bissett, Billy Merrin, Jack Payne and Debroy Somers.

Bert Yarlett

▷ A rather expensive dance band! From the left they are: Humphrey Lyttelton, Steve Race, The Duke of Bedford, Peter Sellers, Norman Wisdom and Larry Adler.

▽ Norman Wisdom was a dance band singer before he began his professional career as a clown, having joined the Army as a musician while still very young. His natural talent surfaced during the war and he quickly realised he could make a living from playing the fool (below) — but he could also sing rather well.

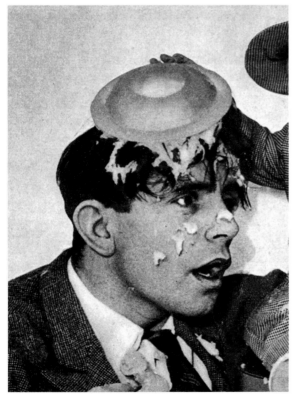

Yana (1932-1989) — Shapely singer whose real name was Pamela Guard. Her ambition to become a dance band singer was realised by the time of her 21st birthday and, after appearing at the West End Astor and Pigalle clubs she branched out into a highly-successful solo career. Married to Channel Islands hotel owner Ronnie Ronald, she was often confused with the wife of another local hotel owner, the whistling-singer Ronnie Ronalde!

Bert Yarlett (1901-1985) — Extremely popular entertainer during the mid-Thirties when he made several recordings with Eddie Carroll, Al Collins, Ben Frankel, Jack Hylton, Henry Hall and Lew Stone. When he married his wife, Aileen, Henry Hall gave away the bride. Went back to live in Canada just before the war and died in Toronto.

Kay Yorston — Singing member of Ivy Benson's All-Girls Band.

Bobby Young (born 1924) — Appeared with Felix Mendelssohn and his Hawaiian Serenaders before joining ENSA in 1941. Joined Oscar Rabin the following year and later recorded with Roberto Inglez.

Jimmy Young (born 1923) — Long before he became a national institution via "The Jimmy Young Show" on BBC Radio 2, this miner's son from the Forest of Dean in Gloucestershire began his singing career with the orchestras of Ronnie Pleydell, Felix King and Ray Martin. Thereafter he became a star of the early-Fifties until rock 'n' roll forced him and most other ballad singers out of the market. His easy style eventually turned him into a successful disc jockey on "Housewives Choice" and other assorted programmes.

Jan Zalski — Wartime singer with Oscar Rabin.

Anne Ziegler (born 1910) — Better-known for her ballad-singing duet role with husband Webster Booth, she recorded alongside him for Carroll Gibbons before the war.

More Singers from the Fifties

Betty Miller

Margaret Bond

Suzi Miller

◁ Peter Lowe, was the younger brother of Dennis Lotis.

▷ Bobbie Britton was renamed by band leader, Ted Heath.

Edna Savage

△ Monty Norman with his wife, Diana Coupland.

▽ Don Lang became famous on the television show "6:5 Special."

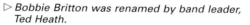

Lorrae Desmond

Toni Eden

Mel Gaynor

Ill-fated Michael Holliday.

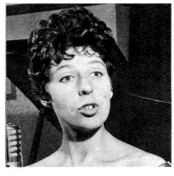

△ *More than 50 years at the top, doyen of them all, evergreen Rosemary Squires. Everybody knew her voice because, in addition to all her other singing, she recorded several well-known advertising jingles for commercial television. A favourite of the Queen Mother who told her to: "Never give up singing".*

Ray Burns sang with Ambrose.

▷ *Robert Earl (left) greeting the American singer, Frankie Laine, in the dressing rooms at the London Palladium.*

◁ *Jimmy Young with Sabrina, who was more famous for her figure than she was for her singing voice! Jimmy became a highly successful radio DJ and presenter, and was still going strong at the BBC as the 21st century unfolded.*

▷ *Australian, Marie Benson, who appeared solo and also with the highly accomplished Stargazers.*

▷ *Janie Marden signing autographs for her fans. Many self-respecting male teenagers wore their school cap on special occasions during the Fifties.*

△ *Jill Day, with film star Terry Thomas.*

Lee Lawrence

Kathryn "Kip" Oldfield

△ *Dick James owned his own music publishing company.*

△ Left: *Alan Dean, founder-member of the Keynotes who later emigrated to America.*

△ Centre: *Benny Lee was extremely versatile and even acted in the popular television programme "Are You Being Served?"*

◁ *Lynette Rae could speak eight languages.*

▷ *Judy Dean, see here with band leader George Evans, was also known as Jan Fraser and Judy Allen.*

△ Sandra Seager sang with many bands, including Maurice Udloff seen here at the piano in 1958. She even persuaded Edmundo Ros to let her have a go while still only a teenager.

◁ Ruby Murray found great fame as a young Irish singer but her later years were marred by unhappiness. Her hit song "Softly, Softly" is the title of her biography published by This England.

▽ This long-range BBC television studio picture was taken during the mid-Fifties and shows Janie Marden singing with the BBC Show Band. The conductor holding the baton is Cyril Stapleton and one of the violinists is wearing a dark eye shade to protect him from the bright lights which necessarily illuminated the singer throughout the live performance.

△ Petula Clark was groomed for stardom from a very young age but actively discouraged her three children from following the same route.

More Band Leaders

This section follows on naturally from the earlier volume *This England's Book of British Dance Bands* first published in 1999, which contained detailed information on all the major band leaders. Since then many new photographs have emerged, several of which have been included here. Readers are therefore recommended to acquire both books in order to allow them to cross-reference the related text, illustrations and captions.

**means the person was pictured in Volume One of *This Englands' Book of Bristish Dance Bands*.
*means the person was mentioned in the text of Volume One.

It is hard to exaggerate the importance of dance band music during the Twenties and Thirties. The exposure of the top bands via records and daily radio programmes meant that many musicians became household names. They were the pop stars of their day and each band leader and singer had a faithful following of fans. Cartoonists employed their skills in portraying the most famous characters and often managed to accurately capture the happy atmosphere of the time.

This picture of Lew Stone's band during the early Thirties consists of eleven top-class musicians (some of whom later became leaders in their own right), plus legendary singer Al Bowlly. Left to right: Harry Berly (clarinet) Ernest Ritte (sax), Bill Harty (drums), Joe Crossman (sax), Jim Easton (sax), Tiny Winters (bass), Al Bowlly (vocal) Eddie Carroll (piano), Lew Davis (trombone), Nat Gonella (trumpet), Joe Ferrie (trombone), Alfie Noakes (trumpet) with Lew Stone conducting.

Harry Acres — Led a late-Twenties and Thirties band which made a small number of recordings and also appeared in the film "Let's Make a Night Of It".

Vernon Adcock (born 1908) — Formerly a pre-war percussionist with Jan Berenska in the Midlands, he formed his own post-war orchestra and played several summer seasons at Bridlington Spa's Royal Hall. During the mid-Fifties he switched to Weston-super-Mare and later retired there.

Johnny Addlestone — Played at the Starlight Ballroom in Leeds during the Fifties and was responsible for the success of Ronnie Hilton.

Archie Alexander (died 1988) — Pre-war band leader in Aberdeen. Discovered both Nat Gonella and George Barclay, taking the latter with him when he moved to London during the early-Thirties. He also played in Cliftonville, a suburb of Margate, a summer seaside resort in deepest Kent.

Gary Allcock — Led his Midland All Stars during the Seventies and Eighties.

Charles Amer — Post-war Managing Director and band leader at the Chatham Hotel, Redcar in North Yorkshire. He appeared regularly at the nearby Butlin's at Filey and also in the 1947 film "Holiday Camp" which launched the Huggett Family, headed by Jack Warner and Kathleen Harrison.

Billy Amstell** (born 1911) — In a career spanning more than 70 years he played with every kind of musician, from classical, right through to dance and jazz. Recognition of his durability, quality and service to jazz came when, in 1978, he was made an Honorary Citizen of New Orleans, a rare award of distinction. He was also a Member of the Guild of Freemen of the City of London – but the award which he treasured most was Honorary Member of the Clarinet and Saxophone Society of Great Britain – not bad for someone who never had a music lesson in his life! He made his last professional appearance in 1994, at the age of nearly 84.

Stanley Andrews (1903-1953) — Post-war band leader at the Orchid Room in Berkeley Square and also deputised for Woolf Phillips with the Skyrockets at the London Palladium. Pre-war hot violinist with Jack Hylton, Spike Hughes, Arthur Rosebery, Howard Jacobs, Jack Jackson, Carroll Gibbons, Lew Stone, Jay Wilbur and Hatchett's Swingtette where he played and became great friends with Stephane Grappelli. During the war he was chief arranger and deputy to Jack Payne. Also chief arranger for many years to Vera Lynn.

Archie Andre — Thirties band which played at Worthing, including a week's spell in the semi-open Parade Bandstand during the summer seasons.

Arthur Anton (died 1980) — More usually known simply as Anton, he led an orchestra at the Paramount cinema in Tottenham Court Road from the mid-Thirties until wartime. Reginald Foort played the accompanying organ until succeeded by Al Bollington.

Billy Arnold — Now largely forgotten, in 1920 his American ensemble was one of those invited to succeed the Original Dixieland Jazz Band (ODJB) at the Hammersmith Palais. The latter had suffered the ignominy of being refused permission to play at the London Hippodrome by George Robey, who objected to their extrovert and brash sound but, like many others, he grossly underestimated this New Orleans-based white group of musicians who went on to become household names just like himself. Meanwhile, Billy Arnold's "Novelty Jazz Band" employed successful on-stage antics and clowning which were extremely popular at the

◁ *Billy Amstell wrote an autobiography entitled "Don't Fuss Mr. Ambrose" in which he detailed an extraordinary life in popular music.*

time but soon faded from public memory. Billy's band, however, did influence the French composer Darius Milhaud, who later moved to Harlem where, in 1923, he wrote his well-known jazz-inspired piece *La Création du Monde* (The Creation of the World).

Reg Arnold — Led a post-war Ambrose-sponsored band which played at the Orchid Room, London.

Sammy Ash — A wartime band which played in Cambridge and Birmingham, and later at the Croydon Palais and the Ritz in Manchester.

Vic Ash — Well-known band leader, clarinettist and saxophonist who, by the end of the century, was playing with the BBC Big Band and also running his own Vic Ash Quartet accompanying Rosemary Squires in her touring show "Day by Day", based on the career of American film star Doris Day. Played with many bands during his career, including Kenny Baker, Johnny Dankworth, and Vic Lewis.

Olly Aston — Sometimes fronted Syd Roy's RKOlians band at the Leicester Square theatre during the early-Thirties, when the whole ensemble, like the theatre organ, was elevated hydraulically from the pit up to stage level. A few years later he became the extrovert musical director at the Empire, Kingston-upon-Thames where he began each performance by jogging down the centre aisle, immaculately dressed in tails wearing a pink carnation and a big smile. He continued playing the piano around the Kingston area up until his death during the Eighties.

Norman Austin — Thirties band leader at the Victoria Cinema, Edinburgh.

Les Ayling — Led a post-war band which was resident at the Lyceum Ballroom on the Strand in London.

Freddy Ballerini — Played with Sydney Lipton, Tommy Kinsman, Frank Weir and others before forming his own band at Quaglinos. Later led one of the branches of the BBC Radio Orchestra.

Freddy Barrett — Trumpet playing band leader based in Birmingham during the early-Fifties.

Ken Beaumont (1913-1996) — Played with his Sextet on "Music While You Work" before moving to America. His daughter Catherine was the voice of Alice in the cartoon film "Alice in Wonderland". He also appeared with Larry Brennan, Henry Hall, Lou Preager, Oscar Rabin, Joe Orlando, Billy Cotton, Harry Leader and Billy Ternent.

Harry Bence (1928-1997) — Initially an experienced clarinet and saxophone player with Joe Loss, Eric Winstone, Ted Heath, Geraldo and Sydney Lipton, he formed his own band in 1953 but, after it foundered financially, joined Harry Leader. After another abortive attempt to go solo it was third time lucky when he established himself back in his native Scotland, where he also promoted his brother Jimmy's musical ensemble. He led the band which played on the final voyage of the liner *Queen Mary*, and then transferred to being musical director on the *QEII*. During the Seventies he led the New Geraldo Orchestra, and in the Eighties the New Squadronaires. Married to singer Elizabeth Batey.

Jan Berenska (born 1905) — His father conducted the Carl Rosa Opera Company and his mother was its leading soprano. It is therefore not surprising that they produced a childhood prodigy who made his first broadcast in short-trousers when only seven years old, playing the violin, cello and piano ... standing on a box to reach the microphone! He later conducted various tea-dance ensembles and led an orchestra in Leamington Spa during which time he became popular as a broadcaster. He also formed a touring Gypsy Orchestra which became very well-known during the Thirties, both on the radio and throughout variety, music and dance halls. He still managed to find time to play with Jack Wilson's Versatile Five, and latterly led an orchestra at Malvern before retiring and swapping his orchestral baton for the role of a music tutor.

△ *Olly Aston*

Al Berlin** — Pre-war band leader in the Midlands but also at the Paramount Dance Salon in London's Tottenham Court Road. Played on the Royal Mail steamship *Atlantis* just before hostilities broke out, then served as a wartime musical director with "Stars in Battledress". Signed by Billy Butlin in 1946 and placed in charge of 11 bands playing at Clacton, Filey and Skegness.

Billy Bevan — Wartime band which played at Southport in Lancashire.

Frank Biffo — Trumpet player with both Stan Greening and Nat Star, who made a few recordings with his own band in the late-Twenties with Maurice Elwin as vocalist.

Dickie Bishop — Bearded guitarist Dickie was a popular member of various bands, including Chris Barber, Monty Sunshine, and Micky Ashman but, briefly during the mid-Fifties, led his own group called the Sidekicks. He was also closely associated with the Vipers Skiffle Group.

Jack Blackman — Post-war band leader in Worcester.

Cyril Blake — West Indian trumpet player who led a wartime ensemble at Jig's Club in Wardour Street, London, often utilising former members of the ill-fated Ken "Snakehips" Johnson's band.

Sidney Bowman — Post-war he appeared regularly on "Music While You Work" and was also a regular broadcaster of old-time dancing on the Light Programme and Radio 2.

Denny Boyce (born 1921) — With his wife June Scott as vocalist, Denny ran a post-war band which toured American service camps and also acted as relief at many provincial ballrooms. In 1955 he began a three-year residency at Purley in Surrey, then succeeded

△ *Sid Bright*

△ *Popular veteran band leader and multi-instrumentalist, Vic Ash.*

Teddy Foster at the Tottenham Court Ballroom before moving on to the Wimbledon Palais and Lyceum in the Strand. He also appeared on television leading a Hawaiian ensemble. In the Sixties he formed the Damon music publishing group and also ran a music and record shop.

Bernard Brent — (see Bernard Ebbing-house).

Sid Bright* (1904-1976) — Bespectacled piano playing twin brother of Geraldo (Gerald Bright) and did much to assist his more famous sibling's cause. He occasionally deputised as the front man and also took over the reins of Ray Starita's band at the Ambassadors Club in 1930. Later the same year he led the Piccadilly Players at the Piccadilly Hotel.

Dave Brook — Glasgow-based band of the Thirties.

Harry Brooker (1927-1967) — Lead guitarist of Felix Mendelssohn's post-war Hawaiian Serenaders until Felix's death in 1952, at which point he formed his own band to play at Southend's prestigious Palace Hotel. Unfortunately the appointment was relatively short-lived, and so was he, because shortly afterwards he collapsed in the street and died from a heart attack, aged only 40.

Trevor Brookes — Popular post-war band leader who spent most winter seasons at Cheltenham Town Hall, where he succeeded Hector Davies. From 1948-1951 he played summer seasons at the Coronation Ballroom, Ramsgate in Kent and the next three years at the Winter Gardens, Weston-super-Mare in Somerset.

△ Percy Bush led the London Aeolian Band which is shown here at the Oxford Galleries, Newcastle upon Tyne in 1925. Left to right they are: Lew Stone (piano), Percy Bush (leader), W. Evans, (trumpet), Vincent Norman (saxophone), C. Cox (trumpet), George Newman (saxophone), F. Neaves (trombone), W. Asplin (brass bass), Tony Hill (banjo) and Leslie Morris (drums). Vincent Norman and Lew Stone both became band leaders in their own right, and it was the latter's first professional appearance outside London.

Derek Bruce — Real name Clive Wells, who had the winter contract at Cheltenham Town Hall during the early-Seventies and also ran a band agency in Evesham.

Ken Bruno — Post-war band leader in the Worcester and Kidderminster areas who continued playing into the Sixties.

Joe Burns — Led a post-war band at the Cumberland Hotel, Marble Arch, London.

Norman Burns (died 1994) — A drummer who, after wartime service in the RAF played with several bands including Ambrose, Geraldo and Lew Stone. During the early-Fifties he formed a jazz group which also played for ballroom dancing. His vocalists included Beryl Wayne, Danny West, and Jerry Warner. With his wife Peggy (Alan Dean's sister) he later emigrated to Australia.

Percy Bush (1893-1945) — Pre-war band leader who played during wartime at Worthing.

Billy Butler — Leading post-war band leader in Aberdare, South Wales.

Frank Butler — Led a wartime band in Ipswich called the Blue Ambassadors which enjoyed a friendly rivalry with Mervyn Dale – both bands earning regular recognition in the annual *Melody Maker* awards.

Jimmy Campbell — Led and sang with his own Paramount band during the mid-Thirties and also sang with Louis Levy. He also provided the music for Lawrence Wright's "On With the Show" on Blackpool's North Pier after the war.

Jack Cannon — Best-remembered for his "olde tyme" broadcasts, he led a conventional dance band at the Devonshire Ballroom in Salford, Lancashire, and also at the Ritz and Plaza further north in Bury.

Eddie Carney — Led a Midlands-based Thirties band called Tony's Red Aces which was resident during the winter months at Tony's Ballroom, in Birmingham, from where they broadcast over the local radio. Summer seasons were usually spent at Payne's Restaurant in Llandudno, north Wales.

Cavendish Band — London-based semi-professional group led by pianist Bob Leach which won the annual *Melody Maker* contest for three consecutive years from 1932-4, all of which were held in Nottingham. One of its early members was Claude Bampton who later became famous with his Bandits.

George Chambers — Manchester-based George won the annual *Melody Maker* contest which was held locally in 1944.

Percy Chandler — Ran an early-Thirties band which made recordings with Al Bowlly, Harry Bentley and Jimmy Messini as vocalists. He also recorded as the Cunard Dance Band and White Star Syncopators.

Jack Chapman — Resident at the Albert Ballroom in Glasgow for many years.

Wally Chapman — Led a post-war band at the Dorchester Hotel.

Glenda Chappelle — An early example of a lady band leader, who operated during the mid-Thirties.

Dick Charlesworth & the City Gents — Dressed in pin-striped suits and bowler hats, the City Gents were a popular traditional jazz band during the late-Fifties and early-Sixties. They took their name from the City of London where many of them worked, and their upper-class image appealed particularly to British universities and to audiences on the continent.

Vic Charters (born 1917) — Londoner who moved to Sussex while still a child and quickly became an accomplished pianist. During the war he played in the Army Dance Band, then became a professional with several orchestras, including Felix Mendelssohn's Hawaiian Serenaders and Melville Christie, with whom he toured the West Country. Spells with Jerry Hoey and Big Bill Campbell's Rocky Mountaineers, with whom he broadcast, were also accompanied by a stint with Tommy Handley's show "Hoopla". Vic then formed his own band and played at various functions in London's West End.

Sydney Chasid — Originally a classical violinist in Newcastle he formed his first dance band called the Californians in 1930. Under contract to ABC cinemas he toured the country in cine variety and later recorded, firstly with his Serenaders, thereafter with his Orchestra.

Melville Christie — Large band with five brass and four saxes which toured the West Country, based at Amesbury near Salisbury.

The City Ramblers — Initially a skiffle and folk group during the mid-Fifties, when fledgling television star Jimmy McGregor, clad in country gear like the rest of the band, occasionally appeared on guitar. They gradually progressed to traditional jazz during the early-Sixties.

Civil family — Northampton-based entourage of three generations, which included George, Harry, Albert, Ernest, Alan, Don, Roy, Adrian, Roland and Peter, who dabbled in all types of music during the 20th century. In pre-decimal days drummer Albert was once informed he was worth only half-a-crown less than the rest of the band so he played a waltz beat throughout the quicksteps and a 6/8 during the tango — he soon got his pay rise!

Tim Clayton — Led a post-war band at London's 400 Club.

Clyde Valley Stompers — Led initially by Ian Menzies but with later changes in personnel this band stomped a passage all the way from Glasgow to London during the traditional jazz boom of the early-Fifties. They eventually relocated in the metropolis, their Scottish name being no bar to a career which encompassed many television appearances.

Leon Cochran — Originally from the Midlands he held a residency at a Torquay hotel during the Fifties.

Percy Cohen — Resident at the Caister holiday camp near Great Yarmouth during the Thirties summer seasons. During the winter he could be found in the ballrooms around Norwich.

George Colborn — Cockney band leader who played with Alan Green at the Hammersmith Palais before branching out on his own at Sherry's in Brighton, then moved to the Streatham Locarno for most of the Thirties.

Gracie Cole (born 1924) — While still only a young teenager, Yorkshire-bred Gracie played her cornet on the radio with the famous Grimethorpe Colliery and Foden Motor Works brass bands. An early invitation to join Ivy Benson was vetoed by her father but, after spells with Gloria Gaye and Rudy Starita's all-female bands, Gracie enjoyed five years touring the world with Ivy's sparkling, but rapidly changing, outfits. Further spells with George Evans, the Squadronaires, Bert Quarmby and

△ *Gracie Cole played with other female bands before forming her own.*

△ *The Bunk Johnson-inspired Crane River Jazz Band from Middlesex were one of the first to set the feet tapping in the post-war traditional jazz revival period. Like most "trad" bands, they pre-dated rock 'n' roll and had dance halls packed out with enthusiasts swinging each other around the floor. Smaller than a conventional big band they created almost as much sound, however, and continued playing until the Sixties.*

Johnny Farley then prompted her to go it alone, and in the mid-Fifties she led a largely female band for four years. In 1955 they had a narrow escape while playing at a Moroccan night club when it was bombed by terrorists. After two brief interludes to give birth, she returned to band-leading before ending her career with Denny Boyce and Sydney Lipton.

Norman Cole — Member of Sydney Kyte's Piccadilly Hotel band from 1931-1936 and broadcast from there with his own band just before the war, with Al Bowlly and Anne Lenner as his singers. The band did not survive the hostilities, however.

Blanche Coleman — One of a number of wartime all-girl bands which firstly did the rounds of the service camps, then one-night stands and summer seasons at the booming post-war holiday camps, especially Butlin's. Later played several seasons in Aberdeen.

Graham Collier (born 1937) — Primarily a jazz composer and musician but learned his trade via dance and military bands. Formed his own orchestra in 1964.

Len Colvin — His Denza Players hailed from South Wales where most of them doubled as coal miners during the day! They were still good enough to broadcast though.

Horace Cook — Cheltenham-based band of the Fifties.

Roy Cooper — Wartime band leader in Scarborough.

Bob Cort (born 1930) — One of the many post-war traditional jazz enthusiasts, he formed his own group at the height of the mid-Fifties skiffle craze, which included Ken Colyer's brother, Bill. Although he continued to record for some years afterwards, the peak of his career came with the BBC popular music programme "Six-Five Special" for which, during the early days, his own recording was used as an introduction, with the steam train bearing down on the camera accompanied by the sound of Bob singing "Over the points, over the points, over the points ..." He played at many dance venues until the mid-Sixties.

118

Mike Cotton — Tottenham-born, he led a popular young traditional jazz band during the early-Sixties when many young people were still leaping around the dance floor to the beat.

Courtley-Seymour Band — Fine jazz orchestra born from the Eric Delaney band in 1956. It was led by trumpeter Bert Courtley (1929-1969) and bass player Jack Seymour but lasted only a short time on the dance band circuit before they both returned to their jazz roots. Their singers included Derrick Francis and Vicki Anderson. Bert was married to Kathy Stobart (*q.v.*) before his premature death at the age of 40, while Jack was a splendid all-round musician who made a big contribution to the Delaney band, especially the arrangement of the famous hit record *Oranges and Lemons*.

Derek Cox — Pianist with Leslie Hopkins and Trevor Brookes who later formed and recorded with his own trio. From the Forest of Dean in Gloucestershire, he was also an expert amateur snooker player and ended up playing music for dancing on cruise liners.

Crane River Jazz Band — An early ensign-waving member of the post-war traditional jazz boom founded by Ken Colyer in 1949 following his visit to New Orleans as a merchant seaman. Monty Sunshine was among its early ranks although the band continued for many years.

Harry Crocker — Led a Thirties band which played at Weymouth in Dorset.

Tony Crombie (1925-1999) — A drummer who appeared with Tito Burns, Eric Winstone, Ronnie Scott and Roy Fox before launching out on his own with a succession of groups which varied from ballroom dancing to rock-and roll, plus all aspects of jazz and modern music. A jazzman at heart, he responded to the mid-Fifties rock 'n' roll craze by forming his own rock band named the Rockets but, comprised mainly of disaffected jazz musicians, they were an unruly bunch who were banned from many venues, taking to bookings under pseudonyms such as "Professor Cromberg and his Students"! He was also an arranger and composer, backed singers Tony Bennett and Jack Jones, and appeared with both Stephane Grappelli and Stan Tracey. In later life he became an antiques dealer.

Austen Croom-Johnson (1909-1964) — Better known as a pianist and singer he briefly led a recording group in the early-Thirties which included Lloyd Shakespeare, Len Fillis, and Rudy Starita. Died in America.

▷ *Alfred Van Dam was a familiar figure both north and south of the River Thames.*

Edna Croudson — Ran an all-girls band during the Twenties and Thirties. One of her residencies was at the Paramount (later the Odeon) cinema in Leeds.

Henry Croudson — Thirties band leader who appeared with the Mills Brothers on their British tour of 1937. In addition to being a successful cinema organist in Leeds he also led an all-ladies band in which it is believed Ivy Benson was an early member.

Mervyn Dale — Led a wartime band in Ipswich which enjoyed a friendly local rivalry with Frank Butler's Blue Ambassadors — both bands earning regular recognition in the annual *Melody Maker* awards.

Alfred Van Dam (1902-1973) — Conducted the Trocadero cinema orchestra at the Elephant and Castle in south London before moving north of the Thames to the newly-opened Gaumont at Kilburn. There he performed under his own name but when cinemas finally turned their back on dance orchestras he re-crossed the river to become musical director at Streatham Hill Theatre, before its eventual demise and conversion into a bingo hall.

Benny Daniels* (born 1913) — Multi-instrumentalist from Hull in Yorkshire, who led his first band at the Peebles Hydro before joining Alex Freer's band at the Glasgow Plaza. In 1934 he joined Jack Hylton with whom he stayed until war broke out in 1939. He then played tenor sax with the RAOC Blue Rockets and took over the leadership when Eric Robinson left after hostilities ceased. In 1949 he became musical director at Stockton Palais, Co. Durham.

D'Arcy's Baby Band was unusual, even for 1925. There is no doubt that it contained many fine young musicians, however, and sitting on the far left of the front row is 14-year-old Billy Amstell, whose career in dance music had few equals. Seated next to him is Sylvia Quick. Frank Davis is surrounded by the sousaphone and Violet Osborne looks as though she means business on the rudimentary drum kit. They proved good enough to travel from London to Glasgow for a successful season in pantomime.

D'Arcy's Baby Band — Billed as "the only juvenile syncopated band in existence", it played with some success around London during the mid-Twenties. The youngest members were only 14 (school-leaving age) but occasionally some of the older ones reached their majority. A very young Billy Amstell cut his professional teeth with the band which, in 1925, entrepreneur Bert D'Arcy (see also The Ramblers) deemed good enough to go on tour to Scotland, where it played a full pantomime season in Glasgow.

Frank Davidson — Great favourite at the Edinburgh Palais during the early-Twenties where among his band were Sydney Lipton, Clem Bernard and Joe Ferrie. He later moved to the Regent Ballroom in Brighton where Billy Cotton quickly picked up all three musicians and whisked them away on tour to Southport.

Hector Davies — Cheltenham-based Hector was extremely well thought of during the Thirties, both locally and nationally and during the war, expanded his activities, deputising for many top bands around the country and continuing to play for many years after hostilities ceased.

Ray Davies — With his Button Down Brass he recorded many strict-tempo records during the late 20th century.

Ben Davis — One time leader of the Carlton Hotel band in London and brother of famous trombonist, Lew Davis.

Al Davison (1889-1936) — Accordionist who led a late-Twenties and early-Thirties band which played at the Astoria, Finsbury Park and various summer venues, including Worthing. He also appeared in the 1932 film "The New Hotel" and was an important musical director who specialised in introducing potential stars to the West End. A band leader with a university degree who died in harness while conducting at Southsea.

Chris Dean — Led the revamped Geraldo Orchestra before taking over the leadership of the Syd Lawrence orchestra during the late-Twentieth century on into the new millennium.

Cliff Deeley — 14-piece band resident at Birmingham's Tower Ballroom from the late-Forties to the early-Sixties, playing six nights a week with a separate Sunday club run by the leader himself. They broadcast several times and also did occasional outside gigs.

Hermanos Deniz — "Hermanos" is Spanish for "brothers" and this Latin American post-war group was led by Frank Deniz, assisted by siblings Joe and Laurie. For many years they were resident at London's Coconut Grove and also played alongside Sydney Lipton at the Grosvenor House Hotel.

Billy Derek — Thirties band which played at Cheltenham Town Hall.

Teddy Desmond — Glasgow-based band of the Thirties.

Louis de Vries (1906-1935) — Dutch trumpeter and band leader who ran an early-Thirties group called the Royal Orpheans.

Myra Deutsch (1914-1982) — Real name Millie Fox, she was born in Birmingham and started her career as a singer in Manchester during 1931, later leading her own all-male band in both Lancashire and the Midlands. She retired from the music scene after her marriage in 1938.

Brian Dike — Gloucestershire-based band of the Fifties.

Jack Doyle (died 1985) — Singing and trumpet-playing member of Billy Cotton's band, who also recorded a few late-Thirties records under his own name. Real name Jack Conn but always known as Jack "Trump" Doyle.

Johnny Duncan (born 1931) — An American serviceman who settled over here after marrying an English girl. A natural Country and Western singer born in Tennessee, he succeeded Lonnie Donegan in Chris Barber's band and soon became a star in his own right. Initially a member of the Vipers Skiffle Group, with his Blue Grass Boys he toured all over the country and appeared many times on television, usually accompanied by crowds of dancing teenagers. He later emigrated to Australia.

Ken Duncan — Led a Southend-based band during the early Thirties.

Michael Eastley — (see Walter Midgley).

Bernard Ebbinghouse — Trombonist, arranger and band-booking agent who also used the name Bernard Brent to lead bands at various small ballrooms, including Slough Palais.

Bill Edge (1902-1982) — Led a band at the Levenshulme Palais, Manchester, from 1948-1959. Also played trumpet with Henry Hall during the war.

Reg Edwards — Popular Thirties band which strayed over the border to play at the Edinburgh Locarno during 1937.

George Elliott (born 1912) — An accomplished guitarist from London who made many records with Ray Noble, Bert Firman, Phil Green, Sid Phillips, Lew Stone, Eric Winstone, Ambrose, and Victor Silvester. In the mid-Thirties he also recorded a number of sides with his own Sweet Music Makers.

Jack Emblow — Initially an accordionist in Ian Stewart's Berkeley Hotel band, he then branched out on his own leading small ensembles. Fame suddenly came his way when he backed the Adams Singers in the popular radio programme "Sing Something Simple", a fixture which lasted almost four decades.

Trevor Emeney — Formed a group called Crescendo in Gloucestershire during the Eighties, specifically to recreate the post-war big band sound of people such as Ted Heath, Count Basie and Duke Ellington.

Harry Engleman (born 1912) — Edgbaston-based pianist and composer who led a small pre-war combination and later a larger band which was popular in the Midlands. He also broadcast regularly with the Aston Hippodrome Orchestra and during the Sixties formed a special Tango orchestra for old-time dancing.

Cecil Epsteid — A pre-war Eastbourne band which featured a very young Paula Green as vocalist.

Charles Ernesco (died 1998) — Led his own post-war orchestra which broadcast and toured throughout the Forties and Fifties.

Grisha Farfel — During the war he toured with ENSA before joining Billy Cotton after hostilities ceased. He then formed a sextet and enjoyed residencies at Richmond, Southend, London and Nairobi before rejoining Billy Cotton, with whom he stayed for many years. He still found time to record separately under the name of Gay Brill, however, and also to combine his Billy Cotton "Wakey, Wakey" activities with occasional club work with his own group.

Harry Farmer* — His pseudonym should have read "Hamilton" but a typist at the Decca studios made a mistake!

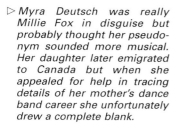

▷ *Myra Deutsch was really Millie Fox in disguise but probably thought her pseudonym sounded more musical. Her daughter later emigrated to Canada but when she appealed for help in tracing details of her mother's dance band career she unfortunately drew a complete blank.*

Five Famous Bands Pictured During the Fifties

△ Ken Mackintosh and his band appeared in the 1955 film "An Alligator Named Daisy" in which they played a crazy number called "Crocodile Crawl". The singers were Don Cameron (sitting on the chair) and on his right, but almost off-picture, Kenny Bardell who was a great friend of Matt Monro. The pianist is Jack Honeybourne who played for Vera Lynn and Harry Secombe, while the trumpeter to the right of Ken Mackintosh's head is Johnny Harris, who scored the arrangements for all Tom Jones' hit songs, including "Delilah" and "It's Not Unusual". Many famous stars appeared in the film, including Donald Sinden, Margaret Rutherford, Frankie Howerd, Gilbert Harding, Stanley Holloway, James Robertson Justice, Jimmy Edwards, Richard Wattis, Patrick Cargill and Diana Dors.

△ Victor Silvester was the master of strict-tempo ballroom dancing and wrote a book about it called "Dancing Is My Life", published in 1958. His son, Victor Silvester junior, was also an extremely accomplished dance band leader but it was never easy following in the footsteps of such an illustrious father.

△ Sid Phillips was one of several musical brothers. His official signature tune was a clarinet solo called "Clarinet Cadenza" but he never recorded it and was more famous for "Hors D'Oeuvres".

△ Edmundo Ros, seen here on the drums, was almost single-handedly responsible for introducing modern Latin American ballroom dancing to Britain. When he arrived just pre-war from Venezuela, he sought advice from Victor Silvester who felt sure the British public would only take to South American rhythms if they were Anglicised first. He was right because Edmundo took him at his word and spawned a whole new dancing genre which is still popular today.

▽ Ted Heath leading his band in the final number of the last swing session show at the London Palladium before his visit to America, which he toured early in 1956.

Sonny Farrar (1905-1979) — Thirties band leader who played at several venues including, Douglas, Isle of Man, Leamington, and in Liverpool at both Lewis's department store restaurant and Reece's Ballroom — which was owned by "PC 49's" family! He was also a comedian, vocalist and banjoist with Jack Hylton and actually deputised for him on a couple of occasions. Toured with ENSA during the war, then went into pantomime — all five foot tall of him! Returned to band leading at the age of 55, playing at the South Parade Pier bandstand in Southsea, Hampshire.

Leonard Feather — Well-known and respected pre- and post-war jazz and music critic who also made a small number of recordings under his own name, leading an all-star band from the piano and celeste.

Al Feld — Wartime and post-war band leader at Sherry's Ballroom in Brighton.

Victor Feldman (born 1934) — Edgware-born, while still only seven he played the drums at the Melody Maker Jazz Jamboree. Until he was 12 he was only allowed to play at charity functions but later made up for this and appeared with Glenn Miller while still a teenager. Although booked to appear with his own sextet at Ted Heath's Sunday Swing Session, he was banned by law from doing so — although weekday sessions were allowed! Feldman's Club in Oxford St. was run by his father so it was no surprise to find Victor playing there with various famous names. In the mid-Fifties he became a member of Woody Herman's band in America.

Stan Fielding — Wolverhampton-based band which ran from the mid-Thirties through the war, and appeared in several All-Britain Dance Band Finals.

Tommy Finnigan — Edinburgh-based band leader who played at the Marine Gardens and Portobello Ballroom during the Thirties through into wartime. Primrose Orrock sang with the band before the outbreak of hostilities.

Howard Flynn (died 1956) — Classically-trained musician who led an early-Thirties recording band which included Stanley Barnett and utilised the vocal talents of Harry Bentley, Cavan O'Connor, Dan Donovan and Phyllis Robins. Managing director of the re-formed Edison Bell company in 1933.

Barry Forgie — Conductor of the BBC Big Band at the turn of the 21st century.

▷ *The 1941* Melodymaker *compared Victor Feldman with Gene Krupa, a famous American jazz drummer.*

Ben Frankel (1906-1973) — As Benjamin Frankel he was an important serious composer of eight symphonies and five string quartets. As a light music and film composer he wrote the famous tune *Carriage and Pair* for the 1950 suspense film "So Long at the Fair". As a dance band leader he led a pre-war orchestra which recorded in 1937, featuring vocalists Eve Becke, Bert Yarlett and Dorothy Carless. He also arranged and played jazz fiddle on numerous recordings with other people, including Fred Elizalde, Roy Fox, Henry Hall, Jerry Hoey, Jack Howard, Percival Mackey, Carroll Gibbons, and Maurice Winnick.

Johnny Franks — Post-war swing violinist who, in addition to touring dance halls and variety clubs, led small bands playing seaside summer seasons.

Alex Freer (1906-1968) — Originally a spool-boy in a local cinema, Alex, who played both alto sax and violin, graduated to running a classy band at the Glasgow Plaza which brightened up the town during the late-Twenties and throughout the Thirties. He also played seasons at the Astoria Ballroom in London's Charing Cross Road, where he shared

OUR 7-YEAR-OLD KRUPA GOES TO TOWN!

This amazing action-picture of the "M.M." seven-year-old drum wizard, Victor Feldman, was taken at the No. 1 Rhythm Club on Sunday, when the child's incredible drumistics had a capacity audience by the ears.

At the conclusion of the show (reported on page one), Harry Parry announced that he is including Victor Feldman and his brothers in an early Radio Rhythm Club programme. He expressed his complete amazement at the child's capabilities—an opinion shared by all who have heard this young genius.

△ *Ben Frankel was unique, being the only British musician to make a living from three quite distinct genres. Beginning as a dance band leader and arranger, he then became a highly-respected post-war composer of both film and serious symphonic music.*

broadcasts with Jack White's band. He also recorded and at one point had a certain film star called Bebe Daniels as his singer. Pianist Eric Spencer went on to become the cornerstone of Edmundo Ros's band, as an instrumentalist and arranger.

Al Freid — During the late-Thirties he was the youngest musical director on the Moss Empire circuit, having previously been MD at several London cinemas.

Oliver Gaggs — The first band leader to serenade tens of thousands of regulars at Blackpool's Tower Ballroom, a position he held until his retirement in 1929 ending a 30-year unbroken association with the Tower.

Larry Gains — Southend-based band leader of the mid-Thirties.

Gale Family — Ran their own band in Devon during the late-Thirties. Billed as the Gales Premier Seven-piece Family Band they played at venues such as Okehampton Drill Hall just before the outbreak of war.

Billy Gammon (1906-1984) — Pre- and post-war band leader in Malvern, Worcestershire. A child prodigy on the piano he graduated to leading Sunday night concerts and often performed at Priory Park and the Winter Gardens. When popular music began to change during the Fifties he swapped his baton for an engineering company which he founded in partnership with one of his band.

Gloria Gaye (born 1910) — Glorious Gloria ran a popular wartime outfit which she called Gloria's Glamour Girl Band. Initially formed in 1938 it toured with ENSA and appeared at numerous variety venues up and down the land. Married to racing driver George Newman she continued playing until the Fifties.

Geoffrey Gelder — Recorded during the late-Twenties with a band called the Kettners Five which was resident at Kettners Restaurant in London. Among its members was a young multi-instrumentalist called George Melachrino.

Harold Geller (born 1917) — Australian who came to study classical music in England but ended learning the clarinet and saxophone and transferring to dance music instead. Served in the wartime RAF and then formed his own band which played at Fischer's Club and Frascati's Restaurant. Regular broadcaster on "Music While You Work" and "Morning Music", and also a composer of such tunes as *The Green Cockatoo* and *The Mocking Bird*.

Al George — Pseudonym used by Metropole to cover various pre-war bands.

Hughie Gibb — Played the Mecca circuit ballrooms in the Isle of Man and north of England from 1940 until his retirement nearly twenty years later.

George Glover — Multi-instrumentalist who played with many bands, including Ray Starita, Billy Mason, Jock McDermott and Billy Cotton, after which he led his own band during the mid-Thirties. He then joined Eddie Carroll, Jack Harris and Harry Roy before emigrating to Australia.

Jan Godowsky — Resident mid-Thirties band at the Astoria Cinema, Southend.

Reggie Goff (1915-1956) — Despite contracting polio when aged 13, within two years he was leading his own band and during the war years played saxophone and featured as a vocalist with Billy Ternent, Stanley Black and George Crow. He also recorded with Ted Heath, Robert Farnon and Felix King. Later he led his own quartet and sextet and guested for Cyril Stapleton. He made several records, both as a vocalist and band leader but died young, the victim of heart disease. Although confined to a wheelchair for much of his career he never stopped enjoying life, and confounded his doctors by touring right up till the end.

Alfie Good — Dundee-based band of the mid-Thirties.

Eddie Gordon — Dundee-based keyboard and band leader of the mid-Thirties.

125

△ *Where it all started — Hammersmith Palais during an unusually quiet spell in the Twenties. Note the rudimentary roof supports which indicate the building's origins as an aircraft factory.*

Jack Gordon — Formerly a drummer with Jay Whidden he became resident at the pre-war Pico (Embassy) Ballroom in New Brighton until it was destroyed by fire. Not to be confused with the same recording pseudonym used by Jack Plant, Billy Scott-Coomber and others!

Hal Graham — Forties and Fifties band based at the Rialto Ballroom in Liverpool.

Kenny Graham (1924-1997) — Best-known for leading a colourful upbeat band called the Afro Cubists which operated on and off throughout the Fifties. In between times he played saxophone for Nat Temple, Ambrose, Nat Gonella and Jack Parnell.

Oscar Grasso** (1914-1982) — Long-time violinist with Victor Silvester, he sometimes broadcast with a small band of his own called Intimate Music.

Al Gray — Part-time band leader who led a group of part-time musicians whose day job was driving taxis! As "Al Gray and his Taxi Band" they broadcast during the late-Thirties.

Glen Gray — Real name Gilbert Gray who led a small wartime group called the Rhythm Kings at Middleton Baths Ballroom in north Manchester.

Art Gregory (1906-1970) — Played many venues pre-war including Sherry's Dance Hall, Brighton and Covent Garden in London. During the war he entertained the troops for ENSA, both at home and in France.

Sim Grossman — Formerly a London band leader he became resident at the Bournemouth Pavilion for most of the Thirties.

Cliff Gwilliam — Led a band at the Imperial Hotel, Torquay during the mid-Thirties.

Johnny Haim — Leader of a young late-Forties revivalist traditional jazz band called the Jelly Roll Kings, with Beryl Bryden as its one-time singer. Just as they were beginning to make an impact, however, Johnny died in his sleep.

Basil Halliday — Post-war band which was resident at the Mayfair Ballroom, Nottingham.

Wilf (died 1936) and **Mary Hamer** — Liverpool-based band resident at the Grafton Rooms. Unfortunately, while doing a summer season at Rhyl, Wilf died suddenly from pneumonia. Mary, already the band's vocalist, then took over as leader and continued throughout the war years and on into the Fifties.

Ord Hamilton (1899-1955) — Pianist, singer, organist and pre-war broadcasting and recording band leader who could also turn his hand to adagio dancing and composing. With his 20th Century Music he deputised for Henry Hall when he made the 1935 film "Music Hath Charms". He was also a musical director for some of George Formby's films and accompanied his wife, Mary, when she sang with ENSA during the war.

△ *A youthful Dan Hopkins before he set sail around the world as a musician.*

Thelma Hammond — Lady band leader during the Forties who played at Skegness, Llandrindod Wells and Streatham. Highly competent on alto-saxophone, clarinet and violin.

Ronnie Hancox — Sutton Coldfield-based post-war band which was popular throughout the Midlands and lasted until the early-Sixties. He also played summer seasons in Eastbourne, Weston-super-Mare and Southsea. Singers included Susan Maugham and Tonia Gale.

Freddy Hargraves — Popular wartime band which hailed from Kent and was based in the Margate area.

Edwin and **Ceres Harper** — For many years they provided the music for summer season concerts at both Bridlington and Southport Floral Halls, and also for diners at prestigious venues such as the Grand Hotel, Scarborough.

Bernard Harris — For many years the resident band on Eastbourne Pier, for the summer of 1935 he replaced Peter Fielding at the Oxford Galleries in Newcastle upon Tyne.

Jack Hart (1910-1973) — Real name Jack Marshall, he led and sang with his own band on the Isle of Man before joining the wartime RAF. During the early-Thirties he recorded on the rare Dominion label with a band which included Harry Hayes and Cecil Norman, with arrangements by Fred Elizalde.

Jack Harvey — Glasgow-based band of the Thirties.

Frank Harwood — Real name Frank Reed he originated from Essex and led a band during the Twenties, before performing on ocean liners sailing out of Tilbury. He eventually settled in Oregon, USA.

Les Haskell — Thirties band which played in the Channel Isles, London, Brighton and Newcastle.

Bill Hawkins — Directed the Ritz Dance Orchestra at the Bury Palais and broadcast occasionally from the BBC studios in Manchester.

Len Hayes — Thirties band which played at the Paradise Club in London.

Fraser Hayes Four — Well-known on radio, particularly with Kenneth Horne in "Beyond Our Ken" and "Round the Horne" . The Fraser Hayes Four (led by guitarist Jimmy Fraser and bass-player Tony Hayes), actually began as a cabaret and resident dance group at a variety of venues including Brighton, Southend, Bristol, Scotland and London. Singers included David Mason June Ellis, Annabelle Lee (formerly Angela Lambert), Lynda Russell and Kerri Simms. Closely associated with them in the early-Fifties was Denny Dennis, then in the twilight of his career.

Scott Henderson — Glasgow-based, his Quintette won the annual *Melody Maker* contest held at Blackpool in 1946.

Charles Hennessy — Resident post-war band at the Rex Ballroom, Stockport.

Art Hickman — Big-name American band leader and drummer whose New York London Five appeared briefly in London during 1920, including future band leaders George Fisher and Jack Howard. So successful was he in the States that Columbia Records paid an enormous sum to hire a Pullman railway carriage to transport his whole band from San Francisco to New York, just for a week's recording session. Another famous member of his band was the unfortunate Bert Ralton who was accidentally shot dead on a hunting expedition in Southern Rhodesia in 1927. Roy Fox also played cornet before he switched to the trumpet and emigrated to England.

Bernard Hilda — Parisian band leader who for a time ran a post-war group at Ciro's Club. If no one was dancing then he would personally approach the nearest lady and request "the pleasure of your company". Other couples would then follow his example.

Billy Hill — Early-Thirties band leader who featured both Al Bowlly and Val Rosing among his recordings.

Eddie Hilton — Led a 10-piece band around Rochdale after the war, several members of whom had played with Freddie Platt before he moved to the Blackpool Tower Ballroom.

Leslie Holmes — Not to be confused with the better-known comedian and variety artist, he ran a post-war dance band called the Londonaires which played at the American Officers' Club in Munich.

Dan Hopkins — Drummer and band leader who played with Art Hickman in America after the First World War, became a full-time CSM in the Cameron Highlanders and then led a highly-successful group at Singapore's famous Raffles Hotel during the early-Twenties. After a brief spell in London with Fred Elizalde he returned to the Orient and played until being ousted by the Japanese invasion of 1942. When hostilities ceased he formed a band of local servicemen in Singapore, eventually ending his career as a percussionist on Radio Malaya.

Leslie Hopkins — Gloucester-based post-war band who played regularly at the Guildhall.

Johnny Howard — Strict-tempo band leader who played all the different styles during the last three decades of the 20th century. He also led a singing group with his orchestra.

Les Howard — Born Leslie Samuel Howarth, and originally a singer with Hal Graham and Eric Winstone, Les formed a mid-Fifties band of his own, based mainly in the North of England, playing successfully for many years.

Stan Hudson — Ran a 10-piece orchestra at Birmingham Palais during the Thirties.

Gil Hume — Ran a band at Southampton's Guildhall and Royal Pier during the Forties and Fifties.

Tom Hunt — Played during the early Fifties at the Seaport Ballroom in Galway, on the west coast of Ireland.

Cecil Hurn — Played with his Esplanade Band at the State Café in Liverpool during the early-Thirties.

Will Hurst — Resident for more than 20 years at the Blackpool Palace.

Leslie "Jiver" Hutchinson* (1906-1959) — Formed his "Coloured Orchestra" in 1944 which he led until rejoining Geraldo five years later. Killed when the minibus carrying his band called the Ebony Knights, overturned *en route* to a booking at Fakenham in Norfolk.

Frank Jagger — Led a wartime band at the Branksome Towers Hotel in Bournemouth.

David Java — Post-war band leader at the New Queen's Restaurant, Leicester Square.

Ronnie Jay — Led a post-war band at the Majestic Ballroom, Wembley.

Tom Jenkins (1910-1957) — Succeeded Leslie Jeffries as leader of Eastbourne's "Grand Hotel" Orchestra in 1938 and was closely associated post-war with the radio programme of the same name.

Bobby Johnson — Formerly a trombone player with Ken Mackintosh, he formed his own band which played at the Tower Ballroom in Edgbaston, Birmingham, during the late-Sixties and early-Seventies.

Johnnie Johnson — Older brother of Laurie Johnson (both nephews of Billy Cotton), who ran a resident band in Radlett, Hertfordshire during the mid-Thirties. Not to be confused with Johnnie Johnston (real name Johnny Reine), founder of the Keynotes.

Robin Jones — Percussionist who arrived from India during the Fifties and was promptly snapped up by Edmundo Ros. He later developed a big following for two bands in tandem, one playing salsa and the other Latin jazz.

Tom Jones (born 1902) — Post-war he became famous as the violin-playing leader of the Palm Court Orchestra in the popular radio programme "Grand Hotel".

Teddy Joyce** (extra text to Volume One) — Real name Edmund John Cuthbertson. Had a long-lasting romance with film star Chili Bouchier.

Harry Kahn — Formerly a pianist and arranger with Joe Loss, Harry ran his own post-war band which also played on cruise liners.

Maurice Kasket — Broadcast from the Royal Bath Hotel, Bournemouth before the war, styled as the director of Harry Roy's Lyricals.

Jimmy Kavanagh — Ran a mid-Fifties band at Hornsey Town Hall in north London.

Cab Kaye** (1921-2000) — Real name Augustus Kwamlake Quaye he was born in Lambeth, of a Ghanaian musician father and English music hall artiste mother. Sang with Billy Cotton while still a teenager and survived both a torpedo attack and a plane crash during the war. After playing in New York he returned to England and in 1948 formed the Ministers of Swing, later renamed the Cabinettes. He then led a number of smaller jazz-style groups, interspersed with singing for others, including Tito Burns, Ronnie Scott and Eric Delaney. Later became entertainments director for the government of Ghana.

Ronnie Keene — After serving a saxophone-playing apprenticeship with Ken Mackintosh, Jack Parnell, Eric Winstone, and Nat Temple, Ronnie formed a long-lasting band which played from the mid-Fifties through to the mid-Seventies, appearing at several venues including the Tottenham Court Royal Ballroom,

△ Three provincial bands from 1935. (Top) Eddie Shaw at the Nottingham Palais, (centre) Eddie Carney conducting his Red Aces at Tony's Ballroom, Birmingham, (bottom) Stan Hudson at the Birmingham Palais.

The Lyceum in the Strand, Welling Embassy, and his own ballroom at Barnewood, near Bexleyheath. Married to singer Marion Davis (Keene).

Jim Kelleher — Alto saxophone player who led a band at London's Piccadilly Hotel in the late-Twenties. Future band leader Jerry Hoey featured in the reed section while vocalists included Cavan O'Connor and Fred Douglas

Hal Kemp — Well-known American band leader who first came over here during the mid-Twenties and later, during the early-Thirties, played at the Café de Paris and London Coliseum.

Johnny Kerrison — Led a post-war rumba band at London's Café de Paris.

Lena Kidd — Took over Gracie Cole's all-female band when Gracie left to give birth to her first child.

Frank King — Fifties band which played at the Jack of Clubs in London.

Tony Kinsey — Popular Fifties modern jazz band which featured among the country's best. Tony had quite a reputation as a drummer.

George Kirchel — London-based George won the annual *Melody Maker* contest held at Wimbledon in 1943.

Krakajax — Mid-Thirties group which played in London's West End and recorded for Parlophone.

Johnny Lambe — Led a 17-piece band from the Sixties to the mid-Seventies. It was similar in composition to Syd Lawrence with several musicians having experience in both, and some also with the BBC Big Band. Broadcast several times and regularly worked with big-name stars, including Cilla Black.

Don Lang (1928-1992) — As Gordon Langhorn he played trombone with Teddy Foster, Vic Lewis, Ivor Mairants and Ken Mackintosh, before shooting to fame overnight with his quickfire playing and singing. As Don Lang and his Frantic Five he became a regular on "Six-Five Special", thereafter touring with great success all over the country.

Harry Lang — Cheltenham post-war band.

Cy Laurie (born 1926) — Traditional jazzman to the core, especially the Twenties Chicago style, Cy eventually opened his own jazz club in London's Great Windmill Street. During a career spanning almost 40 years, he fronted a number of bands, also guesting in many others.

Billy Lawrence — London-based Billy won the annual *Melody Maker* contest held at Blackpool in 1939.

Brownie Lay — Banbury-based drummer who eventually formed his own band in 1956, retiring in 1991.

Bob Leach — (see Cavendish Band).

Lecuona Cuban Boys — Possibly the first Latin-American band to appear in London, when they came over from Havana in 1934. Described by the *Melody Maker* as "the rum rhythm of the real rumba" the band included instruments labelled as "horse's jaw bones and finger drums", the latter being another name for bongos which were tuned over hot spirit lamps! Gave Britain its first taste of Caribbean dance music (later refined by Edmundo Ros), and also introduced the Conga to the dance floor.

Peter Leigh — Resident post-war band leader at London's Regent Palace Hotel.

Reg Leopold (born 1908) — Post-war he became famous as the violin-playing leader of the Palm Court Orchestra in the popular radio programme "Grand Hotel". Pre-war he made a huge number of recordings with many bands, notably Ambrose, Carroll Gibbons, Jay Wilbur and Ray Noble. On his own admission his hobbies were "playing, sleeping and eating"!

Art Lewis — Long-serving band leader from Northampton.

Ted Lewis — Big-name pre-war American band leader who spent a good deal of his time in London and also on the Continent.

Ken Lewtey — Cheltenham-based post-war band.

Monia Liter* (1905-1988) — His real Russian name was Monia Litter but while he was in Singapore he was persuaded to change it by local band leader Dan Hopkins, who felt that Monia Rubbish was not a good idea for a musician!

△ *Cy Laurie during the late-Fifties.*

△ *Despite leading a group called the Dutch Serenaders, Anthony Macari was actually born in Liverpool.*

Malcolm Lockyer (1923-1976) — Pianist with Ambrose, Buddy Featherstonhaugh, Cyril Stapleton and Robert Farnon, Malcolm then founded his own orchestra and smaller groups during the mid-Fifties. In 1964, with Paul Fenoulhet, he shared the leadership of the new BBC Radio Orchestra, formed from the amalgamation of the old Variety and Revue Orchestras.

Lord Rockingham's XI — As the name suggests, this was a band specially created for the rock 'n' roll craze of the mid- to late-Fifties, specifically for the teenage dancers of the ITV show "Oh Boy", a direct rival to BBC's "Six-Five Special". Led by Harry Robinson the band featured saxophonist Red Price and clarinettist Benny Green.

Don Lorusso — Billed as "Britain's Ace Swing Organist" he led Jan Ralfini's band for a short time during the war.

Eddy Lucas — Led a Metropolitan-based group during the early Thirties, called the London Cabaret Band.

Don Lusher (born 1924) — Leading post-war trombonist who ran his own band during the Seventies. A regular participant of several television backing orchestras he was also an important member, and final leader, of Ted Heath's orchestra which was reformed in 1975, six years after the maestro's death. It was the wish of Heath's widow, Moira, that the orchestra would eventually finish while the musicians still sounded young, although in reality they were aged between 65 and 79. In addition to Lusher the final band included original members Jack Parnell (drums), Tommy Whittle (saxophone), Jackie Armstrong (trombone), Duncan Campbell (trumpet), and Lennie Bush (bass), with veteran singer Dennis Lotis also in attendance. Fittingly, the era finally came to an end in December 2000.

Macari and his Dutch Serenaders (born 1896) — Liverpudlian, Anthony Macari came from a circus family and, after appearing as one half of an accordion duo called the Macari Brothers, in 1931 he formed an accordion showband which played in full Dutch costume, usually against a backdrop of painted windmills. His children Larry, Joe and Rose were all members of the band which eventually, like most other show bands, bit the dust when economics squeezed it out after the war. Kept a shop in North London for many years.

Terry Mack — (see Terence McGovern).

Ivor Mairants (1908-1998) — Expert guitarist from Poland who played with many British dance bands, as well as running the Central School of Dance Music. A member of Roy Fox's singing group the Cubs (the others two were Harry Gold and Les Lambert), he later moved to Geraldo where he led the Swing Septet for more than a decade. He later jointly-led the Big Six with Don Lang and also wrote books on guitar playing.

Pete Mandell — American late-Twenties banjo playing member of the Savoy Orpheans and Sylvians, he then made a number of recordings with his Rhythm Masters, featuring drummer Joe Daniels, and vocalists Les Allen, Fred Douglas and Jack Plant. Returned to the States in the early-Thirties.

Robert Mandell — American who took over the running of the Melachrino Strings after George Melachrino's death in 1965.

Charles Marcus — Led a post-war band at the Scala Ballroom, Leeds.

Leigh Martin — Offshoot of Ronnie Jay's band at Wembley which toured American service camps during the early-Fifties.

Dave Mason — Ran a post-war big band for many years before retiring to Brighton.

Archie May — Post-war band which played at the Cricklewood Palais.

Alan Mayo — Gloucestershire post-war band which played regularly at Cheltenham Town Hall.

Jack McCormick — Led a band at Lewis's store and the Rialto Ballroom, Liverpool during the Thirties. "When I set out as violinist, my ambition was to broadcast" — which he achieved with his Ambassadors band by the time he was only 30.

Chas McDevitt — Glaswegian in origin, he settled in London where he joined the Crane River Jazz band. Shot to fame in January 1957, when his Skiffle Group, featuring Nancy Whiskey as singer, recorded *Freight Train*.

Ray McVay — in the jacket — leading the Glenn Miller Band, UK.

Thereafter he became a regular and popular dish for youngsters to dance too, but later returned to folk music, with his daughter, Kerry, as vocalist.

Eddie McGarry — Blackburn-based Eddie won the annual *Melody Maker* contest at nearby Blackpool for three consecutive years from 1936-8.

Terence McGovern — Better known as Terry Mack, he fronted an early-Thirties band playing his piano-accordion. Singers included Jack Plant, Sam Costa and Joe Leigh.

Jimmy McIntosh — Edinburgh-based band during the mid-Thirties.

Ross McManus — Trumpeter, and father of pop singer Elvis Costello, Ross sang for many years with Joe Loss but also ran his own band at the 51 Club in London. In addition, it was later revealed he was the singer David Ross who recorded for the Woolworth brand name Embassy label.

Ray McVay — Typical Palais band which was extremely popular on the long-running BBC television show "Come Dancing". He also directed the Glenn Miller Band (UK).

Eddie Mendoza — Toured during the late-Forties and early-Fifties with his group "The Spivs", broadcasting on "Variety Bandbox" and "Music Hall". A regular at Butlin's during the Fifties, in 1962 he beat the TV panel of "What's My Line" when he appeared as a yo-yo demonstrator which was his winter occupation! A year later he toured down under with the "Black and White Minstrel Show".

Fred Mercer — Midlands-based dance band of the Eighties and Nineties.

John Merrick — Post-war band leader at the Winter Gardens in Droitwich, Worcestershire.

Merseysippi Jazz Band — This Liverpool-based, traditional jazz band was a big attraction during the Fifties and Sixties.

Bobby Mickleburgh — London-based band during the Fifties.

Bob Miller (1923-1993) — Possibly the first big dance band leader to successfully adapt to the rock 'n' roll boom of the mid-Fifties, when he trained his Millermen to stand up *en-masse* and gyrate to the music — quite a change from his early playing days with Stan Atkins, and his own first band at Leeds Locarno. He created such an impression, however, that he was quickly invited to appear regularly on both radio and television, where he became a star attraction.

David Miller — Canadian who introduced many dance music programmes for the BBC. He sometimes fronted a band with the signature tune *The Miller of Dee*. Father of child singer and film star Mandy Miller, of *Nelly the Elephant* fame.

Herb Miller (died 1987) — Glenn Miller's younger brother who originally formed his own band in America while Glenn was still at the peak of his powers. In 1981 he was invited to Britain to recreate the famous Glenn Miller sound with an all-British band. Billed as the Herb Miller Orchestra it toured with great success to packed houses.

John Miller (born 1941) — Succeeded his father as leader of the Herb Miller orchestra, created in 1981 to recreate the sound of Herb's older brother and John's uncle, Glenn Miller. He was also the male vocalist, alongside Fiona Paige.

△ *Malcolm Mitchell Trio*

Ron Miller — With his London band called the Modernists, he won the annual *Melody Maker* contest at Trentham, Gardens, Nottingham in 1935.

Tod Miller — Took over leading Joe Loss's band when the maestro retired in 1989.

Malcolm Mitchell (1928-1998) — In 1955, after many years running a successful trio, Malcolm attempted to make it as a pure vocalist, before forming a short-lived big band which, for a variety of reasons, especially financial, lasted only 12 months. He quickly returned to running a trio and at one point had his own television show.

Ross Mitchell — Appeared regularly on BBC television and at the Hammersmith Palais during the later decades of the 20th century. He also recorded and played at all the major championships.

Billy Monk — Billy's Coventry-based New Rhythm Band won the annual *Melody Maker* contest held at Wimbledon in 1942.

Bernard Monshin — Regular performer with his Rio Tango Band on "Music While You Work".

Gerry Moore (1903-1993) — Closely associated with Victor Silvester's band he made a few recordings under his own name during the late-Thirties, which he directed from the piano. Always a jazz man at heart he played swing piano in many different groups, and recorded with the America Benny Carter when he visited England in 1936.

Joe Morrison (died 1944) — Recording band of the late-Twenties which featured Fred Douglas as vocalist.

Dorothy Morrow (see also Three in Harmony) — Singer who also ran her own band during the Thirties.

Phil Moss — Formerly a sideman with Joe Loss, he enjoyed a long residency at the Ritz Ballroom in Manchester and conducted the band which appeared there in the background ballroom scene featuring Dora Bryan in the film "A Taste of Honey". During the Fifties he spent the summer seasons band leading on his accordion at Douglas, Isle of Man.

Ken Moule — Enjoyed success during the Fifties with his modern jazz band called the Ken Moule Seven. He also acted as accompanist to Hubert Gregg.

Arthur Mouncey — Pre-war trumpet-playing band leader in Aberdeen who was responsible for spotting the singing talent of a young teenage George Barclay, whom he set on his way to stardom.

BLACKPOOL — MECCA OF THE NORTH

△ *Thirties view from the Tower overlooking the Central Pier. There was never any shortage of people for late-night dancing in the local ballrooms.*

◁ *Bertini to the fore but Reginald Dixon also starred on the Wurlitzer.*

▷ *(top) The famous Tower Ballroom which was later destroyed by fire.*

▷ *(inset) Charles Barlow who succeeded Bertini and bravely rescued his band's sheet music from the flames in December, 1956.*

▷ *(bottom) Will Hurst was resident at the Blackpool Palace, next door to the Tower, from 1922 until after the war. The building housed a ballroom, picture house and theatre but was demolished for redevelopment in 1962.*

Joe Muddel — A double bass player who formed his own band in 1952.

Charles Mumford — Led his own band at Southend from the early-Twenties to the mid-Thirties.

Joseph Muscant (1899-1983) — For many years conductor of the Commodore Grand Orchestra from Hammersmith, he then moved to the West End Troxy cinema and later to Paignton, where he led an orchestra under his own name.

Eddie Newport — Popular band leader from the Canterbury area of Kent.

Maxwell Nichols — Post-war band leader in the Malvern area of Worcestershire during the Fifties and Sixties.

Bert Noble — Led a band during the Forties at the Derby Castle Ballroom in Douglas, Isle of Man.

Ossie Noble (1910-1975) — Led an all-Welsh band at Lyons Popular State Café in Manchester during the early-Thirties.

Vincent Norman — Shared a late-night broadcasting session with Billy Merrin in the Nottingham studios during the late-Thirties.

Cyril Ornadel — Although not strictly a dance band leader he deserves a mention because of his role in working as a musical director for Jack Hylton, scoring many top shows and musicals in London's West End.

Bert Osborne — Regular band leader at Southampton's Guildhall during the Fifties and Sixties.

Reg Owen (born 1924) — Saxophonist who played with the Teddy Joyce juveniles whilst still a teenager, then formed his own early wartime band at Ealing before joining Harry Roy and Art Thompson. During the war and afterwards he played for Ted Heath, Jack Parnell, Kenny Baker and Peter Yorke, then became a composer-arranger who also recorded with his own orchestra.

Rex Owen (1905-1985) — Skilled saxophonist from East Ham who played with several bands notably Roy Fox, for whom he made several films while on tour, and also sang occasional comedy vocals. Led his own band as a teenager and later took an early-Thirties trio into the Café Anglais featuring Eddie Carroll on piano and Doug Howson on drums, whom he styled as his Nephews! During retirement he ran a garage in London and later a private hotel in Brighton.

▷ *Vincent Norman played with Percy Bush during the Twenties before branching out on his own.*

Gershom Parkington (died 1952) — Pre-war favourite with his Quintet, which appeared in the 1934 classic film thriller "Murder at Broadcasting House".

Alan Parsons — Drummer who led a band at West Pavilion, Jersey during the early-Thirties.

Jack Paterson — Glasgow-based band of the Thirties.

Sydney Pearce — Led the resident band at the Mecca Locarno Ballroom in Leeds and played at other Yorkshire venues during the war.

Brian Pearsall — One of several local post-war bands operating in the West Midlands, with Stourbridge as his base.

Percy Pease — Played at Stratford-on-Avon immediately post-war.

Lester Pendleton — Well-known across the north Midlands during the Thirties and resident at the Café Mimosa, Skegness, for many years.

Phil Phillips — Semi-professional band which played post-war at Swinton in north Manchester.

Teddy Pitfield — Led the Criterion band which frequented London's East End during the Twenties and Thirties, playing at such venues as YMCAs and youth clubs. Vocals were delivered through a megaphone but, despite the band's big following and, like many others, it broke up with the advent of war in 1939.

Freddie Platt — Enjoyed a stint at the Tower Ballroom, Blackpool after several years as the successor to Geoff Love at the Carlton Ballroom, Rochdale.

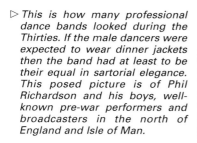

▷ This is how many professional dance bands looked during the Thirties. If the male dancers were expected to wear dinner jackets then the band had at least to be their equal in sartorial elegance. This posed picture is of Phil Richardson and his boys, well-known pre-war performers and broadcasters in the north of England and Isle of Man.

Eric Popperwell — His main claim to fame as an early post-war band leader was discovering Edna Savage, when he allowed her to stand in for his regular vocalist who was taken ill during a dance.

Bob Potter — Toured the Top Rank circuit during the Sixties and was resident at different times at Wolverhampton, Hanley and Birmingham. Broadcast on "Music While You Work", "The Breakfast Show" and Ray Moore's "Night Out".

Jean Pougnet (1907-1968) — Post-war he became famous as the violin-playing leader of the Palm Court Orchestra in the popular radio programme "Grand Hotel". Pre-war he made a huge number of recordings with many bands, notably Ambrose, Harry Bidgood, Debroy Somers and Ray Noble.

Roland Powell — With his Rhythm Aces, he broadcast regularly on Northern regional radio and for many years provided music in Golden Acre Park, Leeds. During the war he led groups called the Octet, and Astoria Players.

△ Joseph Muscant

Ken Prewer — Led a Forties band in Banbury, Oxfordshire.

Wylie Price — Post-war band which played summer seasons at seaside resorts including Worthing, Sussex and Herne Bay in Kent. His most famous vocalist was a young Alma Cogan.

Andy Prior — Singer-band leader who sounded rather like Frank Sinatra, and recorded with his Night Owls, a big band of "young" players which was resident near the end of the 20th century at the Tower Ballroom, Blackpool.

Bert Quarmby — Pianist who, in 1950, teamed up with Ivor Kirchin at Mecca's Tottenham Court Royal Ballroom where they replaced gramophone records with live music. After 18 months they moved to the Lyceum on the Strand and again, after Ivor was involved in a road accident, to the Streatham Locarno where Bert assisted Ivor's son, Basil, in the running of a new band. He also played at the Ilford Palais.

Bernard Rabin (1922-1993) — Eldest son of Oscar Rabin whose dance band he expanded in size when they bought the Wimbledon Palais in 1950, later developing under the leadership of David Ede after Harry Davis left for America in 1951, and even more so when Oscar died in 1958. Together with his younger brothers, Ivor and David, in 1943 Bernard launched the Rabin Agency which booked bands, particularly for touring. In 1968 he sold the Wimbledon Palais to a bingo empire and eventually retired to Rustington on the Sussex coast. Married to singer Diane, who succeeded Beryl Davis with the original Oscar Rabin band.

Michael Rabin — Son of Bernard, and grandson of Oscar, Michael ran his own part-time quintet at Burgh Heath, in Surrey.

Max Raiderman — Took over the running of the former Ambrose band at the Embassy Club when its erstwhile leader was enticed away to the Mayfair Hotel in 1927. Unfortunately the club's owner did not allow live broadcasting so little evidence remains of this period.

Bert Ralton* — His 1927 fatal hunting "accident" near Bulawayo in Southern Rhodesia is still shrouded in mystery and there were incessant rumours that it was not so much an accident as a warning shot which went wrong. Whatever happened, however, nobody pointed the finger and, according to eye-witness Ben Oakley, Bert, with his leg badly-damaged was left to strum his ukelele and sing *I'll Be Loving You, Always* on his way to hospital. He later died from his injuries. It was a particularly sad loss because Ralton rivalled Jack Hylton as the first truly successful professional syncopated dance band to emerge in Britain after the Original Dixieland Jazz Band (ODJB) visited in 1919. Originally a member of the highly-rated Art Hickman band in the USA, Ralton first came to these shores via Cuba, and was an expert on the C-Melody saxophone, a rich-sounding cross between alto and tenor, much favoured by jazz musicians during the Twenties.

△ *Bert Ralton became a legend largely on the strength of his bizarre death in southern Africa. He was, however, a very fine musician.*

Ted Rea — Based in Hartlepool, Co. Durham he was a friend of Chick Henderson, who sang with Ted's All-Star Syncopators during the mid-Thirties. Chick moved south to Slough and lived with Ted's family before his unfortunate demise via a stray shrapnel splinter during the war.

Don Rendell — Fifties modern jazz sextet who also accompanied Billie Holiday.

Harold Rich — Well-known post-war pianist with the BBC Midland Light orchestra who, while still only a teenager, ran a dance band in Coseley, near Dudley in the Black Country.

Phil Richardson — Ran a pre-war band at the Oxford Galleries, Newcastle upon Tyne where one of his members was Teddy Foster, later a famous band leader himself. His catch-phrase was "Always merry and bright". He also played at Douglas in the Isle of Man, and broadcast from Manchester.

Don Rico — Ran a late-Thirties and wartime band which played occasional sessions at Worthing. He also led an all-ladies orchestra.

Wally Robb — Played pre-war with Sim Grossman in Bournemouth before forming his own band in Droitwich after hostilities broke out.

Harry Robinson — (see Lord Rockingham's XI).

Wally Rockett — An early-Fifties band which played at London's Celebrite Club.

Eric Rogers (died 1977) — Multi-instrumentalist wartime fighter pilot who played with Howard Lucraft, Nat Temple and Eddie Calvert before forming his own band in 1949. Thereafter he became a hugely successful music arranger-composer in films, variety and recording studios. During the mid-Fifties he led the Skyrockets at the London Palladium and in the early-Sixties was pianist and deputy-director of Edmundo Ros's band. He wrote both scripts and music for many of the "Carry On" films.

Carlos Romanos — One of the few full-time post-war Latin American band leaders who recorded more than a dozen long-playing records during a career spanning almost four decades.

Peter Rose — Post-war band which played at the Edgbaston Tower Ballroom in Birmingham.

Johnny Rosen** — In addition to playing at Lewis's stores in both Manchester and Liverpool, he regularly performed at balls on board big transatlantic passenger liners while they were docked at the latter. Originally a member of Jack Hylton's band, Johnny once

△ *The post-war Skyrockets with Woolf Phillips on the rostrum.*

employed several ex-Billy Merrin musicians, including Les Cripwell, Nigel Cod Hill and Eddie Pullen, who also played with the BBC Variety Orchestra and broadcast from Manchester.

Andy Ross* — Began his career in Kirkcaldy in Scotland from where Mecca signed him up for the Birmingham Locarno during the late-Sixties. Five years later his talent took him to the London Lyceum where he stayed four years before leaving to go touring in 1977. He led the resident band on BBC television's "Come Dancing" and won many awards for his versatility.

Arthur Rowberry — Turned professional at the Nottingham Astoria Ballroom after winning the 1951 part-time All Britain Dance Band championship. Two years later the band was renamed the New Skyliners.

George Rowe — Booked by Geraldo, who spotted him playing at Rothesay in Scotland, his band became resident at the Rialto Casino, Coventry during the late-Forties.

Jules Ruben — Led a lively trio during the mid-Thirties featuring himself and Jack May (later replaced by Felix King) on two pianos, with Nat Burman on drums.

John Russell — Thirties band leader from London, best-remembered for giving a break to a young accordion player from Derby called Ronnie Binge, who proved so good in his stint at Great Yarmouth that he was encouraged to try his hand in London, which he did most successfully with Mantovani, eventually becoming his full-time arranger.

Bertram Sabey — Led a Watford-based band during the early Thirties.

Jean Salder — Popular Thirties broadcaster from the Midland Hotel, Birmingham who also made sorties into seaside resorts such as the Palace Hotel, Torquay.

Albert (1906-1948), **Harold** and **Jennie Sandler** — Albert was for many years at the Grand Hotel, Eastbourne and ran the BBC Palm Court Orchestra, brother Harold led a band at the Grand Hotel, Sheffield, and sister Jennie had her own pre-war female trio. She also toured South Africa with Bebe Daniels and Ben Lyon.

Santiago — Early wartime singer with Edmundo Ros who formed his own Latin American band in 1945.

Frenchy Sartell — Fronted Carroll Gibbons's post-war band at the Savoy during the time Carroll was designated as the hotel's Entertainments Director.

139

Kenny Baker

George Fisher

Teddy Foster

Harry Davis

John Firman had three musical brothers.

The actor, Roger Moore (later 007 and the Saint) nicknamed Ivy Benson, "Ivy Bunsen and her Burners"!

Ken "Snakehips" Johnson died in the Blitz.

Edmundo Ros

△ Percival Mackey led an accomplished band which did more than just play dance music.

▽ Edgar Adeler, at the piano, had a hand in bringing Al Bowlly to Britain.

▽ Both foreigners, Fred Elizalde (left) and Adrian Rollini played "hot" dance music in the UK.

△ Felix Mendelssohn looked the part but was probably the only band leader who could not play a musical instrument! He more than made up for it in charisma, however.

△ Philip Brown's Revellers. The right hand picture was taken outside the Columbia Graphophone Studio in London EC1, which merged with HMV and Parlophone in 1931 to form EMI. Philip later became the BBC's Controller of Dance Music from 1936-1945, after which he formed a booking agency.

▷ Eric Winstone's signature tune was "Stagecoach" which superseded another hit tune, "Oasis". After the war he was closely associated with Butlin's and appeared at every one of their camps between 1946-1969, most commonly at Bognor Regis. The splendid publicity picture (below) speaks for itself and dates from the time when post-war holiday camps were at their peak during the Fifties.

▽ This fine picture of Henry Hall's New BBC Dance Orchestra can easily be dated to late 1931-1932 because the 16-year-old oboe player is Richard Matthews, fresh out of music school. Henry proudly introduced him to the public on a film extract.

YOUR LAST CHANCE!

Phyllis Robins.

Jack Plant.

Dan Donovan.

Billy Scott-Coomber.

Sam Browne.

Denny Dennis.

Bill Currie.

Elsie Carlisle.

THE CHANCE OF A LIFETIME!

DON'T WASTE A MOMENT—SEND NOW!

ABSOLUTELY YOUR LAST OPPORTUNITY TO GET YOUR EIGHT AUTOGRAPHED PHOTOS OF THE WORLD-FAMOUS CROONERS AND A HANDSOME ALBUM!

This is absolutely your last opportunity to accept the greatest offer ever made in the history of radio. Just imagine your delight when you receive the **Handsome Album** containing **EIGHT** beautiful autographed photographs (postcard size)—autographed portraits of **EIGHT** of the grandest Crooners on the air.

RADIO PICTORIAL is only able to make this stupendous offer as the result of its close association with the radio " stars " themselves. **Nowhere else and never again will such an opportunity arise.**

All you have to do is to fill in your name and address in Reservation Form (No. 1) at the foot of the page, and send it to us **immediately** in a ½d. envelope (unsealed). Your album complete with eight autographed portraits will then be reserved for you.

At the foot of page 38 in this issue will be found " Crooner " Token No. 3. This will appear each week; all you do is to cut out the token from each of six consecutive issues and fix them in the squares indicated in Coupon No. 2 below. When every square has been filled in, tear out the coupon neatly, fill in your name and address and send in a 1½d. envelope with four 1½d. stamps or P.O. for 6d. (to cover cost of postage, packing, etc.) to " Crooner," " Radio Pictorial," Chansitor House, 37/8 Chancery Lane, London, W.C.2.

But you must **act quickly** as this is **absolutely the last time** this magnificent offer will appear. Don't miss this amazing opportunity—send in the reservation form below **immediately**, to-morrow may be too late.

Cut out the coupon No. I immediately below and send to-day in an unsealed envelope to "CROONERS' ALBUM," RADIO PIC., Chansitor House, 37-8 Chancery Lane, W.C.2

Keep this coupon until you have fixed tokens cut from six consecutive issues of RADIO PICTORIAL to it. Fill in your name & address, enclose remittance for 6d., and send in a sealed envelope to "CROONERS' ALBUM," RADIO PICTORIAL, Chansitor House, 37-8 Chancery Lane, W.C.2

POST THIS COUPON TO-DAY!

I Please reserve for me one of your special Albums containing eight autographed photographs of Radio Crooners as below.

I. DENNY DENNIS	5. JACK PLANT
2. ELSIE CARLISLE	6. DAN DONOVAN
3. BILLY SCOTT-COOMBER	7. PHYLLIS ROBINS
4. SAM BROWNE	8. BILL CURRIE

Name ....

Address ....

....

....

3 (BLOCK LETTERS PLEASE)

KEEP THIS COUPON

2 I have affixed coupons cut from six consecutive issues of " RADIO PICTORIAL " in the spaces indicated below and enclose remittance for 6d. to cover cost of postage and packing, etc., for my album of autographed Radio Crooners' Photographs which you have already reserved for me.

Name ....

Address ....

....

....(BLOCK LETTERS PLEASE)

△ *Television had yet to invade the lives of the general public in 1935, when mass entertainment was confined to the cinema, theatre, dance hall and radio. But 78 rpm records were available to all and a picture of your favourite singer added to the attraction. This advert shows who was "Top of the Pops" at the time.*

Mervyn Saunders — Post-war band which broadcast under the name of Sergeant Saunders of the Mounties.

Bill Savill (born 1910) — Played at the Grafton Rooms in Liverpool and broadcast from the BBC studios in Manchester, appearing several times on "Music While You Work".

Joe Saye (1923-1995) — Glaswegian Joseph Schumann was born blind, but quickly learnt to play both the accordion and piano, later becoming friendly with fellow-blind musician George Shearing. Played for Roy Fox while still a young teenager, toured with ENSA during the war and then formed his own small band which performed successfully at various summer seaside resorts and at several London clubs. One time accompanist to Kitty Masters, he also broadcast on radio before emigrating to North America, eventually settling in Toronto.

Les Seager — Native of Colwyn Bay who led and broadcast with the all-Welsh Craigside Rhythm Band from the Craigside Hotel Hydro down the road in Llandudno. He and his two brothers took three of the six individual prizes in the North Wales Dance Band contest held locally in 1936.

Jack Seymour — (see Courtley-Seymour Band).

Anne Shar — Late wartime band which played at Sherry's Ballroom in Brighton.

Ralph Sharon — Pianist and leader of a post-war group which broadcast and enjoyed residencies at London's Fischer's Restaurant and Stork Club. As a solo artist he emigrated to America during the early-Fifties and later became accompanist to Tony Bennett on his world-wide tours.

Eddie Shaw — Popular Thirties attraction at the Nottingham Palais.

Murray Sheffield — Dundee-based band of the mid-Thirties.

Bill Shuttleworth — Band leader who hailed from Preston Palais in Lancashire.

Victor Silvester junior* (1924-1999) — Modest son of a famous father, he actually led the orchestra for almost 30 years, the first eight of which were while his father was semi-retired. An earlier spell in charge came when his father was injured in a road accident during the mid-Fifties. Victor junior had always been associated with the orchestra from an early age and, following a lengthy spell as a BBC recording engineer during the war, when he lost the sight in one eye after an accident during a hand grenade training exercise, he entered the business full-time, becoming its business manager and music arranger. Before assuming full control, as well as working alongside his father he co-operated closely with Oscar Grasso, the orchestra's long-time violin player and co-director.

Percy Simmonds — Led an inter-war band which, in the late-Twenties was packing them in on Ventnor Pier on the Isle of Wight. In 1928, after they won the *Melody Maker* South of England Dance Band Championship at Chelsea Town Hall, they played at Llandudno where they met Ramon Newton, latterly of the Savoy Havana Band fame, who persuaded them to join him in Newcastle billed as the New Havana Band. They later played at Scarborough.

Lou Simmons — Blind London drummer who led a band from the late-Thirties through into post-war. One of his singers was Betty Taylor, with whom he did some live outside broadcasts from the Hotel Burlington in Boscombe near Bournemouth.

Les Simons — Ran a fine band in the early-Fifties which played around south London.

Derek Sinclair — Post-war band which played in Leeds.

Les & Bert Skelton — Ran a post-war Midlands family band called the Skeltonaires.

Arthur Slater — Midlands-based post-war bebop quartet which appeared in several All-Britain Dance Band Finals.

△ *Son of a famous father, Victor Silvester junior never really achieved the status he deserved.*

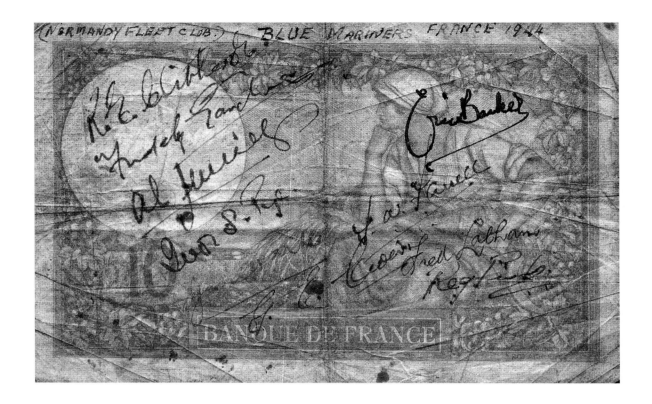

DANCE BANDS AND SINGERS IN WORLD WAR TWO

Many bandsmen and singers enlisted (see the chapter on "Service Bands" in Volume One), and gave invaluable support to the troops. Some worked with "ENSA" which stood for "Entertainments National Service Organisation" while others plied their trade with "Stars in Battledress". Some of the biggest stars toured the world and turned up in distant Asia as well as nearer to home in continental Europe.

The unique souvenir above — a wartime French 10 franc note — is seeing the light of day for the first time since it was ceremoniously autographed by the famous Blue Mariners at the Normandy Fleet Club in 1944. Also there at the time was comedian Eric Barker, whose autograph is clearly visible in the top right corner. The other signatures are (left to right); Fred Clitheroe, Freddy Gardner, Al Jennings, Ivor Pye, George Crow, Billy Farrell, Fred Latham and Reg Pink. A very faded signature in the middle appears to be Eric Barker's first attempt with a failed fountain pen, being turquoise blue as opposed to everyone else who signed in black.

Alec Smith (1901-1976) — Pianist from Wakefield in Yorkshire where, during the Twenties, he led his Black and White band formed of eager amateur musicians like himself, usually at the aptly-named Music Saloon. In the Thirties and throughout wartime he played at the Unity Hall while post-war he moved to the Criterion Ballroom. When the electronic age came along during the Fifties and Sixties he led a smaller group at local village hops before retiring with his wife to Australia.

Betty Smith (born 1929) — Tenor sax and clarinettist who played with Blanche Coleman's all-girls wartime band, then with Ray Starita, Ivy Benson and Freddy Randall. She formed her own small band during the mid-Fifties which, in addition to ballroom dance music also played skiffle and jazz, later expanding in size and proving a great favourite on the continent as well as at home.

Bryan Smith — Versatile band leader who played many instruments, including the organ. Extremely popular from the Seventies until his death in 1995, partly because he played for all types of dancing, including sequence and formation, and never turned down a request or booking. Played on the cruise ship *Canberra* for 25 years and was also closely involved in the Radio 2 ballroom series of programmes which ran from 1976-1988.

Chick Smith — Formerly lead trumpet with Woolf Phillips he emigrated to Ireland in 1953 where he opened a shop in order to finance his touring show band. Initially with ex-Geraldo singer Derrick Francis as his main vocalist he toured all over the country to great acclaim. Also a member of the late-Thirties vocal trio called the Harristocrats who sang with Jack Harris, and recorded for Radio Luxembourg and Carroll Gibbons.

Ronnie Smith (born 1926) — Born Ronnie Smitherman in Croydon, he learned to play the bugle after his family moved to Shoreham in Sussex, and later graduated to the trumpet during wartime service in Birmingham. After forming his own orchestra he won the 1957 Melody Maker South of England dance band championship and then deputised for Harry Leader, whose band he also played with until industrial action by the Musicians Union frustrated their broadcasting work. Back with his own band he played all the holiday camps, often working every night of the week — at the same time as having an ordinary day job! Operating latterly along the south coast, particularly in Sussex, he remembered a period when there were more than 400 full-time musicians based in Brighton alone. His final bow with the Ronnie Smith Big Band came at the Worthing Assembly Hall in January 2000.

Tommy Smith — Led a post-war band at the Savoy Ballroom, Oldham, Lancashire where he featured local teenage pianist Laurie Holloway, who went on to accompany all the top singers in the world.

Judd Solo — Resident for many years at the London Hilton rooftop restaurant, more than 200 feet up in the sky. He could also sing in five different languages.

Geoff Sowden — Trombone player who led a touring dance orchestra during the Fifties.

Charlie Steele — Ran a Thirties band in the restaurant at Lewis's store in Leeds and also played at the Majestic Hotel in Harrogate. Broadcast from Leeds and often supplied musicians to other bands across the county.

Johnnie Stiles — Swindon-based, he won the annual *Melody Maker* contest held at Manchester in 1949.

Kathy Stobart (born 1925) — An outstanding Geordie tenor sax player who was always in demand and played for many different bands, including Don Rico's Ladies' Orchestra (at the tender age 14), Peter Fielding, Canadian Art Thompson (her first husband), Vic Lewis, Ted Heath, and later Humphrey Lyttelton. In between times she formed her own band in 1950 and, following her marriage to Bert Courtley the following year, a number of other short-lived groups. After Bert's early death, however, she resumed guesting for others, especially Humphrey Lyttelton.

▽ *Kathy Stobart's early-Fifties group of young musicians was correctly styled as "Kathleen's" band!*

△ *Richard Valery*

Dick Sudhalter — American who came to England during the early-Seventies when he led a band called the New Paul Whiteman Orchestra.

Rube Sunshine — Led a wartime band at the Victoria Palais, Nottingham.

Hal Swain** — During the war he formed a touring variety group called Hal Swain and his Swing Sisters, consisting mainly of accordionists and dancers.

Ken Sykora — Fan of Django Reinhardt on whom he modelled his Ken Sykora Six, an unusual and well-liked group during the Fifties. Also a popular broadcaster.

Conri Tait — Yorkshire band leader from the Thirties who at different times employed many famous names including Billy Merrin and Helen Clare. Among his residencies was the Grand Hotel, Harrogate.

Geoff Taylor — Outstanding alto sax player who also led his own band in Hornchurch, Essex.

Ted Taylor — Began his career in Manchester before joining ENSA in 1943. After demob he played with Syd Seymour's Mad Hatters and then in 1952, with Bob Rogers, formed the Ted Taylor Four which played at the Manchester Plaza, Streatham Locarno and finally the Strand Lyceum.

George Thomas — Midlands-based quintet which appeared in several All-Britain Dance Band Finals during the Forties and early-Fifties.

Art Thompson (born 1918) — Canadian who joined Harry Roy as a pianist in 1941 before leaving to form his own eight-piece band which played at both the Royal Court Hotel and Embassy Club. In 1948 he went back to Canada but returned briefly to the Embassy Club before moving to Hollywood with the Victor Lombardo band. He also played with Charlie Spivak. Married briefly to Kathy Stobart who did not join him when he returned to North America.

Sydney Thompson — Synonymous with old-time dancing but also played modern dance music. Beginning in 1946 he broadcast on the programme "Take Your Partners" for more than 20 years, during which time he became a household name.

Irven Tidswell — Strict-tempo band from the late 20th century which was the first to be televised from the Empress Ballroom, Blackpool during the 1984 International Team Match. Played all styles of dance music.

Eric Tolley — Veteran band leader who operated in the Oxford and Didcot area right through to the 21st century.

Sheila Tracy (born 1934) — Most unusual female musician who introduced the regular BBC programme "Big Band Special" from its inauguration in 1979 right through until the 21st century. Initially a trombone-playing member of Ivy Benson's All-Girl Band she also formed a vocal duet called the Tracy Sisters but when asked to tour America her partner resigned, saying her husband would divorce her if she disappeared for six months! She then became a radio announcer and in 1974 was the first lady to read the news on Radio 4. Still playing regularly at the turn of the century and occasionally conducting the BBC Big Band. Author of two books based on American big-bands and British big-band players

Ken Turner — Derbyshire brass band player who graduated through the ranks to become the Music Manager of Blackpool's Winter Gardens in whose Empress ballroom he played for many years, also appearing many times at the Tower Ballroom next door. Regularly played for British ballroom dancing championships.

Maurice Udloff — Midlands band during the Fifties.

Richard Valery — Manchester-based composer and band leader during the mid-Thirties.

Vipers Skiffle Group — Formed by Wally Whyton (1930-1997), who later became a regular presenter of radio folk music programmes. They enjoyed a brief but memorable mid to late-Fifties career, playing music which youngsters loved to dance to. Other well-known members of the group were Dickie Bishop and Johnny Duncan.

Charles Vorzanger (born 1908) — Violinist and leader of the Commodore Grand Orchestra in London.

Victor Vorzanger — With his Broadway Band he played and recorded in London during the Twenties, both in the West End and also at the East Ham Palais.

YOUR RADIOLYMPIA PROGRAMME GUIDE

AUGUST | WEDNESDAY 14 | THURSDAY 15

SYDNEY BAYNES AND HIS ORCHESTRA

THE 16 RADIOLYMPIA GIRLS TRAINED BY TONY SMYTHE

COLLINSON & DEAN COMEDIANS | RADIO THREE SWEETHEARTS of SYNCOPATION

NORMAN LONG | HAROLD RAMSAY

The Famous Radio & Vaudeville Sisters
ELSIE & DORIS WATERS
Radio's "Gert" and "Daisy"

CLAUDE DAMPIER Professional Idiot encouraged by BILLIE CARLYLE

"IN TOWN TO-NIGHT"

LEONARD HENRY, Comedian

ELSIE CARLISLE & SAM BROWNE (YOUR RADIO FAVOURITES) | BILLY MERSON COMEDIAN, Assisted By BABS VALERIE

Santos Casani presents THE CASANI CLUB ORCHESTRA
Directed by CHARLIE KUNZ

AUGUST | FRIDAY 16 | SATURDAY 17

SYDNEY BAYNES AND HIS ORCHESTRA

THE 16 RADIOLYMPIA GIRLS TRAINED BY TONY SMYTHE

COLLINSON & DEAN COMEDIANS | RADIO THREE SWEETHEARTS of SYNCOPATION

HAROLD RAMSAY | NORMAN LONG

The Famous Radio & Vaudeville Sisters
ELSIE & DORIS WATERS
Radio's "Gert" and "Daisy"

CLAUDE DAMPIER Professional Idiot encouraged by BILLIE CARLYLE

"IN TOWN TO-NIGHT"

LEONARD HENRY, Comedian

ELSIE CARLISLE & SAM BROWNE (YOUR RADIO FAVOURITES) | BILLY MERSON COMEDIAN, Assisted By BABS VALERIE

Aug. 16.
THE CASANI CLUB ORCHESTRA
SANTOS CASANI presents
directed by CHARLIE KUNZ

Aug. 17.
GAUCHO TANGO ORCHESTRA
GERALDO and his original
by courtesy of the SAVOY HOTEL LTD.

PROGRAMMES YOU WILL HEAR AT RADIOLYMPIA

On this page and on page 30 are given the "Music Hall" bills of the shows which the B.B.C. will present at Radiolympia commencing on Wednesday, August 14. These programmes will be broadcast on Wednesday, August 14, 8-9 p.m. (Regional); Saturday, August 17, 8-9 p.m. (National); Monday, August 19, 8-9 p.m. (National); and Saturday, August 24, 9-10 p.m. (Regional).

△ There was no shortage of dance bands and singers at the 1935 "Radiolympia" held at the Kensington Olympia exhibition hall in west London. At the time it was one of the biggest attractions in the country with several programmes being broadcast live on national radio. Until well into the Fifties, special London Underground trains were run regularly on exhibition days to the nearby Olympia station.

△ When Monte Rey (centre) went on tour in the late-Thirties he was often accompanied by local bands, such as Owen Walters (left) from Stockton-on-Tees in County Durham.

Bob Walker — Started as a pre-war band which played at the Gaiety Ballroom, Grimsby throughout hostilities and beyond.

Willie Walker — Clarinettist with the Stanley Black orchestra who ran his own trio at a large department store in his home town of Newcastle upon Tyne.

Wall City Jazzmen — Chester-based traditional jazz band of the mid-Fifties.

Jack Wallace — Left Nat Gonella to form a wartime band at London's Embassy Club and later, Prince's Restaurant.

Owen Walters — North eastern band which accompanied Monte Rey in 1937.

Hedley Ward — Midlands-based post-war band leader whose rhythm group went on to become the famous Hedley Ward Trio in 1951. Hedley himself, however, was not part of the combination and continued to run his own band which often played at Birmingham's Grand Hotel, also appearing regularly on radio! Although most of his engagements were in central England, the group also travelled as far afield as Newcastle upon Tyne, Weymouth, Cardiff and Minehead.

Tom Ward — Long-serving Birmingham-based band leader who began his career in 1929 and continued right through to the Sixties.

Percy Waterhouse — Directed the Chalet Club Orchestra which broadcast from Northern Ireland during the Thirties.

Billy Watson — Resident post-war and early-Fifties broadcasting band at the Clery Ballroom in Dublin.

Charles Watson — Late-Twenties band leader from London who played at the Piccadilly Hotel, Café Anglais and Kit-Cat Club. This was followed by a residency at the biggest ballroom in the United Kingdom, Green's Playhouse in Glasgow with a young Billy Amstell among his ranks, but not too young to assume charge when Watson returned to London five weeks prior to the engagement ending.

Tommy Watt (born 1928) — Professionally trained musician who became a fine post-war arranger before forming his own band which played at Quaglino's Restaurant and featured vocalists Matt Monro and Margaret Rose. After a six-month spell with the Northern Dance Orchestra in 1960, he returned to London, continuing as a BBC arranger and also fronting a band at the Dorchester Hotel.

Bernard Weeden (died 1979) — Formed his first band during the mid-Thirties in Southend, Essex — where he remained a popular artist for more than a quarter of a century. A pianist with a gift for harmony, he wrote many tunes but never learnt to read music!

Bill Weeden (1913-1984) — Leader of the seven-piece Eltham Studio Band in south London which won the *Melody Maker* All-Britain Championship in 1945. Emigrated to Australia in 1952 and 20 years later founded the International Sinatra Society.

Dennis Wheeler — Trumpet player from Malvern in Worcestershire, who took over the running of Billy Gammon's post-war band, performing in local hotels and at the Winter Gardens. He also appeared at Cheltenham Town Hall.

Teddy White (died 1994) — Led a Fifties band in Littlehampton, Sussex and at the Grand Spa Hotel, Bristol, before graduating to London's West End where he also became a successful music arranger and publisher. Married to singer Janie Marden with whom he moved to Majorca during the Sixties.

Duncan Whyte — Former trumpeter with Jay Whidden and Billy Mason who formed his own largely Scottish swing band in the mid-Thirties which broadcast from Glasgow. After the war he appeared at Dundee's Empress Ballroom.

Wally Whyton — (see Vipers Skiffle Group).

Jay Wilbur** (extra text from Volume One) — Real name James Edward Wilbur Blinco.

Jan Wildeman — Post-war band which was resident at Cricklewood Palais.

△ *This rare picture from "down under" is of clarinet-playing Percy Winnick (younger brother of famous band leader Maurice), who emigrated to Sydney, Australia and ran his own band during the Fifties.*

Corelli Windeatt — Succeeded Albert Ketèlbey as leader of the London Dance Orchestra after the First World War and later made a few records under his own name.

Percy Winnick (1910-1988) — One of ten children and younger brother of famous band leader Maurice, who initially taught him the saxophone. He later joined his big brother at London's Piccadilly Hotel, also playing clarinet and oboe. In 1951 he emigrated to Sydney, Australia, where he ran his own band until retiring from music altogether.

Sonny Winters — Formerly engaged in Harringay, during the early Thirties he was resident at the Tottenham Palais, at the time the largest ballroom in the country with a capacity of 2,000 dancers.

Tiny Winters (1909-1996) — As his name implies he was small in stature but as big-hearted as his double bass, which he played with many pre-war bands including Ambrose, Lew Stone, Ray Noble and Roy Fox. An exponent of "slapped bass" (plucking the strings so hard that they rebounded and slapped against the backboard), he gave extra bounce to the rhythm section and was much in demand for post-war performances, both jazz and commercial. During the mid-Thirties he led an offshoot of the Ambrose band which recorded jazz tracks under the title "Tiny Winters and his Bogey Seven". 50 years later, he formed a band to recreate the classic 1930s dancing at the Park Lane Hotel, London. Called the Café Society Orchestra it recorded an LP shortly afterwards. He also led a trio which played nightly in front of the National Theatre and was a member of George Chisholm's famous Jazzers, an integral and popular part of the televised "Black and White Minstrel Show". Active right up until his death Tiny was at the heart of the dance band and early British jazz eras.

Arthur Wood (1875-1953) — Best-remembered for his light music compositions, especially *Barwick Green*, the familiar signature tune to the Radio 4 programme "The Archers", but he also directed a number of strict-tempo dance band recordings for the Gramophone Company's "house band" around the time of the First World War. It was named the Mayfair Orchestra for HMV recordings and the Peerless Orchestra on Zonophone.

Harry Wood — An early-Twenties band who recorded a small number of titles, including *I'm Just Wild About Harry*.

Jimmy Wooding — Long-serving band leader from Northampton.

Nat Younkman (1892-1957) — Originally from Latvia he toured all over the country with his Czardas band, especially as a music hall act.

▷ No, you are not seeing things and yes, it really is Margaret Thatcher holding — but not playing — the clarinet. The occasion was a fund-raising event for the Conservative party in Fulham and Hammersmith. On the left is Chris Barber, who perhaps more than anyone else, popularised the traditional jazz scene during the Fifties. He also set the short-lived skiffle boom going after what was meant to be a bit of private recording fun with Lonnie Donegan on "Rock Island Line" turned out to be a best-seller. On the right is trumpeter Kenny Ball, another top "trad" man while the second trombonist is Peter Sellers look-alike, Dave Morgan.

△ The Jelly Roll Kings was a relatively short-lived late-Forties band led by Johnny Haim .
◁ An undated post-war picture of Jan Ralfini, who enjoyed a long and colourful career as a band leader. Among his one-time musicians were singer Tony Blackburn and saxophone-player, Tommy Trinder!

▷ This picture captures more top band leaders in close proximity than perhaps any other known photograph. From the left: Bill Harty, Phil Green, unknown, Lew Stone (holding the double bass), Christopher Stone (Britain's first disc jockey but before they were called that during the early-Fifties), Carroll Gibbons, Harry Roy, Geraldo, Ray Noble, Henry Hall, Jack Hylton (with trumpet), Jack Jackson, Ambrose and Howard Jacobs.
The lady is Christopher Stone's wife and the photograph was taken at their Silver Wedding in November, 1933, three years before Howard Jacobs went to Australia and became a largely forgotten figure. He later emigrated to America where he changed his name to Howard Jones. Whatever the joke, it must have been funny!

BRIAN
LAWRENCE

150

EVE BECKE

WYNNE AJELLO

PEGGY COCHRANE

BERTHA WILLMOTT

THE CARLYLE COUSINS

PAUL ROBESON

△ Carlyle Cousins — left to right: Cecile Petrie (founder), Lilian Taylor and Helen Thornton.

CIGARETTE CARDS

You knew you had really arrived when you appeared on a "Faggie" during the Thirties. All the singers seen here were household names.

LESLIE HOLMES AND LESLIE SARONY

OLIVE GROVES

ANONA WINN

Bebe Daniels

LEONARD HENRY

Snippets from Billy Amstell

Edward, Prince of Wales was a great friend of Bert Ambrose, as was Prince George, the Duke of Kent, who was killed in an air crash in 1942. During the early Thirties Prince Edward regularly attended West End restaurants and night clubs, often with Wallis Simpson whom he later married. He fancied himself as a percussionist and occasionally would try out the drum kit of the resident band — which some leaders tolerated, including Ambrose — while others, especially Billy Cotton, found it difficult to conceal their displeasure. Edward was the subject of rigorous security but delighted in giving his bodyguards (appointed by his mother, Queen Mary) the slip, often going to ground at Ambrose's flat. He also appeared when British dance bands were on tour in southern France, especially at Monte Carlo and Biarritz, where he once plunged into the sea to save a boy from drowning — much to the astonishment of his bodyguards. The incident was necessarily kept top secret to save them any embarrassment.

*   *   *

When playing with Ambrose during the early-Thirties, Ted Heath was blowing his trombone minus his dentures. Unfortunately, when he pulled a handkerchief out of his top pocket to mop his brow, he was dismayed to see, and hear, his false teeth bounce across the dance floor.

△ *Ambrose*

*   *   *

Many musicians were practical jokers, known as "lumberers" because they "lumbered" the recipient of the joke with an awkward situation. On one occasion, saxophone player Billy Amstell was making his debut with Geraldo and was informed by drummer Maurice Burman that his tenor sax predecessor always played solos in front of the band — and that the audience expected it. When his solo turn came round, Harry duly got up out of his seat and stepped forward, creating a puzzled look on Geraldo's face. When he sat down, amid rapturous applause, Maurice casually remarked that it was a pity Harry's predecessor had never thought of going out front like that!

*   *   *

In 1935 an enlarged Ambrose band played at the Royal Opera House — the first and last time this occurred. Sponsored by the *Melody Maker* music magazine, the full house of more than 2,000 came from all over Europe for the occasion.

*   *   *

While the London Blitz was at its height Ted Heath always carried a suitcase around with him. When challenged by some of his closest friends as to what was in it, after swearing them to secrecy he revealed the contents to be tightly-packed rolls of bank notes. If Hitler was going to kill him then he reckoned he might as well take his money with him!

*   *   *

On another occasion, while in Paris on a wartime tour with Geraldo, Ted Heath dabbled in the black market and exchanged cigarettes, soap, tea and coffee for several expensive-looking fur coats … but which turned out to be made from cat skins!

*   *   *

Despite his sometimes sombre expression Sir Malcolm Sargent was occasionally seen applauding live dance music — professional musicians often acknowledging their colleagues from a different genre. On the same theme, Geraldo once conducted the BBC Symphony Orchestra and Chorus, the RAF Orchestra and his own band, all together at the same time in the Albert Hall.

*   *   *

Jack Hylton once offered to conduct any piece with Sir Dan Godfrey's orchestra which the conductor cared to choose, if Sir Dan, in turn, would reciprocate with Jack Hylton's band. Geraldo did exactly the same thing with Sir Malcolm Sargent. In both cases the classical maestros declined!

On his introduction to Ambrose's band, singer Alan Dean "borrowed" Billy Amstell's cap from his tenor saxophone — but when he came to sing Alan was forced to hold his hand over his throat for more than an hour. Ambrose could not understand why until, at the interval, Billy returned Alan's bow-tie!

*　　　*　　　*

During the freezing winter months of 1947, the worst weather for many years, live dance music business was down on its luck. Ambrose was playing at Ciro's Club but on 19th March, when the maestro walked in to conduct his waiting band, he found there was no audience. He went straight to the glum-looking patron, Captain Nathan, who was sitting at his usual table on the balcony and, while the band waited for their cue, was heard to say above the silence "You don't need us here any more, Nathan, do you?" "Not really" was the reply... and that ... as they say... was that! The end of the Golden Age of British Dance Bands.

*　　　*　　　*

Cyril Grantham related how the band once played a joke on Geraldo. Their boss had just bought a brand-new Humber Snipe limousine, so they superimposed a realistic looking scratch all down the side. When he saw it Geraldo was horrified, until he realised he was the only one not laughing.

Snippets from Ken Mackintosh

When travelling to a one-night stand in the West Country, Ken stopped to give a lift to an RAF serviceman hitch-hiking back to his base near Gloucester. The topic of conversation turned to the young man's appreciation of various entertainments put on by the camp authorities and how much he had enjoyed the visits of Joe Loss, Johnny Dankworth and Ted Heath. There was one band which he could not stand, however, and that was Ken Mackintosh who he thought was "lousy". Before the aircraftsman departed at the gates, Ken handed over his card — whereupon the car was vacated rather rapidly!

*　　　*　　　*

At rehearsals one day, the girl singer was out of tune. "What's the matter with you today?" said Ken. "Sorry I'm flat" came the response "... I forgot to clean my teeth this morning!"

*　　　*　　　*

While introducing the boys in the band, Ken said "This is a special day for Bobby in the trumpet section whose wife gave birth to a baby boy this morning. I think the proud father should stand up", at which point — to howls of laughter and applause — the whole band stood up and took a bow!

*　　　*　　　*

A trombone player had his expensive leather jacket stolen while working at the Hammersmith Palais. He immediately reported it to the police station next door. At the end of the show the police produced the jacket and explained how a man had come in saying he was a stranger and could they help him find accommodation. The sergeant noticed what he was wearing and said "We've got just the place for you. Come inside!" He did and was locked in a cell for the night!

*　　　*　　　*

During a weekly show on Radio Luxembourg for Lyons Mint Chocs, a lady sent in a letter saying she had listened to the show throughout her pregnancy during which she craved for, and ate, several mint chocs every day. "You'll never believe this Ken, but the baby was born with a brown birthmark in the middle of his hand, the size and colour of a Lyons Mint Choc!"

*　　　*　　　*

While practising for a 9am BBC broadcast early one morning, a trumpet player bowled in late. When Ken challenged him, he replied: "Sorry, I'm late but the goldfish jumped out of the bowl and I had to give it the kiss of life". "Pull the other one" said Ken, "Let's get on with the show."

General Index

Please note that only important dance band entries have been indexed and that people have not been included where the reference is en passant, for example "Ambrose" is mentioned more than 90 times in the text! All references to non-band singers and players have been ignored except for photographs and illustrations.

Bibliography

Ballad Years, 1945-60, The — Don Wicks (published privately 1990s)
Band Leaders — Julien Vedey (Rockliff 1950)
Billy Cotton Band Show — John Maxwell (Jupiter 1976)
Blackpool Tower — Bill Curtis (Terence Dalton 1988)
British Dance Bands on Record 1911-1945 — Brian Rust & Sandy Forbes
   (Gramophone 1987)
Cavalcade of Variety Acts (Who's Who in Light Entertainment) — Roy Hudd
   (Robson 1997)
Dance Band Era, The — Albert McCarthy (Spring 1971)
Dancing Is My Life — Victor Silvester (Heinemann 1958)
Don't Fuss Mr. Ambrose — Billy Amstell's autobiography (Spellmount 1986)
Fascinating Rhythm — Peter Cliffe (Egon 1990)
Georgia On My Mind (Nat Gonella Story) — Ron Brown (Milestone 1985)
Hollywood, Mayfair and All That — Roy Fox's autobiography (Leslie Frewin 1975)
Housewives' Choice (George Elrick's autobiography) — (Mainstream 1991)
I'll Sing You 1000 Love Songs (Denny Dennis Story) — Mike Carey (Pinnacle 1992)
Jazz Away from Home — Chris Goddard (Paddington 1979)
Lew Stone — Kenith Trodd (Joyce Stone 1971)
Musician At Large — Steve Race's autobiography (Eyre Methuen 1979)
Oxford Companion to Popular Music — Peter Gammond (Oxford 1991)
Showbiz Goes to War — Eric Taylor (Robert Hale 1992)
Stars of Melody — Jack Payne (Thames circa-1955)
This England's First Book of British Dance Bands — Edmund Whitehouse
   (This England 1999)
Vocal Refrain — Vera Lynn's autobiography (Star 1976)
We Said It With Music — Peggy Cochrane (New Horizon 1979)
World of Big Bands, The — Arthur Jackson (David and Charles 1977)
World of Jazz, The — Jim Godbolt (Studio Editions 1990)

The following periodicals were also of great assistance:-

Beat — popular music journal of the Forties and Fifties
Journal Into Melody — quarterly magazine of the Robert Farnon Society
Memory Lane — quarterly magazine of musical nostalgia — PO Box 1939,
   Leigh-on-Sea, Essex, SS9 3UH
Melody Maker — long-running popular music journal
Radio Magazine — short-lived monthly magazine first published in 1934
Radio Pictorial — weekly magazine popular throughout the 1930s